An **ABeCeD**arian of Sacred Trees

An **AB**e**C**e**D**arian of Sacred Trees

Spiritual Growth through Reflections on Woody Plants

MARK G. BOYER

WIPF & STOCK · Eugene, Oregon

AN ABECEDARIAN OF SACRED TREES
Spiritual Growth through Reflections on Woody Plants

Copyright © 2016 Mark G. Boyer. All rights reserved. Except for brief quotations in critical publications or reviews, no part of this book may be reproduced in any manner without prior written permission from the publisher. Write: Permissions, Wipf and Stock Publishers, 199 W. 8th Ave., Suite 3, Eugene, OR 97401.

Wipf & Stock
An Imprint of Wipf and Stock Publishers
199 W. 8th Ave., Suite 3
Eugene, OR 97401

www.wipfandstock.com

PAPERBACK ISBN: 978-1-5326-0447-8
HARDCOVER ISBN: 978-1-5326-0449-2
EBOOK ISBN: 978-1-5326-0448-5

Manufactured in the U.S.A.   DECEMBER 7, 2016

Dedicated to St. Meinrad School of Theology Class 1976
Ronald Ashmore, Richard Bennett, David Bergs,
Kenneth Bohlinger, Gilles Brault, Kevin Bryan,
Conrad Cambron, Noah Casey, Henry Cecil,
Stephen Churchwell, Robert Cushing, Richard Daunhauer,
Roger Dorcy, James Dvorscak, Richard Faulk,
G. Patrick Garrity, Mark Gottemoeller, William Haegelin,
Christian Hearing, H. Michael Hilderbrand, David Hillier,
James Holmer, Robert Hull, C. David LeSieur,
John McCaffrey, Ramon Marrufo, David Martin,
Jerome Martinez, Thomas Morrison, Francis Murd,
Joseph Scheib, Ernst Schuler, Benedict Swiderek,
Stephen Tripey, and Walter Verbish

"On the first day [of the festival of the LORD]
you shall take the fruit of majestic trees,
branches of palm trees,
boughs of leafy trees,
and willows of the brook;
and you shall rejoice before the LORD your God for seven days."
(Lev 23:40)

"All the trees of the field shall know
    That I am the LORD,
I bring low the high tree,
    I make high the low tree;
I dry up the green tree
    And make the dry tree flourish."
(Ezek 17:24)

Do you not see how all things in heavens and the earth,
the sun, the moon, the stars, the mountains, trees and beasts,
and men in abundance, pay homage to God?"
(Quran 22:18)

"Many for refuge go

To mountains and to forests,

To Shrines that are groves of trees—

Humans who are threatened by fear."

(Dhp 14:188)

"Let the woods

and all the trees of the field

praise the Lord. . . ."

(*D&C* 110:23)

"A tree gives glory to God by being a tree.

For in being what God means it to be

it is obeying him.

It 'consents,' so to speak, to his creative love.

It is expressing an idea which is in God

and which is not distinct from the essence of God,

and therefore a tree imitates God by being a tree.

The more a tree is like itself, the more it is like him.

If it tried to be like something else

which it was never intended to be,

it would be less like God

and therefore it would give him less glory."

(Thomas Merton, *New Seeds of Contemplation*)

Contents

Abbreviations | xi
Notes on Sacred Texts | xv
Introduction | xix

Acacia | 1
Almond | 6
Apple | 9
Ash | 22
Bramble | 24
Broom | 27
Burning Bush | 29
Cross | 33
Cypress | 38
Dry (Bad) Tree / Green (Good) Tree | 42
Elder | 48
Fig | 50
Fir | 55
Fruit | 58
Glastonbury Hawthorn | 62
Hemlock | 65
Holm | 74
Incense (Myrrh, Aloes) | 77
Joshua | 82
Kadam | 85

Laurel | 87
Mastic | 92
Mulberry | 95
Myrtle | 101
Nest for Birds | 104
Oak | 106
Olive | 112
Palm | 120
Pine | 127
Plane | 132
Pomegranate | 135
Poplar | 140
Red Cedar | 143
Sycamore | 153
Tamarisk | 157
Terebinth | 163
Vine (Vineyard) | 167
Willow | 197
Yew | 206
Zaqqum | 212
Conclusion and Trees in Film | 215

Other Books by Mark G. Boyer | *241*
Bibliography | *243*

Abbreviations

Aesop	**Aesop's Fables**
Analects	**The Analects of Confucius**
CB (NT)	**Christian Bible (New Testament)**
Acts	Acts of the Apostles
1 Cor	First Letter of Paul to the Corinthians
Gal	Letter of Paul to the Galatians
Heb	Letter to the Hebrews
Jas	Letter of James
John	John's Gospel
Jude	Letter of Jude
Luke	Luke's Gospel
Mark	Mark's Gospel
Matt	Matthew's Gospel
Rev	Revelation
Rom	Letter of Paul to the Romans
Dhp	**The Dhammapada**
D&C	**The Book of Doctrine and Covenants**
Grimm	**Grimm's Complete Fairy Tales**
HB (OT)	**Hebrew Bible (Old Testament)**
Amos	Amos
1 Chr	First Book of Chronicles

2 Chr	Second Book of Chronicles
Dan	Daniel
Deut	Deuteronomy
Eccl	Ecclesiastes
Esth	Esther
Exod	Exodus
Ezek	Ezekiel
Ezra	Ezra
Gen	Genesis
Hab	Habakkuk
Hag	Haggai
Hos	Hosea
Isa	Isaiah
Jer	Jeremiah
Job	Job
Joel	Joel
Josh	Joshua
Judg	Judges
1 Kgs	First Book of Kings
2 Kgs	Second Book of Kings
Lev	Leviticus
Mal	Malachi
Mic	Micah
Nah	Nahum
Neh	Nehemiah
Num	Numbers
Obad	Obadiah
Prov	Proverbs
Ps	Psalm
1 Sam	First Book of Samuel
2 Sam	Second Book of Samuel
Song	Song of Songs (Canticle of Solomon)

Zech	Zechariah
Zeph	Zephaniah
Mormon	**The Book of Mormon**
Al	Alma
He	Helaman
Jac	Jacob
Mos	Mosiah
1 Ne	First Book of Nephi
2 Ne	Second Book of Nephi
3 Ne	Third Book of Nephi
OT (A)	**Old Testament (Apocrypha)**
Bar	Baruch
Jdt	Judith
1 Macc	First Book of Maccabees
2 Macc	Second Book of Maccabees
4 Macc	Fourth Book of Maccabees
Sir	Sirach (Ecclesiasticus)
Sus	Susanna (Daniel)
Tob	Book of Tobit
Wis	Wisdom (of Solomon)
Proto-Jas	**Proto-Gospel of James**
Pseudo-Matt	**Gospel of Pseudo-Matthew**
Quran	**The Quran**
RV	**The Rig Veda**
Thos	**Gospel of Thomas**

Notes on Sacred Texts

The Analects of Confucius

THE ANALECTS OF CONFUCIUS contains twenty numbered books. In notating texts from this book, abbreviated *Analects*, the first number refers to the book, and the second number refers to the paragraph within the book. Thus, *Analects* 13:19 means that the quotation comes from book 13, paragraph 19.

The Bible

The Bible is divided into two parts: The Hebrew Bible (Old Testament) and the Christian Bible (New Testament). The Hebrew Bible consists of thirty-nine named books accepted by Jews and Protestants as Holy Scripture. The Old Testament also contains those thirty-nine books plus seven to fifteen more named books or parts of books called the Apocrypha or the Deuterocanonical Books; the Old Testament is accepted by Catholics and several other Christian denominations as Holy Scripture. The Christian Bible, consisting of twenty-seven named books, is also called the New Testament; it is accepted by Christians as Holy Scripture. Thus, in this work:

— Hebrew Bible (Old Testament), abbreviated HB (OT), indicates that a book is found both in the Hebrew Bible and the Old Testament;

— Old Testament (Apocrypha), abbreviated OT (A), indicates that a book is found only in the Old Testament Apocrypha and not in the Hebrew Bible;

— and Christian Bible (New Testament), abbreviated CB (NT), indicates that a book is found only in the Christian Bible or New Testament.

Unless otherwise noted, the *New Revised Standard Version* (NRSV) of the Bible is used throughout this work.

In notating biblical texts, the first number refers to the chapter in the book, and the second number refers to the verse within the chapter. Thus, HB (OT) Isa 7:11 means that the quotation comes from Isaiah, chapter 7, verse 11. OT (A) Sirach 39:30 means that the quotation comes from Sirach, chapter 39, verse 30. CB (NT) Mark 6:2 means that the quotation comes from Mark's Gospel, chapter 6, verse 2.

Book of Doctrine and Covenants

The *Book of Doctrine and Covenants* contains 140 numbered and named sections, each of which is subdivided into numbered paragraphs. In notating texts from this book, abbreviated *D&C*, the first number refers to the section in the book, and the second number refers to the paragraph within the section. Thus, *D&C* 12:1 means that the quotation comes from the *Book of Doctrine and Covenants,* section 12, paragraph 1. Older editions of this book do not always correspond with newer editions or online editions due to the renumbering of sections and paragraphs.

The Book of Mormon

The Book of Mormon contains fifteen named books. In notating texts from this book, abbreviated *Mormon*, the first number refers to the chapter in the named book, and the second number refers to the verse within the chapter. Thus, 1 Ne 6:9 means that the quotation comes from the First Book of Nephi, chapter 6, verse 9.

The Dhammapada

The Dhammapada contains twenty-six named chapters, each of which is subdivided into 423 continuously numbered paragraphs. In notating texts from this book, abbreviated *Dhp*, the first number refers to the chapter, and the second number refers to the paragraph within the chapter. Thus, 26:383 means that the quotation comes from chapter 26, paragraph 383.

The Quran

The Quran contains 114 numbered and named books. In notating texts from this book, abbreviated *Quran*, the first number refers to the book, and the second number refers to the verse within the book. Thus, 23:34 means that the quotation comes from book 23, verse 34.

The Rig Veda

The Rig Veda contains ten numbered books, each of which is subdivided into numbered hymns, and each hymn is subdivided into numbered verses. In notating texts from this book, abbreviated *RV*, the first number refers to the book, the second number refers to the hymn within the book, and the third number refers to the verse within the hymn. Thus, 3:30:4 means that the quotation comes from book 3, hymn 30, verse 4.

Introduction

Title of Book

THIS BOOK IS TITLED *An Abecedarian of Sacred Trees: Spiritual Growth through Reflections on Woody Plants*. As we look at each part of the title, keep in mind that this book is designed to foster the spiritual growth of people through reflections on forty trees arranged in alphabetical order.

Abecedarian

An abecedarian, as its onomatopoetic sound (a, b, c, d) suggests, is a book whose contents are in alphabetical order. For our purposes here, trees are chosen to coincide with the letters of the alphabet. Thus, the first entry begins with a, the second with b, the third with c, etc. While there are only twenty-six letters in the alphabet, there are forty entries in this tome; this means that some letters get more than one entry, and q, u, and x have no entry.

Sacred

The word *sacred* means *dedicated to a deity* or *religious purpose*. All across religions trees are used in religious worship in some way. The type of tree deemed sacred depends upon the place on the earth where it grows. The HB (OT) Book of Leviticus names trees with which the Israelites were familiar: majestic, palm, and willow (Lev. 23:40). Using those trees, the people are instructed to keep a seven-day festival in honor of the LORD their God. In other parts of the world, trees indigenous to specific areas are considered sacred, as will be seen in the entries that follow. A tree is considered sacred because of where it grows on the third planet from the sun and with whom or with what event it is associated over time. For example, the bo tree is considered a sacred tree because the Buddha was enlightened while meditating under one.

Trees have religious significance in most, if not all, cultures. If it is not the tree itself that is honored, then it is an aspect of the human that is applied to the tree. In other words, trees are personified; people are like trees. However, trees are also compared to people. A tree sings or bows in adoration of God. Thus, knowing sacred trees fosters self-knowledge and social cohesion in the universal context of life, especially the spiritual movement in the broader cosmos.

Trees tell us about ourselves and about the divine. God's spirit is in all things; God's fingerprints can be seen on every tree. The intangible inner spirit or sacredness of a tree is the universal divine—no matter what name one gives to him, her, or it—and how all things spirit or sacred are both connected to and flow from the one pervading source. While the power and divine nature of God are invisible, they can be seen in the trees he made.

In other words, the word *sacred* indicates that there is spirituality to be learned from trees. Because we share the planet with trees, they are not objects to be exploited; they have the ability to help us reach (w)holeness if we learn their wisdom and integrate it into our lives. Spirituality demands that the intangible God be made tangible in some way; this quest for the sacred can be somewhat satisfied by reflecting on various trees through the use of this book.

Tree

The word *tree* is being used in its broadest understanding as a woody plant that grows to a height of several feet to many feet and typically has a single erect main stem with side branches. More will be said about this below, but suffice it to be said now that humans are connected to trees intimately.

Once we are focused on learning from trees, then we begin to realize that they can serve as guides, leading us deeper and deeper into the divine life we share with them. The stories that abound about trees reveal the fascination that humans have with trees.

Thus, a sacred tree is one that sparks the spiritual in people. The tree discloses something, such as essence, being, or spirit, about its creator in a degree that is less than human, but nevertheless divine. Trees are not just growing plants that produce fruit, lumber, or wood; they are bearers of the spirit, just like people are. Griffith quotes Sieman, stating, "If God is embedded in the natural world, then all creation is sacred."[1] Because trees share this spiritual connection with each other and with people on the planet, they can teach them spirituality.

In other words, trees are carriers of the Spirit; they are manifestations of the God who created them. While all of creation is an overflowing of God's Spirit, our focus in this book is limited to trees. Some spiritual writers refer to this as concrescence, the experience of the world through prehension, total perception by the senses. If this concept is applied to God, then he—in terms of spirit or divinity—becomes the concrescent subject, in whom everywhere at once the many of the universe are perceived as being one. Thus, a tree can be a revelation; it attracts a person and speaks to him or her about spirit, participating in God's own truth and inexhaustibility. Burt writes, "When viewing life from a spiritual perspective, we see ourselves connected—to the unknowable and to something far greater than we are."[2] In other words, a person sees a tree as an expression of grace.

Because divinity is disguised by the bark of a tree, a spiritual guide is needed to get under that bark. This book functions as a spiritual guide, helping us to experience transcendence through immanence. The spiritual guide leads us to the divine. While the sacred is often defined in opposition to the profane, it is better to think of trees as manifestations of the divine. Consolmagno says that we find "the unexpected hidden among the mundane" which "is the pattern of how we experience God in the real world."[3] A spiritual guide leads a person to see a connection between the mundane human and the unexpected divine. "What appears in the world as immanent is at the same time a representation of what we take to be the transcendent."[4]

Spiritual Growth through Reflections on Woody Plants

Trees surround us. They grow in our front and back yards. They grow along our streets. We see them in fields and group them into forests. They are woody plants. Standing trees are collectively called "timber," especially

1. Griffith, "Organic Habits," 16.
2. Burt, "Healing Gardens," 23.
3. Consolmagno, "Sci-fy Guy," 36.
4. Eicher-Catt, "Signs," 231.

when they can be cut and sawed into building materials. Most people are not aware that most—if not all—of their homes is made from sacred trees.

In order for humans to see trees as manifestations of spirit, they have to stop looking at them as items to be consumed. That for what we look is what we find. Being present, mindful of the here and now, resting in awareness, enables one to see trees as ancient people saw them: bearers of spirit. Contacting this deeper understanding or plumbing the depths of the universal spirit is one way to see trees as inspirited or sacred. Tarrant says that "the core of spirituality is to experience and entrust [one]self to processes that are bigger than the things [one] can manage and manipulate and scheme about every day."[5] This book can facilitate our viewing of this manifestation of divinity and the development of our spirituality through its reflections on a variety of woody plants from around the world.

The Universal, World, or Cosmic Tree

Before the sixteenth-century Copernican revolution—which proposed that the earth was one of several planets rotating around the sun—ancient cosmology conceived of the universe as being a three-story building. Above the top story, usually called the dome of the earth, lived God or the gods. On the plate-like middle story lived people. And on the first story, usually referred to as the underworld, lived the dead. One way to imagine the three stories of the world united as one was the universal or world tree. With its roots firmly planted in the first story and with its trunk in the second story its branches reached up to the top story. Thus, a tree that connected the three stories of the universe was considered sacred because it functioned as a portal on earth to either the story above where the divinity lived or to the story below where the dead lived.

This same three-story universe is found in Norse mythology. "On the top was Asgard, where the gods lived in their magnificent halls . . . . On the level below was Midgard, the world of men . . . . Down below, on the third level, was Niflheim, [the] world of the dead . . . ."[6] Likewise, the Meso-

---

5. Mowe, "Why Play," 66.
6. Littleton, *Mythology*, 280.

american Maya presumed a three-story universe; they lived on the middle story. "... [T]he realm of heaven was one of permanence; its stability was assured by massive cosmic trees that anchored it in place."[7] At the base of their cosmic world "lay the gloomy underworld kingdom, [which] ... was simply the final home of everyone who had not come to a violent end."[8] The North American Native "... Haida believed that the universe was divided into three separate zones."[9] There was the underworld, from which souls emerged at birth; the sky world, the realm of the dead; and in between those two was the flat disk of the earth supported by a giant cedar pole.[10] Hinduism believed that one of the five trees located at the center of Indra's paradise was the kalpa-vriksha.[11]

The best presentation of the world tree in the Bible is found in the prophet Daniel, who records the Babylonian King Nebuchadnezzar's dream of a tree at the center of the earth (Dan 4:10a). "The tree grew great and strong, its top reached to heaven, and it was visible to the ends of the whole earth," records the prophet (Dan. 4:11). In order to further emphasize its cosmic function, Daniel notes its beautiful foliage, its abundant fruit, its ability to provide shade for animals and nesting space for birds, and how from it all living beings were fed (Dan 4:12). Because the tree unites all three stories of the universe, someone comes from heaven to earth and announces that the tree is to be cut down, and its branches chopped off, but its stump and roots are to be left in the ground (Dan. 4:14–15a). In other words, the unity between heaven, earth, and the underworld is to be dissolved.

In other mythologies, the world tree has branches that reach as high as the heavens and its roots plunge deep into the underworld. In Norse mythology the world tree is named Yggdrasil. In Hungarian mythology it is known as the Sky Tree. And in Baltic mythology it is called the Dawn Tree; it is "depicted with a golden trunk, copper roots, and silver leaves."[12] According to Davies, "The trunk represented life in the present, while the past was embodied in its roots (life that has passed). The branches, however, represented future choices yet to be made."[13]

The Maya's universe was also a tripartite structure. The realm of heaven was anchored in place by massive cosmic trees. In the middle of the universe

7. Ibid., 516.
8. Ibid.
9. *Spirit*, 159.
10. Ibid.
11. Witcombe, "Trees and the Sacred."
12. Davies, "Sacred Trees."
13. Ibid.

was the earth. And at the base lay the underworld. Both the heaven and the underworld were subdivided into levels. All three parts of the Maya universe were connected by a world tree, usually depicted in Mayan art as a cross.[14]

Axis Mundi

Besides serving as a link or portal between the three stories of the universe—heaven, earth, and underworld—the universal, world, or cosmic tree is often called an *axis mundi*, that is, a point of connection between sky, earth, and underworld where the four compass directions meet. The spot is sometimes referred to as the navel of the universe, the point of the world's beginning. It becomes a sign of growth (eternity), death (immortality), and rebirth (fertility). Besides being a tree, an *axis mundi* can be a mountain, a tower, a pillar, or a pole that marks the center for a group of people; that center is considered sacred.

As we will see in the entries that follow, around the world there are various people who consider a universal, world, or cosmic tree an *axis mundi*. For example, some Celtic tribes often took a tree trunk or a whole tree and planted it into a pit dug into the ground and placed their offerings around it. The idea was that the tree would be the means for the offerings on earth to be sent to the gods above. In Norse mythology, according to Littleton, "The different worlds were linked by the central column of the World Tree, the great ash Yggdrasil, whose tree roots reached all three levels and whose branches extended above them all providing shelter and sustenance."[15] Bulfinch states, "The mighty ash tree Yggdrasil was supposed to support the whole universe."[16] In China, it is the tree of Jianmu that unites heaven and earth.[17] In Native North American mythology, people lived in the sky in a village "at whose center grew a tree with huge white flowers."[18] Once the tree is uprooted, it sinks through the hole in the sky to the world below. Tane Mahutia is the name of New Zealand's largest kauri tree; it is named after the god of the forests: Tane. According to Littleton, as "[a] tall straight hardwood, it forms a living link between earth and sky."[19] The *Rig Veda* alludes to the world tree as a source of life in hymn 24 of book 1: "Varuna, King, of hallowed might, sustains erect the tree's stem in the

14. Littleton, *Mythology*, 516–17.
15. Ibid., 280–81.
16. Bulfinch, *Mythology*, 330.
17. Littleton, *Mythology*, 405.
18. Ibid. 488.
19. Ibid., 665.

baseless region" (*RV* 1:24:7). Varuna is the Hindu god of water, which, in the underworld, supplies the cosmic tree with life-sustaining nutrients. Native North American Sioux, Cheyenne, and other Plains Indians regard a tree in South Dakota's Bear Butte State Park "as the center of their universe."[20] Native North American Haida constructed their houses around a central pole that represented the center of the universe. The pole, planted in the earth, reached through the house and into the sky; thus, it connected the underworld, the earth, and the sky world.[21] Likewise, the Delaware Indians narrate the institution of the Big House with a center post, which "represented the World Tree that ascended to heaven from soil deposited on the back of a great turtle to form the earth."[22]

The concept of the *axis mundi* has not disappeared. It is still present in the tall wooden pole erected as a part of some European folk festivals held in the spring. It is known as a maypole; it may be a remnant of the Norse reverence for sacred trees. The pole appears in Joseph Jacobs's "Jack and the Beanstalk" fairy tale. As Tatar states, "The beanstalk has a certain whimsical inventiveness, for beanstalks are notoriously unstable and usually require staking to remain propped up."[23] The rather lengthy tale begins with a certain Jack selling the family cow for five beans. The buyer tells Jack, "If you plant them overnight, by morning they grow right up to the sky."[24] Once Jack gets home and tells his mother how he bartered the cow for five beans, his mother takes the beans and throws them out of the window. The next morning, Jack wakes up and looks out the window to see that the beans "had sprung up into a big beanstalk, which went up and up and up till it reached the sky."[25] Jack climbs the beanstalk into the sky and discovers a giant from whom he steals gold and climbs down the beanstalk. Taking an ax, he chops down the beanstalk. Thus, he destroys his link with the world above. However, with the gold he and his mother are able to live happily ever after.

No Axis Mundi Permitted

Because Moses instructs the Israelites to "demolish completely all the places where the nations . . . serve their gods . . . under every leafy tree" (Deut 12:2), and not to "plant any tree as a sacred pole beside the altar . . . for the

20. *Spirit*, 87.
21. Ibid.
22. Ibid., 164.
23. Jacobs, "Jack," 131.
24. Ibid., 134.
25. Ibid., 135.

LORD" (Deut 16:21), there is to be no universal, world, or cosmic tree; there is to be no *axis mundi* in Israel because the LORD God is the *axis mundi*, the center and creator of the Hebrew world. Furthermore, any sacred tree or sacred pole would represent Asherah, a mother goddess who is also known as Ashratum, Ashtaroth, Ashtoreth, etc. and may even be Ishtar, the goddess of fertility and sex. According to Bar, "For pagans, trees probably symbolized the protection and fertility the worshiper hoped to receive from the deity."[26] In the HB (OT), Asherah is found under trees (1 Kgs 14:23; 2 Kgs 17:10), is made by human hands (1 Kgs 14:15), is worshiped under green trees (2 Kgs 16:4; 2 Chr 28:4), and erected by people (2 Kgs 17:10). The goddess is usually represented by a sacred pole, that is, a phallus, to represent fertility. According to Ions, in Ur (Babylon), the tree of life was a sign of Ishtar; it was meant "to achieve and attest the king's potency in fertility rites."[27] Sometimes the tree of life was depicted as a date palm from which Ishtar "grant[ed] the king his power to promote fertility . . . ."[28] Bar states that in Israel there is the prohibition against planting an asherah, pole, or tree besides God's altar because it was "associated with Canaanite worship and the Canaanite goddess Asherah."[29]

In Israel, only the LORD God gives life. This is why the prophet Jeremiah refers to Israel's idolatry as "sprawled and play[ing] the whore . . . under every green tree" (Jer 2:20b; Jer 3:6, 9, 13). Later, Jeremiah writes: "The sin of Judah is written with an iron pen; with a diamond point it is engraved on the tablet of their hearts, and on the horns of their altars, while their children remember their altars and their sacred poles, beside every green tree . . . (Jer 17:1–2). The prophet Ezekiel, too, narrates God declaring that after he brought his people to the land that he had promised them "wherever they saw . . . any leafy tree, there they offered their sacrifices and presented the provocation of their offering; there they sent up their pleasing odors, and there they poured out their drink offerings" (Ezek 20:28).

Because neither sacred trees nor sacred poles are permitted in Israel, in the HB (OT) Book of Genesis, the LORD God plants a garden. "Out of the ground the LORD God made to grow every tree that is pleasant to the sight and good for food, the tree of life also in the midst of the garden, and the tree of the knowledge of good and evil" (Gen 2:9). It is important to note that even though there are two trees in the middle of the garden, neither one of these is an *axis mundi*. The LORD God is the *axis mundi*; he created the three-story

26. Bar, "Trees," 390.
27. Ions, *World's Mythology*, 20.
28. Ibid.
29. Bar, "Trees," 390.

universe (Gen 2:4b); he planted a garden of delight (Gen 2:8); and he made everything—including the tree of life and the tree of the knowledge of good and evil—grow in the garden (Gen 2:9). If the man eats from the tree of life, he will be given immortality; if he eats from the tree of knowledge, he will be given wisdom. The two trees present two aspects of the same image; each tree confers a boon. One tree gives life; the other tree gives wisdom.

Tree of Life

The man and the woman, after she is created, have free access to the tree of life, but they do not approach it. After they have eaten of the tree of wisdom, however, the LORD God fears that they might "take also from the tree of life, and eat, and live forever" (Gen 3:22). So, after driving the couple out of the garden, God places winged creatures—cherubim—and a sword flaming and turning to guard the way to the tree of life (Gen 3:24).

In biblical literature the tree of life is not mentioned again until the HB (OT) Book of Proverbs. According to Ryken, "the tree of life becomes a general image of blessing and fulfillment, a touchstone for what one would desire."[30] In 3:18, the author of Proverbs states that wisdom "is a tree of life to those who lay hold of her; those who hold her fast are called happy" (Prov 3:18). Later, the writer reflects that the fruit of the righteous is a tree of life (Prov 11:30), that a desire fulfilled is a tree of life (Prov 13:12), and that a gentle tongue is a tree of life (Prov 15:4).

The last mention of the tree of life in the Bible is found in the CB (NT) Book of Revelation in which it "connects the creation of the world to the re-created world that is to come."[31] In other words, according to Ryken, "In Revelation the tree of life is the supreme image of future splendor and paradise regained."[32] In the letter to the church in Ephesus, the Son of Man tells John of Patmos that to everyone who conquers in his or her battle against evil he will give permission to eat from the tree of life that is in the paradise of God (Rev 2:7). The next time the tree of life appears in Revelation is in the last chapter. In the new Jerusalem that has come down from heaven, on either side of the river flowing from God's throne "is the tree of life with its twelve kinds of fruit, producing its fruit each month; and the leaves of the tree are for the healing of the nations" (Rev 22:2; cf. Ezek 47:12). According to Ryken, "the tree of life is the supreme image of future splendor and

---

30. Ryken, *Dictionary*, 890.
31. Ibid., 889.
32. Ibid., 890.

paradise regained."³³ Using a beatitude, John of Patmos writes, "Blessed are those who wash their robes, so that they will have the right to the tree of life and may enter the city by the gates" (Rev. 22:14). In other words, the tree of life is accessible once again. Ryken states, "With the death of death, access to the tree of life is restored."³⁴

Thus, in biblical literature, the tree of life represents paradise, wisdom, and paradise regained. However, the tree of life is referenced in literatures other than the Bible. For example, Davies writes that "a tree of life belongs to the goddess Iusaaset, who was said to have conceived the lineage of Egyptian gods through the tree's life-giving properties."³⁵ Iusaaset is also associated with the acacia tree, which was considered a tree of life. Bar states, "In ancient Egyptian literature [the tree of life] appears as a tall sycamore on which the gods sit, eating its fruits in order to enjoy eternal life."³⁶ Polizzi writes, "The oak tree, specifically the red oak and white oak, was so important to the first people of California and Oregon that they called it 'The Tree of Life.'"³⁷

The Book of Mormon contains many references to the tree of life. In the First Book of Nephi, the writer records that he "beheld a tree, whose fruit was desirable to make one happy" (1 Ne 8:10) and that he partook of it, discovering that "it was most sweet, above all that [he] ever before tasted" (1 Ne 8:11). "It filled [his] soul with exceeding great joy" (1 Ne 8:12). A few chapters later, Nephi describes his vision of a tree whose "beauty . . . was far beyond, yea, exceeding of all beauty" (1 Ne 11:8); it was "precious above all" (1 Ne 11:9). Then, Nephi identifies the tree as "the tree of life" and "a representation of the love of God" (1 Ne 11:25). The Book of Alma, which equates the tree of life with the word of God (Al 33:37–42), records the invitation to "partake of the fruit of the tree of life" (Al 5:34; cf. 5:62); in order to do so, a person must "nourish the tree as it begins to grow, by . . . faith with great diligence, and with patience, looking forward to the fruit thereof; it shall take root; and behold it shall be a tree springing up unto everlasting life" (Al 32:41). Those who do this reverse God's cutting off of the first parents from the tree of life (Al 42:2–31).

In *The Rig Veda*, the tree of life is referred to as "the tree of treasure" (*RV* 2:39:1). In a hymn dedicated to the Asvins, the gods representing sunrise and sunset, the gods are said to be "like two misers to the tree of treasure" (*RV* 2:39:1); just as misers come to dig up the gold they have buried at the

---

33. Ibid., 890.
34. Ibid.
35. Davies, "Sacred Trees."
36. Bar, "Trees," 389.
37. Polizzi, "Sacred Medicine Trees."

foot of a tree, so do the gods of sunrise and sunset come to drink the sacred soma juice. Likewise, the chief Hindu god Indra is asked to shake "the tree for ripened fruit, for wealth to satisfy [the singer's] wish" (*RV* 3:45:4). In another hymn, Indra, "invoked by many," is praised for the "manifold aids" he gives to his worshipers; the gifts are "like branches of a tree," which when shaken yield fruits (*RV* 6:24:3).

Schwartz narrates a tale titled "The Tree of Life" concerning the Baal Shem Tov, who leads three rabbis into a pristine forest. One gets distracted by a tall and magnificent tree. One dallies at a pond reflecting an angelic presence. The third tarries before trees that seem to be on fire but are not consumed. After suddenly becoming aware that they have all returned to their study, the Baal Shem Tov addresses them: ". . . I brought you with me into paradise. And the further we went, the fewer were those who followed. And when I came to the tree of life, I found that all of you had lagged behind."[38] The tale is meant to emphasize the importance of following the directions of the master in his teaching so as not to get left behind. Echoing Proverbs 3:18 above, the tree of life refers to wisdom, and according to Schwartz, "has traditionally been understood to refer to the Torah."[39] Thus, "the tale serves as an allegory about how the master leads his disciples to the real treasure of the Torah."[40]

Tree of Knowledge of Good and Evil

The other tree in the garden of delight is "the tree of the knowledge of good and evil" (Gen 2:9). The LORD God tells the man that he may eat freely of every tree in the garden; "but of the tree of the knowledge of good and evil [he] shall not eat, for in the day that [he] eat[s] of it [he] shall die" (Gen 2:17). After God creates the woman she enters into dialogue with the serpent and repeats God's command (Gen 3:3). The serpent explains to her that if she eats of the tree of the knowledge of good and evil that she will not die, but that her eyes will be opened and she will be like God, knowing good and evil (Gen 3:5). The woman understands that the tree will give her wisdom to be like God (Gen 3:5–6). So, she eats its fruit and gives some to the man. Thus, both the woman and the man attain wisdom or enlightenment, and they do not die. According to Bar, "Eating from the tree of knowledge caused [Adam and Eve] to hunger for the tree of life; they could

---

38. Schwartz, *Gabriel's Palace*, 193.
39. Ibid., 328.
40. Ibid.

now distinguish ephemeral life from eternal life and wanted to be like God and live forever."[41] He continues:

> Eating from the tree of knowledge is the transitional stage, the beginning of choice, of subjective discrimination, and of the self-consciousness that spoils natural innocence but replaces it with broader understanding and with emotional conflict. Adam [and Eve] wished to be like God in knowledge, but lacked the tools to overcome the difficulties of the outside world.... Adam [and Eve], who [were] endowed with knowledge, attempted to be like God by means of rebellion and disobedience.[42]

The attainment of wisdom becomes a theme that runs through sacred literatures, even though the above biblical references are all that appear in the Bible about the tree of knowledge of good and evil. For example, the Buddha gains wisdom or enlightenment under the bo tree. Moses is enlightened by a burning bush. Druids are often inspired under an oak tree. Odin finds enlightenment under Yggdrasil. We will delve more deeply into these and discover others when we cover specific trees later in this book.

On the British Columbia West Coast, the Salish nation honors the arbutus tree as a tree of knowledge because it knows how to find the sun.[43] "It twists and turns and somehow knows to drop one branch when there is not enough sunlight and it is shaded, and it will grow a new one where the sun can reach it."[44] Olafson, a poet, narrates a native legend about the arbutus that illustrates its cosmic aspect: "The tree's webbed roots hold the splintered earth together."[45] Thus, if the arbutus should ever disappear, the planet would fly apart and be utterly destroyed. Like the arbutus, the Australian aborigines believe that the force their ancestors left latent within the earth is accessible to their descendents in the form of djang, "a type of stored-up primal power which collects in certain sacred places."[46] Djang can be held "in a particular tree" and can be released "at a word or a touch to instill strength or confer cunning on the initiate, or to bring much-needed sunshine or rain."[47] The aborigines consider the creative energy of djang to be that by which the world was originally formed. Thus, its continued presence in a tree allows the aborigines to tap into their ancestors's whole spiritual

41. Bar, "Trees," 389.
42. Ibid.
43. "Sacred Trees: Arbutus (Madrone) Tree."
44. "Sacred Trees: Arbutus (Madrone) Tree."
45. Ibid.
46. Littleton, *Mythology*, 646.
47. Ibid.

resource. As such, any tree functions as one of wisdom or the knowledge of good and evil.

Using the image of a tree as an archetypal sign of life, *The Quran* narrates the biblical account from Allah's point of view. To Adam God says, "Both you and your spouse live in the garden; eat freely to your fill wherever you like, but approach not this tree or you will become transgressors" (*Quran* 2:35). After repeating the same line in 7:19, the narrator suggests that the sin of Adam and Eve has to do with nakedness. He states:

> ... Satan suggested (evil) to them, in order to reveal their hidden parts of which they were not aware (till then), and said: "Your Lord has forbidden you (to go near) this tree that you may not become angels or immortal." Then he said to them on oath: "I am your sincere friend;" and led them (to the tree) by deceit. When they tasted (the fruit) of the tree, their disgrace became exposed to them; and they patched the leaves of the garden to hide it. And the Lord said to them: "Did I not forbid you this tree? And I told you that Satan was your open enemy." (*Quran* 7:20–22)

In 17:60 God refers to "the accursed tree of the Quran" and in 20:120–121 re-narrates the sin of nakedness, stating, "... Satan tempted [Adam] by saying: 'O Adam, should I show you the tree of immortality, and a kingdom that will never know any wane?' And both [Adam and Eve] ate of (its fruit), and their hidden parts were exposed to one another, and they patched the leaves of the garden (to hide them). Adam disobeyed his Lord, and went astray." Thus, in *The Quran*, eating from the tree of knowledge of good and evil results in the man and woman being conscious of their nakedness.

In a Tree

Because the universal, world, or cosmic tree serves as an *axis mundi* connecting the three stories or levels of the universe, it is also a portal, a door that opens from one level to another level. Thus, Adonis, in Greek mythology the annually-renewed and ever-youthful god of vegetation, has a mother—Smyrna—who was attracted to her father and becomes pregnant with his child. As Segal narrates the story, once her father finds out he draws his sword in order to kill her. "She fled, and he pursued her. On the verge of being overtaken, she prayed to the gods to become invisible, and they, taking pity, turned her into a myrrh (smyrna) tree. Ten months later the tree burst open, and Adonis was born."⁴⁸ Not only does the tree protect the child and his mother, but it connects him to the three-story universe. He is a god who comes from the heaven to the earth, where he dies at a young age and enters the underworld, from which he is reborn. According to Segal, "Adonis's gestation takes place in the tree, and his birth requires his breaking out of it."⁴⁹ Through the portal that the tree provides, the god from heaven enters the earth. Through death, he enters the underworld, from which he breaks out to become the god of vegetation.

Mythology narrates the Egyptian tale of the trickery Seth used to murder Osiris:

> Seth ordered the making of an exquisitely crafted chest, to the exact height and width of his brother. Then he threw a great banquet for Osiris, at which he displayed the chest to the admiration of all.... [O]ne by one the guests tried the chest for size. But none matched its measurements—except Osiris himself. And the moment the unsuspecting king lay in the chest, Seth and his fellow-plotters promptly nailed the lid shut, sealed it with molten lead, and cast the chest upon the waters of the Nile Delta.
>
> Isis at once set off to find her husband's body. But by the time she learned where Seth had put the great chest, it had floated far out to sea. It finally came to land at Byblos in the Lebanon. There, the washed-up chest gave root to a sapling which magically grew into a vast tree big enough to enclose Osiris and his coffin within its trunk. Impressed by the size of the tree, the king of Lebanon had it cut down and used as a pillar for his new palace—with Osiris still within.⁵⁰

The tale concludes this way: "In time, of course, Isis tracked the coffin down, and to the astonishment of the king and his court, cut open the great roof-pillar and removed her husband's body."⁵¹ The tree which enclosed Osiris and his coffin connects all three levels of the universe to demonstrate that Osiris is a god, that he lived on the earth, that he was buried in the chest-coffin, and that he was set free to live again by his wife, Isis.

The Aztec myth explaining the origin of the alcoholic beverage known as pulque also features gods using a tree as a portal between the stories of the universe.

---

48. Segal, *Myth*, 6.
49. Ibid., 110.
50. Littleton, *Mythology*, 56.
51. Ibid.

> Travelling to the heavens, Quetzalcoatl found the lovely Mayahuel, the granddaughter of one of the tzitzimine, a group of malevolent female spirits transformed into star demons who held a grudge against the living, and persuaded her to come down with him to earth. When they reached the earth, the couple transformed themselves into a single gigantic tree. Mayahuel was one fork and Quetzalcoatl the other. When the grandmother tzitzimitl discovered that Mayahuel was missing, she was enraged. She summoned the tzitzimime and together they swooped down to earth in pursuit of the errant granddaughter. As the star demons arrived on earth, the tree composed of Mayahuel and Quetzalcoatl split in two. Recognizing Mayahuel in one of its great branches, the grandmother tzitzimitl ripped the offending bough to pieces and fed it bit by bit to the other tzitzimine. Sorrowfully, Quetzalcoatl buried what was left of the beautiful Mayahuel's fleshless bones, and from these sprang the original maguey cactus that would later produce the joyfully intoxicating drink pulque.[52]

The gods, coming from the heavens, use a single, gigantic tree in which to hide on the earth. Once the tree splits in two, one part of it gives birth to the maguey cactus.

In Australian mythology, there are two opposing winds, named Bara and Mamariga. Like the Aztec gods transform themselves into a tree, Mamariga seizes Bara and imprisoned it "in a giant hollow tree on a headland above the sea."[53] Every year some aborigines "assemble before the place of captivity, sing sacred incantations and exhortations, and use their axes to strike deep cuts in the bark. Through these apertures . . . the . . . wind may once more be released into a welcoming world."[54]

In India, the ghosts of Brahmans are believed to live in fig trees, pipal (bo) trees, or banyan trees while awaiting liberation or reincarnation.[55] Likewise, the North American Mesquakie "believed the spirits of their ancestors dwelled within the trees of their Iowa homeland."[56] The members of the tribe thought that the murmur of the wind passing through the trees was the voices of their ancestors. Thus, all wood and all objects made from wood were considered sacred. According to *The Spirit World*, "The wooden feast bowls used as ritual vessels during religious ceremonies were thought to contain the very essence of a tree's spiritual substance. . . . Because their naturally rounded

52. Ibid., 552.
53. Ibid., 658.
54. Ibid.
55. Witcombe, "Trees and the Sacred."
56. *Spirit*, 90.

shape suggested the swelling of pregnancy, burls [, the dense knotty outgrowths on tree trunks,] were looked upon as symbols of fertility. The bowls, which were endowed with the same associations, represented birth and were revered as symbols of hope for the continuity of the tribe."[57]

Not to be forgotten, of course, is the tale of Merlin (also called Myrddin and Taliesin); in one version of Niviane's (also known as Niniane, Nimue, Vivaine, Vivien, etc.) spell, the wizard is placed in a tree, climbs a pine tree, or is confined in a hawthorn tree, where he experiences a profound revelation and never returns to the world.[58] In *The Meaning of Trees: Botany, History, Healing, Lore*, Hageneder explains why he thinks it is a pine tree which Merlin climbs:

> According to Breton legend, the legendary wise man Merlin climbed the Pine of Bareton (from *bel nemeton*, Sacred Grove of Bel), just as shamans climb the World Tree. Here, he had a profound revelation and he never returned to the mortal world. In later versions, Merlin's *glas tann* was mistranslated as a *glass house*. It is actually a living tree (from the Cornish *glas (ever) green*, and *tann*, *sacred tree*), and from these words the name of Glastonbury, in Somerset, England, is sometimes derived. Hence, according to legend, it is a sacred tree in which the soul of Merlin awaits his return.[59]

In Alfred Lord Tennyson's "Idylls of the King," Vivien imprisons Merlin in a deep sleep in an oak. Tennyson writes: "Then, in one moment, she put forth the charm / Of woven paces and of waving hands, / And in the hollow oak he lay so dead, / And lost to life and use and name and fame."[60] In ABC's TV series "Once Upon a Time," it is Emma Swan who frees Merlin from the tree.

Caldecott records a story about Merlin witnessing the horrors of battle and fleeing "to the great forests of Scotland," where he lives for many years in "a kind of holy madness." She continues: "At this stage he lived with the trees and drew strength and wisdom from them. Later he reached a stage when he became one with them—he became tree—and freed thus from having to express himself in words that could be so easily misunderstood and distorted, he communicated as trees communicate: wordlessly, but profoundly."[61]

Schwartz narrates a tale titled "The Voice in the Tree" about an old rabbi who attends a funeral and sits under a tree while the grave is being

57. Ibid.
58. Caldecott, *Myths*, 178.
59. Hageneder, *Meaning of Trees*, 149.
60. Goodrich, *Merlin*, 248.
61. Caldecott, *Myths*, 179.

dug. A voice speaks to him from within the tree and seeks his help. The voice identifies itself as that of his neighbor of years past and explains how after death a soul undergoes four transformations. It is the second one that concerns us here. The tree explains: ". . . [T]here are the souls that cross the ocean and pass above the trees. If the soul falls and enters a fruit-bearing tree, and if those fruits are later picked and blessings pronounced on them, that soul . . . enters the garden of Eden, its sufferings at an end."[62] The voice within the tree then tells the rabbi that his soul has undergone three of the four transformations. In the near future, a sheep will eat the crop into which the neighbor's soul has entered. He needs the rabbi to buy the sheep, have it slaughtered, and set him free from suffering; the rabbi does as requested and learns in a dream that his neighbor has made it to the garden of Eden. As a reward, the neighbor reveals where a treasure is buried at his old house.

People Are Like Trees, and Trees Are Like People

Grimm's Complete Fairy Tales contains a story about "The Three Green Twigs" which compares people to trees. A hermit who lives in a forest witnesses a poor sinner being taken to the gallows and declares that he is getting what he deserves. God reveals his displeasure with the hermit through a speaking bird who becomes an angel in the story. The hermit's penance is to carry a dry branch with him "until three green twigs sprout out of it."[63] At night he is instructed to put it under his head. After accepting the dry piece of wood, the hermit goes begging from door to door until he enters a forest where he finds a cave with an old woman sitting in it. He asks her if he can spend the night there, and she permits him to do so. However, she tells him that she has "three sons who are wicked and wild; if they come home from their robbing expedition, and find [him], they will kill" both him and their mother.[64] When the hermit proceeds to lie down beneath the stairs and put the wood under his head, the woman asks him about it, and he tells her how it is his penance for having offended the Lord by what he said about the man on his way to the gallows. "Then the woman began to weep and cried, 'If the Lord thus punishes one single word, how will it fare with my sons when they appear before him in judgment?'"[65] Around midnight the sons return home, ask their mother about the hermit sleeping under the stairs, and hear her tell them how he is doing penance for his sin. The story continues:

62. Schwartz, *Gabriel's Palace*, 177.
63. Grimm, 401.
64. Ibid.
65. Ibid.

> The robbers were so powerfully touched in their hearts by this story, that they were shocked with their life up to this time, reflected, and began with hearty repentance to do penance for it. The hermit, after he had converted the three sinners, lay down to sleep again under the stairs. In the morning, however, they found him dead, and out of the dry wood on which his head lay, three green twigs had grown up on high. Thus the Lord had once more received him into his favor.[66]

While the hermit did not ever realize it, the piece of tree he carried with him represented the three sons of the woman in the cave who needed to be converted.

The Native American Cherokee refer to trees as the "Standing People." "Each tree has its properties and attributes with the ability to share these with the people . . . ."[67] According to "Tree Symbols," "A tree symbolizes permanence, longevity, and its firm base symbolizes the concept of roots and an ongoing relationship with natural surroundings."[68] The members of many Native American tribes thought that the qualities of each type of tree brought specific medicine to them and contained a sacred spark of the Great Spirit. Thus, when trees were used to make sacred objects, "the wood was carefully chosen for its strength and spirituality."[69] It was taken from a tree that had special meaning" to the person making the object, and the person sought permission from the tree spirit to take the wood from the tree.

The OT (A) Book of Sirach compares the high priest Simon son of Onias to several trees. He is like an olive tree laden with fruit, and like a cypress towering in the clouds (Sir 50:10); he is like a young cedar on Lebanon surrounded by the trunks of palm trees (Sir 50:12). The prophet Isaiah records that "when the house of David heard that Aram had allied itself with Ephraim, the heart of Ahaz and the heart of his people shook as the trees of the forest shake before the wind" (Isa 7:2; cf. 2 Ne 17:2). The prophet Jeremiah compares himself to a tree and declares what his enemies are saying: "Let us destroy the tree with its fruit, let us cut him off from the land of the living, so that his name will no longer be remembered!" (Jer 11:19c).

Later, Jeremiah describes those who trust in the LORD to be "like a tree planted by water, sending out its roots by the stream. It shall not fear when heat comes, and its leaves shall stay green; in the year of drought it is not anxious, and it does not cease to bear fruit" (Jer 17:8). The prophet's

---

66. Ibid., 402.
67. "Tree Symbols."
68. Ibid.
69. Ibid.

words echo Psalm 1, which states that those who delight in the LORD's law and meditate on it day and night "are like trees planted by streams of water, which yield their fruit in its season, and their leaves do not wither" (Ps 1:3a). *The Dhammapada* echoes both Jeremiah and Psalm 1 when it states that the non-virtuous person's lack of virtue is "like the maluva creeper" spreading over "a sala tree" (*Dhp* 12:162). The creeper captures water with its leaves when it rains and completely overwhelms the sala tree by pulling it down. *The Dhammapada* notes that a person does this to himself or herself, "just as a foe wishes [to do] to him [or her]" (*Dhp* 12:162). In other words, craving that is not disciplined is self-destructive.

There is also the declaration of the blind man that Jesus heals in Mark's Gospel. After taking the man out of the village of Bethsaida, Jesus puts saliva on his eyes and lays his hands on his head. He asks the man if he can see anything, and the man replies that he can see people, but they look like trees, walking (Mark 8:24). So, Jesus puts his hands on the man again, and then he can see clearly.

The prophet Isaiah portrays Assyrian rulers as trees, which "the Sovereign, the LORD of hosts, will lop [off] the boughs with terrifying power; the tallest tress will be cut down, and the lofty will be brought low" (Isa 10:33). The prophet states that the LORD "will hack down the thickets of the forest with an ax, and Lebanon with its majestic trees will fall" (Isa 10:34).

The prophet Ezekiel portrays Egyptian rulers as trees, asking: "Who are you like in your greatness?" (Ezek 31:2b) Then, Ezekiel, echoing Isaiah, writes:

> Consider Assyria, a cedar of Lebanon, with fair branches and forest shade, and of great height, its top among the clouds. The waters nourished it, the deep made it grow tall, making its rivers flow around the place it was planted, sending forth its streams to all the trees of the field. So it towered high above all the trees of the field; its boughs grew large and its branches long, from abundant water in its shoots. All the birds of the air made their nests in its boughs; under its branches all the animals of the field gave birth to their young; and in its shade all great nations lived. It was beautiful in its greatness, in the length of its branches; for its roots went down to abundant water. The cedars in the garden of God could not rival it, nor the fir trees equal its boughs; the plane trees were as nothing compared with its branches; no tree in the garden of God was like it in beauty. I made it beautiful with its mass of branches, the envy of all the trees of Eden that were in the garden of God. (Ezek 31:3–9)

Following this detailed description of the cosmic tree, the LORD God decrees that it is to be cut down. Thus, its top among the clouds (Ezek 31:10) will fall; its branches will be broken off (Ezek 31:12); and birds will settle on its fallen trunk (Ezek 31:13). Ezekiel specifically mentions how its roots reach to the underworld, commonly called Sheol (Ezek 31:15–17). Thus, the cosmic tree that united the three stories of the universe is no more. God has abandoned his people to their enemies!

Isaiah decrees that it is the LORD of hosts who will be lifted up and high; he will be against all the cedars of Lebanon, lofty and lifted up, and against all the oaks of Bashan (Isa 2:12c–13). The LORD will be lifted up above the highest trees because he is greater than any sacred tree. Then, one day "a shoot shall come out from the stump of Jesse, and a branch shall grow out of his roots" (Isa 11:1). In other words, one day after the Jews return from Babylonian captivity God promises to restore the line of David.

If it is true that people are like trees, it is also true that trees are like people. *The Quran* tells its readers, "It was not in your power to make trees germinate" (*Quran* 27:60); just as Allah gives life to trees, so, too, does God give life to people. In *The Rig Veda*, the god Indra is the originator of all life. In narrating the creation of the world, hymn 89 notes that after Indra created the mountains "the tall trees followed" (*RV* 10:89:13). In book 2, hymn 14 declares that Indra "with the lightning smote like a tree the rain-witholding Vrtra," the water monster (*RV* 2:14:2a). In book 7, hymn 8, Indra is asked to "smite down the sinner like a tree with lightning-flash" (*RV* 7:8:5b). The singer of hymn 57 exhorts his hearers to cling closely to Indra's love "as to a tree's extended bough" (*RV* 6:57:5). And hymn 95 of book 7 requests Indra's protection as people approach "a tree for shelter" (*RV* 7:95:5b), while hymn 13 of book 8 implores Indra to accept the zealous worshipers's songs, which are "like branches of a tree up-grows what they desire" (*RV* 8:13:6).

In hymn 1 of book 5 of *The Rig Veda*, Agni's flames are "like young trees shooting up on high their branches . . . rising to the vault of heaven" (*RV* 5:1:1b). Agni, the god of fire and lightning, descends as rain into the trees. Thus, hymn 91 declares that "the forest trees . . . bear him within them and produce him evermore" (*RV* 10:91:6b). The blessings that Agni bestows spring from the god of fire like "branches from a tree" (*RV* 6:13:1).

The unmatched devotions of the singers of hymns "are like a tree's branches part[ing] in all directions" (*RV* 7:43:1b). In other words, just like trees have branches, the gods and people have arms.

According to *The Quran*, "the trees bow [to God] in adoration" (*Quran* 55:6). According to the prophet Isaiah, the "forest and every tree in it" is to sing God's praises (Isa 44:23) while "all the trees of the field shall clap their hands" (Isa 55:12b). According to the First Book of Chronicles, on the day that David brought the ark of the LORD to Jerusalem the trees of the forest sang for joy before the LORD (1 Chr 16:33). This verse comes from Psalm

96 in which the singer declares: "Then shall all the trees of the forest sing for joy before the LORD; for he is coming, for he is coming to judge the earth" (Ps 96:12b–13a).

In a hymn dedicated to the god Indra in book 8, hymn 4, *The Rig Veda* states "the very trees were joyful" at Indra's coming (*RV* 8:4:21). In book 10, hymn 65, the forest trees are among those that "generated prayer" (*RV* 10:65:11). Or as hymn 12 in book 9 states: "The tree whose praises never fail yields heavenly milk among our hymns" (*RV* 9:12:7).

While the Q (from Quelle meaning *source*) parable found in Matthew's Gospel and Luke's Gospel about a mustard bush does not yield heavenly milk, it does portray Jesus' use of hyperbole to stress his point that the kingdom of heaven "is like a mustard seed that someone took and sowed in his field; it is the smallest of all the seeds, but when it has grown it is the greatest of shrubs and becomes a tree, so that the birds of the air come and make nests in its branches" (Matt 13:31–32). Luke records the parable in a slightly different way, writing that the kingdom of God "is like a mustard seed that someone took and sowed in the garden; it grew and became a tree, and the birds of the air made nests in its branches" (Luke 13:19).

There is another version of the parable found in Mark's Gospel. Jesus says that the kingdom of God "is like a mustard seed, when, when sown upon the ground, is the smallest of all the seeds on earth; yet when it is sown it grows up and becomes the greatest of the shrubs, and puts forth large branches, so that the birds of the air can make nests in its shade" (Mark 4:31–32). In The Gospel of Thomas, Jesus states that the kingdom of heaven "is like a mustard seed. It is [the] smallest of all seeds, but when it falls on tilled ground, it puts forth a great branch and becomes a shelter for the birds of the sky" (Thos 20).[70]

Hedrick states:

> In Mark the seed produces a shrub with large branches so that the birds can build nests in its shade. In Matthew and Luke the seed produces a tree in whose branches birds build nests. In Thomas the earth produces a large branch providing shelters for birds. All four versions contrast the small beginning (the seed) and the large result (tree/large branches or branch).[71]

It is important to note that no one sowed mustard seed in a field, a garden, or tilled ground because it was considered a weed in the ancient world![72] In other words, mustard was pulled up and tossed aside. It is also important to note that mustard grows into a scraggly bush and not into

---

70. Ehrman, *Apocryphal Gospels*, 315.
71. Hedrick, *Unlocking the Secrets*, 54.
72. Dart, *Unearthing the Last Words of Jesus*, 52.

a tree! However, from ignominious beginnings springs surprising results. Jesus shocks his hearers by declaring that the great God's reign is like the smallest weed seed known to people and pulled up by farmers that grows into a tree. Today it would be like comparing God's reign to a dandelion seed, which when sown in the lawn is a small seed, but after it is sown and grows it becomes a great tree with large branches in which birds build nests in its shade! The large tree represents God's kingdom.

We conclude this background on trees with a statement from the Mormon *Book of Doctrine and Covenants*. In a revelation given in December 1833, the unidentified recipient records that "an infant shall not die until he is old, and his life shall be as the age of a tree" (*D&C* 98:5). The prophet Isaiah records God declaring something similar once he creates new heavens and a new earth: ". . . [L]ike the days of a tree shall the days of my people be, and my chosen shall long enjoy the work of their hands" (Isa 65:22). Because trees were thought to live long lives and be older than most people, the life span of a tree is used as the measure of the life span of a person.

Organization of this Book

A five-part exercise is offered for every one of the forty entries in this book.

1. The name of a tree indicates the focus of the chapter. As indicated above, the entries are arranged in abecedarian format. The picture is meant to represent the tree under consideration, not to be an exact copy of it.

2. A few verses or sentences from a text are provided. The text may be from the Bible (Hebrew Bible [Old Testament], Old Testament [Apocrypha], Christian Bible [New Testament]), from a world religion (*The Book of Mormon, The Quran, The Dhammapada, The Rig Veda, The*

Analects of Confucius), from a fable, a tale, a legend, or a story (Aesop, Grimm), or from some other source that illustrates a truth about the tree under consideration.

3. A reflective study follows the text. The reflection presents some of the context for the text, attempting to surface its meaning. It also presents other references to the tree in other sources. The reflective study is not be understood as exhaustive of the presence of the tree in biblical, world religions, fables, tales, legends, stories, or other texts. The study is a sampling, a sketch of the sacred tree across religions and cultures. It is designed to get the reader to stop and consider the wondrous works of God (Job 37:14). Some entries go into more detail than others. Thus, some reflective studies are longer than others, and some are shorter than others.

   When I use some Egyptian, Greek, and Roman mythology involving a particular tree, I rely on the English translation of ancient texts prepared by others. Some of these mythologies are common knowledge, whereas some may be new to the reader. When mentioning Greek gods and goddesses, I usually give the names of their Roman counterparts in parentheses where necessary.

4. The reflection is followed by a question for journaling and/or personal meditation. The question functions as a guide for personal appropriation of the message of the reflective study, thus leading the reader into journaling and/or personal prayer. The journal/meditation question is designed to foster a process of actively applying the reflection to one's life. The question gets one started; where the journal/meditation goes cannot be predetermined. It may be a single statement or an idea with which one lingers for a few minutes, a few hours, or a few days. The process has no end; the reader decides when he or she has finished exploring the topic because he or she needs to attend to other things.

5. A prayer concludes the exercise and summarizes the original theme announced in the title, which was studied and explored in the reflection and which served as the foundation for the meditation. The prayer is written in a Christian form. The non-Christian reader may use the prayer as it is presented or ignore it and write his or her own prayer in his or her journal.

Using This Book

This book can be used at any time a person desires to develop further his or her spiritual life. It can be used in one's home as a daily exercise for a month, or the parts of each entry may be spread over several days or a week. A reader may take it outside and, while sitting on a bench under a tree, read the entry and reflect upon the spiritual truths learned from woody plants. In warmer climates, one can sit in the back yard while listening to the wind blow through the trees and read an entry, or a reader may choose to go to a park, forest, or conservation area, observe some of the trees there, and read the entry in this book about the tree in which one has an interest. This book can also be used during a retreat or on days set aside for reflection. Small groups of people might use it, reading its entries, sharing their reflections, and closing with its concluding prayer.

Shapiro encourages people to "talk about the sacred, the wondrous, and the awe-inspiring."[73] He urges people to "[s]hare with each other [their] respective sense of wonder and see if that doesn't open into different conversation about life, meaning, and purpose."[74] While he limits his remarks to reading the HB (OT), his words hold true for reading other sacred and profane writings, which are ways "to deepen [our] understanding of who [we are] and of what—for better and for worse–[we are] capable of."[75]

The book is designed to help the reader grow in spirituality through reflecting on sacred trees. The woody plants on the earth reveal the divine to us if we but open our eyes to see. Some of our human ancestors have recorded the truths learned from trees, and we are enriched by what they have left us. May our reflections further this spiritual journey and process for our descendants.

Mark G. Boyer
Arbor Day
April 29, 2016

---

73. Shapiro, "Roadside Assistance," 19.
74. Ibid.
75. Ibid., 20.

Acacia

Text: "... [T]he LORD said to [Moses], 'Carve out two tablets of stone ... and make an ark of wood. I will write on the tablets ..., and you shall put them in the ark.' So I [, Moses,] made an ark of acacia wood, cut two tablets of stone ..., and went up the mountain with the two tablets in my hand. Then he wrote on the tablets ..., and the LORD gave them to me. So I turned and came down from the mountain, and put the tablets in the ark that I had made ...." (Deut 10:1–5)

Reflection: The acacia tree is the most sacred tree in the Bible, because the ark of the covenant, the altar of sacrifice, and the altar of incense are made out of acacia wood. Commonly known as a thorn tree, the acacia features gnarled bark with orange-brown wood that is dense or hard grained. It lives for thirty or forty years, repelling insects, and producing fragrant clusters of yellow, white, cream, or reddish-pink blossoms from which three-inch-long, locust-like seed pods form. The seeds turn from green to brown when they ripen; the seed pods may split open to release the seeds or fire may be required to get this to occur. The wood, because of its hardness, is used for handles for tools, pegs, small boxes, spear shafts, and other items in the ancient world.

In the above passage from the HB (OT) Book of Deuteronomy, Moses recounts for the Israelites his making of the two tablets of stone upon which God wrote the ten commandments. Those tablets were placed in the ark, made out of acacia wood. In the Book of Exodus, Moses receives the offerings of the people among which is acacia wood (Exod 25:5). The LORD instructs Moses to make an ark of acacia wood (Exod 25:10); the ark was a container for the tablets of stone and functioned as a throne or footstool for the divine presence. Bezalel, the chief artisan for the ark's construction, made the ark of acacia wood (Exod 37:1a). The LORD also tells Moses that the ark is to be carried with poles of acacia wood (Exod 25:13) which are inserted into two gold rings on each of its sides; Bezalel made the poles (Exod 37:4). Also constructed out of acacia wood by Bezalel is a table (Exod 25:23; 37:10) with poles for carrying it (Exod 25:28; 37:15); upon the table was set the bread of the presence, a sign of hospitality to God.

The LORD instructs Moses that he is also to construct the tabernacle, a tent into which the ark is placed. The upright frames were to be made of acacia wood (Exod 26:15); Bezalel and Oholiab, Bezalel's assistant, made the frames (Exod 36:20). The two artisans were also instructed to make ten bars of acacia wood (Exod 26:26), five for each side of the tabernacle, which they did (Exod 36:31), and four pillars of acacia wood (Exod 26:32)—which they did (Exod 36:36)—upon which to hang curtains. A screen for the entrance to the tent was also to be constructed of five pillars of acacia (Exod 26:37; 36:37–38).

Besides the ark, the table, and the tabernacle, the LORD also instructs Moses to use acacia wood to make two altars from the items he collected from the Israelites (Exod 35:7, 24). The altar upon which sacrifice or burnt offering is offered is made of acacia wood (Exod 27:1; 38:1) along with the poles used to carry it (Exod 27:6; 38:6). Likewise, the altar on which to offer incense is made of acacia wood (Exod 30:1; 37:25), as well as the poles used to carry it (Exod 30:5; 37:28).

Besides being used to make the ark, the table, the tabernacle, the altar of burnt offering, and the altar of incense, the acacia tree also represents the burning bush. According to Taylor, "the burning bush was an acacia."[1] He adds, "The bush was on fire but was not destroyed, and therefore, acacia bushes also represent the immortality of the soul."[2] However, the more likely association of the acacia with the burning bush is the fact that the burning bush represents the divine presence to Moses, and so the acacia tree wood was chosen for the items both needed to represent the divine presence—the ark and the tabernacle—and the items used to minister to the divine presence—the table, the altar of sacrifice, and the altar of incense.

The acacia tree is a sign of immortality. According to Tresidder, "The red and white flowers suggest life-death dualism."[3] The Egyptians believed that because of its hardness, durability, resistance to decay, and evergreen nature, the acacia tree was a sign of immorality and innocence. Caldecott narrates the Egyptian myth of "The Two Brothers," one named Anpu, the

---

1. Taylor, *How to Read a Church*, 201.
2. Ibid.
3. Tresidder, *Dictionary of Symbols*, 11.

elder, and Bata, the younger. Bata leaves Anpu to go "live in the land of the acacias."[4] Before he leaves, he tells is brother, "I will house one part of my soul in the top of an acacia tree, and if I die, the beer you drink will go cloudy."[5] Bata leaves, and many years pass. "In the land of the acacias, Bata built a great house for his body, but one part of his soul remained in the topmost flowers of a particularly tall acacia tree."[6] Caldecott notes that "[t]he theme of the soul kept outside the body in an apparently safe place while the body goes on about its everyday business . . . is based on a very strong belief that the body and the soul are two separate entities and that one can survive without the other."[7] She adds, "The ancient Egyptians believed that the person consisted of nine different parts, each capable of separate identity and capable of functioning separately."[8] The acacia tree represents "the stable, beautiful, more ethereal side [of Bata], creating shade and comfort for others, nonthreatening."[9]

The next part of the story resembles the second account of creation in the HB (OT) Book of Genesis, especially the creation of woman (Gen 2:18–25). One day as the Egyptian gods were walking in the acacia grove, they noticed that Bata was alone; so, they created a woman for him. Although he warned her never to go near the river, she went anyway. While standing on the riverbank, the watery god Hapi ripped off a lock of her hair, which floated to where the pharaoh lived. He wanted to know from whom the lock of hair had come. "At last, word came that a woman living in an acacia grove was undoubtedly the owner of the lock."[10] The woman was persuaded to leave "the rough and lonely life of the acacia grove for the rich and luxurious life of the court."[11] In order to keep Bata from finding her, the pharaoh sent soldiers to destroy the tree that housed his soul by cutting it and burning it. Thus, "Bata, in his house a distance away, died as the tree was consumed by the flames."[12]

While drinking beer, Anpu noticed that it was cloudy and remembered what his brother had told him. He found his brother's corpse in the house among the acacia trees after looking for it for three years. The reader

---

4. Caldecott, *Myths*, 52.
5. Ibid.
6. Ibid.
7. Ibid., 56.
8. Ibid., 56.
9. Ibid., 57.
10. Ibid., 53.
11. Ibid.
12. Ibid.

notes that the number three indicates divine intervention is about to occur in a story. And so Anpu "noticed an acacia seed on the ground. He placed it in a cup of water, and almost immediately the body of his brother began to revive."[13] Caldecott notes that "[t]he acacia seed becomes the revived man,"[14] representing rebirth, immortality, and innocence. "Through transformation, through dying to this world, [Bata is] born again."[15]

Before the acacia was associated with immortality, in Egyptian mythology the gods were thought to be born under the acacia tree of Saosis. Functioning as a tree of life, Isis and Osiris, the first couple, emerged from the acacia tree. Likewise, Horus was supposed to have emerged from the branches of the acacia tree. Thus, it signifies both birth and rebirth. The bulk of the Egyptian pantheon was said to have been born beneath the branches of the goddess Saosis's acacia tree north of Heliopolis. And after Osiris was betrayed and murdered, his coffin was thrown into the river; it lodged in the rocks where an acacia tree grew around it, enveloping it completely. This made the acacia tree one in which both life and death is enclosed.

Tresidder notes that "Freemasonry uses an acacia bough as an initiation symbol and funerary tribute."[16] The use of the acacia as an initiation sign flows from it being a sign of immortality. Just as the acacia is perpetually renovated, so is the human renovated when the incorruptible soul is freed from the corruptible body. This is why a sprig of acacia is placed on the grave of a departed loved one or friend. Furthermore, the seemingly incorruptible nature of the hardwood adds to its representation of the incorruptible nature of the soul. In Greek, the word for acacia signifies innocence and purity of life; in fact, the name *Acacia*, often given to girls, means *guileless* and *honorable*. Because initiation of any kind represents new life, the acacia is a Freemasonry sign of initiation both into the organization and into immortality through mortality.

Tresidder also notes that "by tradition, acacia spines formed Christ's crown of thorns."[17] In the gospels, the Roman soldiers twist some thorns into a crown and place it on Jesus' head before they crucify him (Mark 15:17; Matt 27:29; John 19:2, 5); however, the gospels do not specify the source of the thorns. This legend links the thorns of the acacia tree, itself a sign of immortality, innocence, and initiation, to Jesus, who dies innocently (Luke 23:4, 14–15, 22, 41, 47) on the cross, and is initiated simultaneously

---

13. Ibid., 54.
14. Ibid. 59.
15. Ibid., 56.
16. Tresidder, *Dictionary of Symbols*, 11.
17. Ibid.

into immortal or resurrected life (Matt 27:52–53). This legend also ties into the prophet Isaiah's statement about the messianic restoration of the land. The LORD declares that he will put the acacia in the wilderness (Isa 41:19). Through his death and resurrection, Christ not only restores eternal life to people, but he also restores life to the land, signified by the acacia tree and the crown of thorns he wore woven from it.

Thus, because sacred objects were made from the hardwood of the acacia tree—the ark, the table, the tabernacle, the altar of burnt offerings, the altar of incense, and the poles needed to carry all of them—it became a very sacred tree. Furthermore, because the ark represented God's presence, it did not take long before the burning bush of the LORD's revelation to Moses became an acacia tree. With such association, the acacia tree came to represent immorality in the Israelite world. Similarly in the Egyptian world, gods and goddesses emerged from the acacia tree or were born innocently under it. Freemasonry brings together all these signs, declaring that the acacia represents immortality, innocence, and initiation. A sprig is employed for funerals, representing the immortality of the soul, the new innocence of the deceased, and his or her initiation into new life on the other side of death. The legend of Jesus' crown of thorns being made from an acacia tree Christianizes the sacred tree's sign of immortality, innocence, and initiation.

Journal/Meditation: What tree best represents immorality, innocence, and initiation for you? What tree do you consider to be the most sacred? Why?

Prayer: As a sign of your presence, O LORD, you instructed your servant Moses to make an ark of acacia wood along with a table, a tabernacle, and altars of burnt offering and incense to honor you living among the Israelites. Through the beauty of the trees around me, give me a greater awareness of your presence in my life. I ask this in the name of Jesus Christ, your Son, who lives and reigns with you and the Holy Spirit, one God, forever and ever. Amen.

Almond

Text: "The word of the LORD came to me, [Jeremiah,] saying, 'Jeremiah, what do you see?' And I said, 'I see a branch of an almond tree.' Then the LORD said to me, 'You have seen well, for I am watching over my word to perform it.'" (Jer 1:11–12)

Reflection: According to the notes on Jeremiah 1:11–12 in *The Access Bible*, the Hebrew word for almond tree, *shaqed*, is similar to the word for watch, *shoqed*. What God says through the prophet Jeremiah will happen. However, McKenzie states that the word in Hebrew is *saked* and means *waker* because "the name comes from the early blossoming of the tree in late January or early February."[1] When Jeremiah sees the almond branch in blossom, he concludes that God is awake, *soked*.[2] The white-with-a-tinge-of-pink flowers of the almond tree, thus, indicate that God is awake, watching, and ready to execute his word through the prophet Jeremiah. Thus, the almond becomes a sign of wakefulness and watchfulness.

In the HB (OT) Book of Genesis, Jacob uses almond rods in his primitive genetic engineering of sheep and goats. After taking the "fresh rods of . . . almond" and peeling "white streaks in them, exposing the white of the rods" (Gen 30:37), Jacob places the almond rods in front of the watering places where the sheep and goats come to drink and breed. Seeing the streaked rods, "the flocks produced young that were striped, speckled, and spotted" (Gen 30:39). Jacob's assumption is that whatever the sheep and goats see when they are breeding would determine whether their offspring would be a solid or a spotted color. Since Laban, Jacob's future father-in-law,

---

1. McKenzie, *Dictionary*, 21.
2. Ibid.

had promised to give Jacob all the sheep and goats that were spotted or black (Gen. 30:32–33), through his primitive genetic engineering, Jacob grew exceedingly rich (Gen 30:43) because of almond rods. Thus, the almond rod is a sign of fertility.

When Jacob's (Israel's) sons make their second trip to Egypt to purchase grain during the famine, they bring almonds with them, among other things, as a present for Joseph (Gen. 43:11). According to McKenzie, "the almond . . . was . . . esteemed as a delicacy in the Near East . . . ."[3] This helps to understand why in the HB (OT) Book of Exodus the almond blossom serves as the model for the lampstand placed in the tabernacle. The pure gold menorah was made with three branches attached to each side of a central shaft. On the top of each of the six branches were "cups shaped like almond blossoms, each with calyx and petals" (Exod 25:33; cf. 37:19). Furthermore, "On the lampstand itself there [were] four cups shaped like almond blossoms, each with its calyxes and petals" (Exod 25:34; cf. 37:20). In the evening on each tip of the lampstand fresh oil lamps were placed to burn throughout the night, thus keeping watch with God in the tabernacle. Clifford writes, "The lampstand seems to have symbolized the fertility that comes from God; it may even represent a sacred tree, a common motif of ancient Near Eastern art."[4]

Both of Clifford's insights come to bear in the HB (OT) Book of Numbers's description of the staff of Aaron for the house of Levi having sprouted buds, produced blossoms, and bore ripe almonds (Num 17:8). Not only do the almond blossoms and nuts vindicate the priesthood of Aaron, they also represent the future ministry of the Levite priesthood. According to Taylor, the almond tree is a sign of divine favor.[5] Furthermore, Aaron's staff is a sacred pole or staff (world tree) connecting the world above, where God lives, to the world below, where people live. It is God who makes Aaron's staff blossom and produce almonds (Num 17:1–11).

The last mention of the almond is found the last chapter of the HB (OT) Book of Ecclesiastes. Eight verses of images are strung together as a reflection on aging and death (Eccl 12:1–8). Among the many images is the blossoming of the almond tree (Eccl 12:5). Because "the almond blooming is the last event of winter and is white,"[6] it may represent the gray hair of aging. It may be used also as the opposite of its fertility understanding; as a person's life is coming to an end, he or she should be wakeful and watchful for death.

3. McKenzie, *Dictionary*, 21.
4. Clifford, "Exodus," 57.
5. Taylor, *How to Read a Church*, 201.
6. Wright, "Ecclesiastes," 495.

Thus, the almond tree signifies wakefulness, watchfulness, and fertility. Almonds were a delicacy for ancient people; so, the almond tree was considered sacred. The lampstand for the tabernacle was shaped in the form of a blossoming almond tree not only to signify wakefulness and watchfulness, but to represent the fertility that comes from God when a tree or staff connects the world above to the world below.

Journal/Meditation: What aspect of the sacred almond tree catches your attention the most: watchfulness, wakefulness, fertility, world tree, or aging? Why?

Prayer: Just as the almond tree is the last event of winter, O LORD, keep me watchful and wakeful that I may recognize your presence in the daily events of my life. Make me blossom with good works through the inspiration of the Holy Spirit. I ask this through Christ, my Lord. Amen.

Apple

Text: "A peasant had an apple tree growing in his garden, which bore no fruit, but merely served to provide a shelter from the heat for the sparrows and grasshoppers which sat and chirped in its branches. Disappointed at its barrenness he determined to cut it down, and went and fetched his ax for the purpose. But when the sparrows and the grasshoppers saw what he was about to do, they begged him to spare it, and said to him, 'If you destroy the tree, we shall have to seek shelter elsewhere, and you will no longer have our merry chirping to enliven your work in the garden.' He, however, refused to listen to them, and set to work with a will to cut through the trunk. A few strokes showed that it was hollow inside and contained a swarm of bees and a large store of honey. Delighted with his find he threw down his ax, saying, 'The old tree is worth keeping after all.'"[1]

Reflection: Appended to "The Peasant and the Apple Tree" fable above is this moral: "Utility is most men's test of worth."[2] In other words, once the peasant discovers that his non-bearing apple tree is producing honey, he decides to keep it because it is valuable after all. Caldecott puts the same idea this way: "Enlightenment is not always achieved by the direct approach; it is more likely to come upon us from the direction least expected."[3] She adds: "It is not surprising the apple tree has . . . significance in myth and legend. It is beautiful with blossoms in spring, like a young bride entering into her most fertile and reproductive phase. Its fruit is delicious and sustaining."[4]

1. Aesop, 58.
2. Ibid.
3. Caldecott, *Myths*, 100.
4. Ibid., 101.

The apple, a deciduous tree, has been grown for thousands of years and, as Caldecott points out, has religious and mythological significance. Its Latin name, *malum domestica*, has given rise to its placement in the Garden of Eden in popular presupposition. However, it does not appear in that story (Gen 3:1–13). The association of the apple tree with the myth in the HB (OT) Book of Genesis is due to the apple's Latin name; *malum* is also the word for *evil*. Since the woman and the man engage in evil by eating the forbidden evil fruit, many depictions of the deed feature an apple tree bearing red fruit! Thus, the apple tree became a sign of knowledge, immortality, temptation, and the fall of man and woman into sin, not to mention sexual seduction. It was not long thereafter that Jesus Christ is portrayed holding an apple to represent that unlike the first Adam who brought death, the second Adam brings life (Rom 5:12–21; 1 Cor 15:45). Sill notes that when an apple is depicted as being near or "held by Mary or the Christ Child, the apple signifies acceptance of man's sins and salvation."[5] She adds, "Mary is looked on as the second Eve and Christ as the second Adam: Christ and Mary take away the original sin of the first Adam and Eve and restore to man [and woman] the promise of eternal life."[6]

There are over 7,500 known varieties of apple trees, which grow from six to fifteen feet tall; today the height depends on the trimming method employed. The leaves are dark green ovals with serrated margins and slightly downy undersides. The blossoms, which appear in early spring, are white with a pink tinge, and the fruit matures in late summer or early fall, depending on the variety. Thus, the fruit is ripe when it turns red, yellow, green, pink, or russet, or it may be ripe when two or more colors appear. In most depictions, apples are usually red, and the flesh is usually white or very pale yellow.

The apple tree's sensuality is best illustrated in the HB (OT) Song of Songs. In the poem, the woman declares: "As an apple tree among the trees of the wood, so is my beloved among young men. With great delight I sat in his shadow, and his fruit was sweet to my taste" (Song 2:3). The erotic imagery continues, as the woman tells her lover to refresh her with apples because she is faint with love (Song 2:5). Later in the poem, the man expresses his desire to touch the woman, who is delectable as fruit. He tells her that the scent of her breath is like apples (Song 7:8b), and she tells him, "Under the apple tree I awakened you" (Song 8:5b). The poem's use of the apple tree echoes the supposed apple tree in the Book of Genesis as a place for satisfying sexual desires. Tresidder confirms this, writing, "The apple was widely used as a

---

5. Sill, *Symbols in Christian Art*, 54.
6. Ibid.

symbol for love, marriage, springtime, youth, fertility, longevity, and sexual happiness—and therefore suggested temptation in Christian tradition."[7] He adds, "Its fertility and sexually-related symbolism is perhaps linked with the seeds within the vulva-shaped (in long section) core."[8]

In Norse mythology, the goddess Idunn possesses "precious apples of eternal youth."[9] The trickster Loki, taken captive by a giant, who wants Idunn and her apples, has no choice but to conceive a plan to put the goddess in the giant's hands. ". . . [H]e told Idunn that she must come and see some apples in the forest which she was bound to think were precious."[10] Once in the forest, the giant swooped down on her in the form of an eagle and took her to his home. The rest of the gods were immediately affected because they lost the youth-giving fruit. After discovering that Idunn was last seen with Loki, the gods threatened him with death "if he did not recover [Idunn] and her apples."[11] Loki did, and managed to save his life. Caldecott comments on this myth, stating, "the Norse goddess of spring who gave the gods the apples of youth has to spend some time each year in the storm-giants dark mansion."[12] This is how the Norse explained the difference between winter and summer.

Not to be forgotten is one of Herakles (Hercules) labors, namely, "getting the golden apples of the Hesperides."[13] According to Bulfinch, this was "the most difficult labor of all."[14] Bulfinch explains, "These were the apples which Juno had received at her wedding from the goddess of the earth, and which she had entrusted to the keep of the daughters of Hesperus."[15] Caldecott adds, "At the marriage of Zeus [Jupiter] and Hera [Juno], the mighty earth goddess, Gaia, had given them a gift of a tree that bore golden apples."[16] This tree was precious to Hera, who planted it beyond the reach of mortals; it "was cherished and guarded by the three beautiful daughters of Atlas and Hesperus, the Hesperides."[17] Because the location of the garden was secret,

---

7. Tresidder, *Dictionary of Symbols*, 42–3.
8. Ibid., 43.
9. Littleton, *Mythology*, 308.
10. Ibid.
11. Ibid.
12. Caldecott, *Myths*, 86.
13. Bulfinch, *Mythology*, 145.
14. Ibid.
15. Ibid.
16. Caldecott, *Myths*, 96.
17. Ibid.

Herakles had first to find it. This required a long journey to where the apples grew on an island. Caldecott narrates:

> On this island were flowers that never died and trees that never withered. In the center was the tree he had come so far to seek, and dancing in the meadow around it were the beautiful daughters of Hesperus. They laughed when he asked for some apples to take to his master Eurystheus and said that the apples were not in their power to give, for Hera had put a guardian on them that even they could not defeat.[18]

After defeating the giant serpent that guarded the apple tree, Herakles "snatched the golden apples and made all speed back to Eurystheus."[19] The reader cannot help but notice the parallel structure between this myth and the talking serpent in the Garden of Eden. Caldecott notes that "the garden of the Hesperides represents that mythical land, that garden of Eden, that new Jerusalem, that shining, timeless realm in which mortals believe they will find their higher selves."[20] Tresidder refers to the fruit as "the golden apples of immortality."[21]

Herakles makes haste with the three golden apples to Eurystheus, who looks at the apples but never touches them. "[T]hey can be held only by the one who has sought them out and won against all odds to achieve them," states Caldecott.[22] Herakles lays the golden apples at the feet of Athene (Minerva), who had championed Herakles on several occasions. "Athene then returns them to the garden, for there—and only there—they must be."[23] What is important is not that Herakles possesses them, but that he has completed the quest to get them. The apples represent immortality.

In another version of this myth, Atlas, the father of the Hesperides, was sent by Herakles to seek the apples. He found them and brought them to Herakles, who gave them to Eurystheus, who had commanded Herakles to "bring him three golden apples from the garden of the Hesperides."[24] The reader will note that in all the stories there are three apples signifying some type of divine intervention.

In another myth about a golden apple, Eris (Ate), the goddess of discord, was not invited to the marriage of Peleus and Thetis, even thought all

18. Ibid., 98.
19. Ibid.
20. Ibid., 100.
21. Tresidder, *Dictionary of Symbols*, 43.
22. Caldecott, *Myths*, 99.
23. Ibid.
24. Ibid., 96.

the other gods were. "Enraged at her exclusion, the goddess threw a golden apple among the guests, with the inscription, 'for the fairest.' Thereupon [Hera] Juno, [Aphrodite] Venus, and [Athene] Minerva each claimed the apple."[25] Jupiter delegated Paris, the Trojan prince, to make a decision. "Paris decided in favor of Venus, and gave her the golden apple, thus making the two other goddesses his enemies."[26] According to Littleton, the Trojan War "started because the gods found a golden apple that was said to belong to the most beautiful goddess of all."[27]

There is the myth of Atalata, a virgin huntress, who "would marry only a man who could beat her in running [a race], and the penalty for failure was death."[28] A certain Milanion, according to Cavendish,[29] or Hippomenes, according to Bulfinch,[30] decided to race Atalata.

> ... Hippomenes addressed a prayer to [Aphrodite] Venus: "Help me, Venus, for you have led me on." Venus heard and was propitious. In the garden of her temple, in her own island of Cyprus, is a tree with yellow leaves and yellow branches and golden fruit. Hence she gathered three golden apples, and, unseen by anyone else, gave them to Hippomenes, and told him how to use them.[31]

Just when his breath was about to fail him during the race, he threw down one of the golden apples. While Atalata stopped to pick it up, Hippomenes shot ahead. When she got close, he tossed another golden apple, and Atalata stopped to gather it. Then, he threw the third apple. Atalata looked at it and hesitated, but picked it up just as Hippomenes passed her and won the race.[32] Milanion or Hippomenes won the footrace with the virgin huntress because of three golden apples.

Another tale featuring golden apples is that of King Atlas, whose "chief pride was in his gardens, whose fruit was of gold, hanging from golden branches, half hid with golden leaves."[33] When Perseus came to visit the king, claiming Jove (Jupiter) as his father, Atlas remembered "that an ancient prophecy had warned him that a son of Jove should one day rob him of his golden

---

25. Bulfinch, *Mythology*, 211.
26. Ibid., 211–12; cf. Herzberg, *Myths*, 187.
27. Littleton, *Mythology*, 169.
28. Cavendish, *Legends*, 163.
29. Ibid.
30. Bulfinch, *Mythology*, 141.
31. Ibid., 142.
32. Ibid.
33. Ibid., 117.

apples."³⁴ Likewise, there is King Midas, who asked Bacchus "that whatever he might touch should be changed into gold."³⁵ After changing an oak twig, a stone, and sod into gold, "He took an apple from the tree; you would have thought he had robbed the garden of the Hesperides."³⁶ Obviously an emblem of fruitfulness and a sign of immortality, druids's wands were often made of apple wood. Maybe the HB (OT) Book of Proverbs captures it best: "A word fitly spoken is like apples of gold in a setting of silver" (Prov 25:11).

"The Golden Bird," one of Grimm's fairy tales, begins by describing a king "who had at the back of his castle a beautiful pleasure garden, in which stood a tree that bore golden apples."³⁷ The tale continues, "As the apples ripened they were counted, but one morning one was missing."³⁸ In two successive nights, another apple goes missing each evening until the traditional number of three apples cannot be accounted for. One by one the three sons of the king are sent to spend the night in the garden in an attempt to see who is taking the apples, but the two oldest fell asleep. Only the youngest discovers that it is a golden bird that is stealing the apples. With a fox as his guide, the youngest son finds a castle with the golden bird and the missing three golden apples. The lengthy tale continues with domino-like quests one built upon another, but the golden apples are not mentioned again.

Golden apples are mentioned in "One Eye, Two Eyes, and Three Eyes," a tale about a woman who has three daughters. One daughter has one eye; one daughter has two eyes; and one daughter has three eyes. It is the daughter with two eyes who, while tending the goat, receives a bit of wisdom from another woman. Once the goat is slaughtered for food, the wise woman tells Two Eyes to bury its entrails. The next morning "a strangely magnificent tree with leaves of silver, and fruit of gold hanging among them," appears.³⁹

Neither One Eye nor Three Eyes is able "to get hold of one of the golden apples."⁴⁰ However Two Eyes "climbed up and the golden apples did not get out of her way, but came into her hand of their own accord, so that she could pluck them one after the other, and she brought a whole apron full down with her."⁴¹ As in all good fairy tales, a prince appears and asks for a branch from the golden apple tree, but the two odd-eyed sisters are not

---

34. Ibid., 118.
35. Ibid., 46.
36. Ibid.
37. Grimm, 493.
38. Ibid.
39. Ibid., 180.
40. Ibid., 181.
41. Ibid.

able to break off one and give it to the prince. However, Two Eyes rolls out "a couple of golden apples from under the barrel to the feet of the knight."[42] When he saw the apples, he was astonished and asked about their origin. Two Eyes explained; then she climbed into the tree "and with the greatest ease broke off a branch with beautiful silver leaves and golden fruit and gave it to the knight."[43] The knight took Two Eyes with him and married her.

A famous American myth features John Chapman (1774–1845), better known as Johnny Appleseed. According to Cavendish, he is the "unofficial patron saint of the apple orchards."[44] Furthermore, "In American folk tradition he has become a type of St. Francis [of Assisi], or the Voice in the Wilderness . . . ."[45] According to Peck, Appleseed began his mission of planting apple seeds after his fiancée died unexpectedly. "[Appleseed's] grief unbalanced his mind, and in his delirium he thought he was called by the Lord as a harbinger of peace to the west and that his special mission was to plant apple seed along the way, that those who followed might reap the benefit of his sowing."[46] Carola states that Chapman died while sleeping in an apple orchard near Fort Wayne, Indiana, at the age of seventy-one. "He was a pioneer nurseryman who provided apple tree seedlings for early settlers in the Midwest," states Carola. "He collected unwanted apple seeds from Pennsylvania mills that processed apples to make cider. Then he dried the seeds and gave them to pioneers who were heading west."[47]

According to Haley, "The first reliable trace of our modest hero finds him in the territory of Ohio, in 1801, with a horse-load of apple seeds, which he planted in various places on and about the borders of Licking Creek . . . in what is now Licking County in the State of Ohio."[48] According to Peck, "In 1806 he planted sixteen bushels of seed on an old farm on the Walhonding River, he planted in . . . Richland Country, and had other nurseries further west."[49] Haley continues:

> [Chapman] would shoulder his bag of apple seeds and with bare feet, penetrate to some remote spot that combined picturesqueness and fertility of soil, and there he would plant his seeds, place a slight enclosure around the place, and leave them to

---

42. Ibid.
43. Ibid., 182.
44. Cavendish, *Legends*, 334.
45. Ibid., 335.
46. Peck, *North American Folktales*, 108.
47. Carola, "Johnny Appleseed," 213.
48. Haley, "Johnny Appleseed," 215.
49. Peck, *North American Folktales*, 104–5.

grow until the trees were large enough to be transplanted by the settlers, who, in the mean time, would have made their clearings in the vicinity.[50]

Cavendish describes Chapman as "a bearded, kindly hermit, barefoot, with a tin pot on his head and a coffee sack on his back."[51] Haley notes that

> his enthusiasm for the cultivation of apple trees in what he termed "the only proper way"—that is, from seed—was the absorbing object of his life. . . . He would describe the growing and ripening fruit as such a rare and beautiful gift of the Almighty with words that became pictures, until his hearers could almost see its manifold forms of beauty present before them. . . . But he denounced as absolute wickedness all devices of pruning and grafting, and would speak of the act of cutting a tree as if it were a cruelty inflicted upon a sentient being.[52]

Closely associated with Johnny Appleseed, according to Cavendish, is "Mountain Mary (Die Berg Maria), who grafted Good Mary apples." Cavendish notes that she "was a more genuinely saintly character."[53] Maria Jung was a German anchorite, who lived in Oley Hills, Pennsylvania, and died in 1819.

In biblical literature the apple is "used figuratively to show how precious [people] are to God, and how extremely sensitive God is to [their] needs."[54] The phrase, "apple of his eye," first appears in the HB (OT) Book of Deuteronomy. Moses recites the words of a song to the whole assembly of Israel in which he reminds the Israelites of how the LORD guarded them as the apple of his eye (Deut 32:10b). In another song, the psalmist echoes these words as he sings to God: "Guard me as the apple of the eye" (Ps 17:8). The teacher in the Book of Proverbs urges his students, "Keep [the] commandments and live, keep [his] teachings as the apple of [their] eye" (Prov 7:2). The prophet Zechariah reminds the Jews in Babylonian exile that the LORD has declared that whoever touches them touches the apple of his eye (Zech 2:8). In the wisdom Book of Sirach in the OT (A), the author reminds his readers that the Lord "will keep a person's kindness like the apple of his eye" (Sir 17:22b).

A withered apple tree represents profound loss. The prophet Joel states that the apple tree, among others, has dried, and people's joy has withered away (Joel 1:12). Such loss is also found in the Grimm fairy tale known as

---

50. Haley, "Johnny Appleseed," 216.
51. Cavenish, *Legends*, 334–5.
52. Haley, "Johnny Appleseed," 218–9.
53. Cavenish, *Legends*, 335.
54. Murphey, *Dictionary of Biblical Literacy*, 30.

"Snow White and the Seven Dwarfs." In her unsuccessful attempts to get rid of her stepdaughter, Snow White's stepmother goes "to a secret lonely chamber, where no one was likely to come, and there she [makes] a poisonous apple."[55] The tale continues: "It was beautiful to look upon, being white with red cheeks, so that anyone who should see it must long for it, but whoever ate even a little bit of it must die."[56] Tatar notes that "the physical description of the apple coincides with the description of Snow White" earlier in the story.[57] Once the apple is ready, the stepmother brings it to Snow White, who lives with the dwarfs. The dwarfs have warned her not to open the door and let anyone in. Her stepmother disguised as a peasant woman selling apples offers one to Snow White through the window, but Snow White refuses. The stepmother says, ". . . [L]ook here, I will cut the apple in two pieces; you shall have the red side, I will have the white one."[58] The narrator states: "For the apple was so cunningly made, that all the poison was in the rosy half of it. Snow White longed for the beautiful apple, and as she saw the peasant woman eating a piece of it, she could no longer refrain, but stretched out her hand and took the poisoned half. But no sooner had she taken a morsel of it into her mouth than she fell to the earth as dead."[59] The dwarfs return home and find Snow White dead. So, they put her in a glass coffin and put the coffin on a mountain. One day a king's son finds the coffin and gets permission from the dwarfs to take it. As the son's servants are carrying it away, they stumble "and with the shaking the bit of poisoned apple [flies] out of [Snow White's] throat."[60] Snow White is revived. The king's son marries Snow White, and they live happily ever after. The trickster stepmother ends up tricked by the king's son.

There is also "The Juniper Tree" tale about a rich man and his childless wife; this tale also features the loss occasioned by an apple. After praying one winter's day, the wife stood beneath a juniper tree in the courtyard in front of their home and, while paring an apple, cut her finger, and the blood fell upon the snow. Seeing the blood upon the snow, she prayed for a child as red as blood and as white as snow. Nine months later, she bore a son and died. Her husband buried her under the juniper tree. Then, he remarried; his second wife bore him a daughter, named Marjory.[61]

55. Grimm, 335.
56. Ibid.
57. Tatar, *Classic Fairy Tales*, 90.
58. Grimm, 335.
59. Ibid.
60. Ibid., 336.
61. Ibid., 268–9.

The tale continues:

> Once, when the wife went into the room upstairs, her little daughter followed her, and said, "Mother, give me an apple." "Yes, my child," said the mother, and gave her a fine apple out of the chest, and the chest had a great heavy lid with a strong iron lock. "Mother," said the little girl, "shall not my brother have one too?" That was what the mother expected; and she said, "Yes, when he comes back from school." And when she saw from the window that he was coming, an evil thought crossed her mind, and she snatched the apple, and took it from her little daughter, saying, "You shall not have it before your brother." Then she threw the apple into the chest, and shut the lid.[62]
>
> Then the little boy came in at the door, and she said to him in a kind tone, but with evil looks, "My son, will you have an apple?" Then she spoke kindly as before, holding up the cover of the chest, "Come here and take out one for yourself." And as the boy was stooping over the open chest, crash went the lid down, so that his head flew off among the red apples. . . . She . . . took a white handkerchief out of the nearest drawer, and fitting the head to the neck, she bound them with a handkerchief, so that nothing should be seen, and set him on a chair before the door with the apple in his hand. . . . Marjory . . . said, "Brother, give me the apple." But as he took no notice, she gave him a box on the ear, and his head fell off, at which she was greatly terrified, and began to cry and scream, and ran to her mother, and said, "Oh mother! I have knocked my brother's head off!" and cried and screamed, and would not cease. "Oh Marjory!" said her mother, "what have you done? But keep quiet, that no one may see there is anything the matter; it can't be helped now; we will put him out of the way safely."[63]

The mother took the dead boy, cut him in pieces, and cooked him for dinner. When his father came home, he asked where his son was. His wife explained that his son had gone to visit his great uncle for a while. Meanwhile, unknowingly, the father ate his son, throwing the bones under the table. After the meal, Marjory gathered the bones into a handkerchief and placed them on the grass under the juniper tree.

> Then the juniper tree began to wave to and fro, and the boughs drew together and then parted, just like a clapping of hands for

---

62. Ibid., 269–70.
63. Ibid., 270.

joy; then a cloud rose from the tree, and in the midst of the cloud there burned a fire, and out of the fire a beautiful bird arose, and, singing most sweetly, soared high into the air; and when he had flown away, the juniper tree remained as it was before, but the handkerchief full of bones was gone.[64]

The bird flies to the goldsmith's house, where it got a gold chain, and then the shoemaker's house, where it got a pair of red shoes, and, finally, the mill, where it got a millstone. At each stop, the bird sings: "It was my mother who murdered me; / It was my father who ate of me; / It was my sister Marjory / Who all my bones in pieces found; / Them in a handkerchief she bound, / And laid them under the juniper tree. / Kywitt, kywitt, kywitt, I cry, / Oh what a beautiful bird am I."[65]

After finishing the song, he spread his wings and flew to his father's house. He carried the chain in one claw, the red shoes in the other, and the millstone around his neck. While his father, his father's wife, and Marjory were sitting in the parlor, he flew to the juniper tree and perched there. Then, he sang the song again. The father went outside to see the bird, and he gave him the golden chain. After Marjory went outside the bird gave her the pair of red shoes. And when his father's second wife went outside, the bird dropped the millstone on her head (cf. Matt 18:5–6). Then the three survivors—the bird turned back into the man's son, the father, and Marjory—went into the house to eat dinner.[66]

The reader must keep in mind that all this occurred because the boy's mother had paired an apple under the juniper tree. Tatar notes that the apple peeled by the man's first wife "reappears as the object of desire that leads to the boy's death."[67] This tale resembles the episode in the Snow White tale when the stepmother gives the poisoned apple to Snow.[68] Tatar also notes:

> The stepmother's serving up of the boy in a stew is reminiscent of the Greek myth in which Atreus prepares a banquet for his enemy Thyestes, who unknowingly feasts on his own sons. Her deed is also reminiscent of dismemberment scenes in other fairy tales.... The powerful resurrection scene at the end forges a connection with the dismemberment of the Egyptian god

---

64. Ibid., 271.
65. Ibid., 271–74.
66. Ibid., 275–76.
67. Tatar, *Classic Fairy Tales*, 160.
68. Ibid.

Osiris as well as the Greek poet Orpheus, who is torn to pieces by the maenads.[69]

Apples play a role in a variety of folk tales. For example, the larynx in the human throat is called the Adam's apple because of the myth that the bulge was caused by the forbidden fruit sticking in the throat of Adam. There is a tale about Conle, who receives an apple which feeds him for a year, in Celtic mythology. Swiss folklore narrates that William Tell shot an apple off of his son's head with his crossbow.[70] Irish folklore holds that an apple peeled in one continuous ribbon and tossed behind a woman's shoulder will reveal her future husband's initials. And of course, Isaac Newton witnessed an apple fall from a tree and was inspired to conclude that gravitation attracted the moon to the earth and kept it from flying off into space.

Various phrases also refer to the apple. For example, New York City is called the big apple. "Avalon is the Isle of the Blessed of the Celts. It is the Isle of Apples, a name reminding one of the Garden of the Hesperides's . . . with its tree of golden apples . . . ."[71] When one compares apples to oranges, he or she is focused on the differences that exist between two ideas or things. And everyone has heard the English proverb's wise advice: An apple a day keeps the doctor away.

Thus, the apple tree has both religious and mythological significance. It serves as a sign of knowledge, immortality, temptation, sin, and sexual seduction. While there are many varieties of apple trees and colors of fruit, the red apple is used most often because of its association with passion and sensuality. Apples also represent eternal youth, while golden apples represent immortality. Being precious to gods and goddesses, they signify beauty and wealth. In fairy tales and folklore, apples represent the quest for truth and innocence. They are considered a gift of God, who considers each person to be the apple of his eye. A withered apple tree is a sign of profound loss, as is a poisoned apple. With such a starring role is so many stories, the apple is indeed a sacred tree.

---

69. Ibid., 163.
70. Baring-Gould, *Curious Myths*, 51–52.
71. Ibid., 137.

Journal/Meditation: When you see or picture a red apple, with what do you associate it? Does the apple represent knowledge, immortality, temptation, sensuality, beauty, fertility, quest, or loss? How is this sign a truth in your life?

Prayer: As the apple of your eye, LORD God, keep me safe. Give me the strength of your Holy Spirit so that I may accomplish the work entrusted to me. Let me learn from the example of your Son, Jesus Christ, who lives and reigns with you and the Holy Spirit, one God, forever and ever. Amen.

Ash

Text: "A woodman went into the forest and begged of the trees the favor of a handle for his ax. The principal trees at once agreed to so modest a request, and unhesitatingly gave him a young ash sapling, out of which he fashioned the handle he desired. No sooner had he done so than he set to work to fell the noblest trees in the wood. When they saw the use to which he was putting their gift, they cried, 'Alas! Alas! We are undone, but we are ourselves to blame. The little we gave has cost us all; had we not sacrificed the rights of the ash, we might ourselves have stood for ages.'"[1]

Reflection: In Aesop's "The Trees and the Ax," the trees sacrifice the ash tree without thinking that the woodman may use the handle he makes from the ash for his ax and use the ax to cut down the noblest trees. In other words, those who do the sacrificing have not thought far enough ahead to consider that the one they sacrificed may be the cause of their own sacrifice!

    The ash tree, which signifies peace of mind, sacrifice, sensitivity, and higher awareness, features prominently in Norse mythology. According to Herzberg: "In the midst of the world stood a gigantic tree, Yggdrasil, at the foot of which the gods held their assemblies. It was an ash, the largest and best of trees; its branches spread over the whole world and rose high into the heavens."[2] As already noted in the introduction, Yggdrasil is a universal, world, or cosmic tree uniting the three stories—heaven, earth, and underworld—of the universe. Bulfinch narrates that after the three Norse god-brothers Odin, Vili, and Ve slew the frost giant, Ymir, Yggdrasil "sprang

---

1. Aesop, 148.
2. Herzberg, *Myths*, 264.

from the body of Ymir."[3] Out of Ymir's hair the three god-brothers created all the trees,[4] the most important being the ash from which they created a man, named Ask(e);[5] they gave him breath, life, consciousness, movement, a face, speech, hearing, and sight. Thus, the ash tree signifies peace of mind, sensitivity, and higher awareness.

The sensitivity represented by the ash tree is found in British, Celtic, and Scottish fairy lore. The ash tree is one of the three primary magical woods, along with oak and thorn, both of which are treated below. People often refused to cut sacred ash trees, even when wood was scarce, for fear of having their homes consumed in flame. Ash pods were used in divination, and ash wood had the power to ward off fairies. The sap of the tree was often used as medicine.

The ash tree represents sacrifice, but the person making the sacrifice needs to consider the cost of the offering; otherwise, like Aesop's fable, he or she may discover that the price is more than originally determined. The ash tree signifies the peace of mind, sensitivity, and higher awareness of people in Norse mythology, because man was created from a sacred ash tree.

Journal/Meditation: What specific aspect of the sacred ash tree catches your attention in the above reflection? What application does that aspect have for your spiritual life?

Prayer: Of all the trees you made, heavenly Father, your people in Northern Europe considered the ash the most sacred. Give me the peace of mind, the sensitivity, and the high awareness with which the ash is associated. I ask this through Christ, my Lord. Amen.

---

3. Bulfinch, *Mythology*, 330.
4. Herzberg, *Myths*, 263.
5. Littleton, *Mythology*, 278; Bulfinch, *Mythology*, 329; Herzberg, *Myths*, 265.

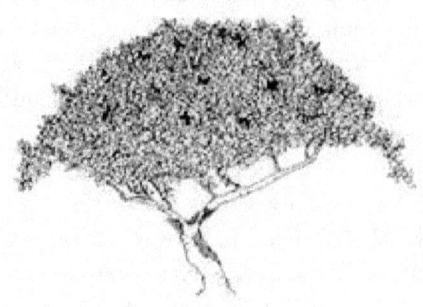

Bramble

Text: "The trees once went out to anoint a king over themselves. So they said to the olive tree, 'Reign over us.' The olive tree answered them, 'Shall I stop producing my rich oil by which gods and mortals are honored, and go to sway over the trees?' Then the trees said to the fig tree, 'You come and reign over us.' But the fig tree answered them, 'Shall I stop producing my sweetness and my delicious fruit, and go to sway over the trees?' Then the trees said to the vine, 'You come and reign over us.' But the vine said to them, 'Shall I stop producing my wine that cheers gods and mortals, and go to sway over the trees?' So all the trees said to the bramble, 'You come and reign over us.' And the bramble said to the trees, 'If in good faith you are anointing me king over you, then come and take refuge in my shade; but if not, let fire come out of the bramble and devour the cedars of Lebanon.'" (Judg 9:8–15)

Reflection: Jotham's fable from the HB (OT) Book of Judges above presents the judge Gideon as a useful plant and kingship as a waste of good plants. The worthless bramble, representing Abimelech, who, like Gideon, is not mentioned in the fable but is clearly intended, is prickly and provides only meager shade; it is even a fire danger! According to O'Connor, "The . . . bramble may claim to offer 'protection' but it hardly affords any real 'shade,' being a ground cover of the sort that propagates forest fires."[1] The irony of the fable emerges as the reader recognizes that it is a prickly shrub (Abimelech, one of Gideon's sons), who wants to be anointed king over the Israelites, when the good trees (Gideon) had refused it. Furthermore, the

---

1. O'Connor, "Judges," 140.

fable itself is being told by Jotham, the youngest of Gideon's sons and Abimelech's brother, who had escaped the murder of all of Gideon's seventy sons by Abimelech! (Judg 9:1–6)

The bramble evokes negativity. This is emphasized by Jesus in his sermon on the plain in Luke's Gospel. Jesus tells his disciples, "Figs are not gathered from thorns, nor are grapes picked from a bramble bush" (Luke 6:45). In other words, bad trees, like thorn trees, do not produce good fruit, like figs. Likewise, bad bushes, like brambles, do not produce good fruit, like grapes. Jesus gives the application of his words, stating, "The good person out of the good measure of the heart produces good, and the evil person out of evil treasure produces evil . . ." (Luke 6:45).

Aesop uses the bramble negatively in four fables. In "The Fir Tree and the Bramble," the fir tree boasts to the bramble, stating, 'You poor creature; you are of no use whatever. . . . I am useful for all sorts of things, particularly when [people] build houses . . . .' The bramble replies, 'Ah, that's all very well, but you wait [u]till they come with axes and saws to cut you down, and then you'll wish you were a bramble and not a fir.' Aesop appends a moral to this fable, writing, "Better poverty without a care than wealth with its many obligations."[2]

In a vein similar to the fable found in the Book of Judges above, "The Pomegranate, the Apple Tree, and the Bramble" illustrates the same message. After the pomegranate and the apple dispute about the quality of their respective fruits and each claims that its own is the better of the two, a bramble breaks up the quarrel when it "impudently pokes its head out of a neighboring hedge and says, "There, that's enough, my friends; don't let us quarrel.""[3]

In "The Bat, the Bramble, and the Seagull," Aesop presents the mythology of the bramble. After the bat, the bramble, and the seagull form a partnership and set off on a trading voyage together, the bramble lays in a stock of clothes. However, a great storm sinks their boat with all the cargo onboard, but the travelers manage to reach land. The mythology of the bramble is stated this way by Aesop: ". . . [T]he bramble catches hold of the clothes of everyone who passes by, hoping some day to recognize and recover the lost garments."[4] Aesop appends a moral to this fable, writing, "All men are more concerned to recover what they lose than to acquire what they lack."[5]

The last of Aesop's fables featuring a bramble is "The Fox and the Bramble." A fox misses his footing and catches at a bramble while making

2. Aesop. 28.
3. Ibid., 83.
4. Ibid., 177.
5. Ibid.

his way through a hedge. "Naturally, he got badly scratched, and in disgust he cried to the bramble, 'It was your help I wanted, and see how you have treated me! I'd sooner have fallen outright.' The bramble replied, 'You must have lost your wits, my friend, to catch at me, who am myself always catching at others.'"[6]

Thus, the bramble carries a negative connotation. Abimelech, the biblical royal usurper, is compared to a bramble by his brother, Jotham. Jesus equates the bramble with what is bad. And Aesop emphasizes the negativity of the bramble, comparing it to poverty and its thorny ability to catch clothes. This negativity makes the bramble a sacred tree to be avoided!

Journal/Meditation: Given the above reflection on the bramble, can you prove from experience that good comes from good and evil comes from evil? Give specific examples. With what tree do you associate negativity?

Prayer: LORD God, through his teaching, your Son, Jesus Christ, made it clear that grapes are not picked from a bramble bush; bad bushes, like brambles, do not produce good fruit, like grape vines. Grant that from the good measure of my heart I may produce good fruit to the glory and praise of your name. Inspire me with the Holy Spirit. I ask this through Christ, my Lord. Amen.

---

6. Ibid., 212.

Broom

Text: "[Elijah] . . . went a day's journey into the wilderness, and came and sat down under a solitary broom tree." (1 Kgs 19:4)

Reflection: The mention of the solitary broom tree in the passage from the HB (OT) Book of First Kings is part of a much longer narrative (1 Kgs 17:1–19:21) which includes Elijah besting the prophets of Baal—the leading male deity in Canaanite fertility religion—on Mount Carmel with a theophany of fire by the LORD. After seeing the LORD consume the bull, the wood, the stones of the altar, the dust, and the water in a trench, Elijah kills the "four hundred prophets of Asherah" (1 Kgs 18:19), that is, the sacred pole or the leading female deity in Canaanite fertility religion.

After killing the pagan prophets, their sponsor, Jezebel, wife of King Ahab of Israel, promises Elijah that she will take his life as soon as she can find him. Thus, Elijah journeys into the wilderness and sits down under a solitary broom tree. The solitary broom tree represents that Elijah is feeling all alone. While under the broom tree, the prophet asks the LORD to take his life. When he finishes his prayer, he lies down under the broom tree and sleeps (1 Kgs 19:5). When he awakens, he experiences another theophany; an angel brings him food and water. After sleeping again and being fed again, Elijah continues his journey to Mount Horeb.

The broom tree, more properly identified as a shrub with a broad canopy, represents shelter. Elijah uses the broom tree to shelter himself from the wilderness sun. It also serves as a hiding place from Queen Jezebel, who is searching for him. Because Elijah is fed by God under the broom three, the shrub signifies renewal. The prophet's vigor is restored; he is given a freshness that enables him to walk for forty days and forty nights (1 Kgs 19:8).

His exhaustion is refreshed with sleep. His depression and readiness to die are given new purpose, as he makes his way to Mount Horeb.

The Book of Job in the HB (OT) mentions the broom tree. In his last and longest speech in the whole book, Job declares that people "warm themselves [with] the roots of broom" (Job 30:4). Psalm 120 confirms that broom tree roots were burned, because it compares a deceitful tongue to "a warrior's sharp arrows, with glowing coals of the broom tree!" (Ps 129:4)

Thus, the solitary broom tree, which sports white flowers with the fragrance of honey, represents the aloneness Elijah is feeling before he makes his forty-day pilgrimage to Mount Horeb and encounters God there. The broom tree is a sign of shelter, for it protects the prophet from the wilderness sun and from Queen Jezebel. Finally, under the sacred broom tree Elijah receives from God food and water which renew him and strengthen him to continue his journey.

Journal/Meditation: When have you felt like a solitary broom tree? Where did you find shelter? Were you renewed? How was God involved in providing you with shelter and renewal?

Prayer: LORD God, you provided your prophet Elijah with shelter under a solitary broom tree and renewed him with food and drink. Shelter me from all that would harm me, and renew me with your grace. I ask this through my Lord Jesus Christ, who lives and reigns with you and the Holy Spirit, one God, forever and ever. Amen.

Burning Bush

Text: "Moses . . . led his flock beyond the wilderness, and came to Horeb, the mountain of God. There the angel of the LORD appeared to him in a flame of fire out of a bush; he looked, and the bush was blazing, yet it was not consumed." (Exod 3:1–2)

Reflection: Because the Israelites are forbidden to construct sacred poles or to plant sacred trees (see Introduction), the story of Moses' encounter with God in the HB (OT) Book of Exodus features a bush. According to Ryken, this theophany "is primarily concerned with God's revelation of himself."[1] The "angel of the LORD" becomes God (Exod 3:6). The LORD's revelation of himself as fire is a frequent biblical image, as seen in the account of God entering into covenant with Abram (Gen 15:17). Ryken states that the "fire is an image of [God's] holiness."[2] He explains: "Fire is often pictured biblically as a purifying and refining instrument of God's holiness."[3] The LORD instructs Moses to remove his sandals because the place upon which he stands is holy ground (Exod 3:5). Fire is also an image of God's glory. ". . .[T]he burning bush is meant to convince Moses of the majesty of God and to stand as a visible reminder in the many dark times ahead," states Ryken.[4]

In addition to being a sign of God's holiness and glory, the fire of the burning bush is also a sign of enlightenment. Not only does God reveal his name to Moses—I AM WHO I AM (Exod 3:14)—but he also enlightens Moses on several important issues. First, God tells Moses that he has observed

---

1. Ryken, *Dictionary*, 130.
2. Ibid.
3. Ibid.
4. Ibid.

the misery of his people in Egypt, and he intends to deliver them from their slavery (Exod 3:7-8). Second, God is sending Moses to Pharaoh to lead the people from Egypt (Exod 3:10-12). And third, because Pharaoh will be reluctant to let the people leave slavery, God will strike the land with his wonders (Exod 3:19-20). Thus, since Moses is considered Israel's greatest prophet, he is like the second founder of Judaism, Abraham being the first.

Schwartz narrates a tale about the Baal Shem Tov who takes three rabbis with him to the forest, where two of them "came to trees that seemed to be shimmering as if they were on fire, yet they were not consumed by the flame."[5] One of the two rabbis remembers the biblical story of Moses and the burning bush and stays behind "trying to discern the mystery of that fire."[6] In another tale narrated by Schwartz, the Baal Shem Tov is again traveling through the forest with several of his disciples who speak to each other about enduring the cold until they reach the place where the Baal Shem Tov wants to pray. "[The Baal Shem Tov] approached a tree that was covered with ice and snow, and he touched it with his finger. And the instant he did, the tree burst into flames and burned with a fire that did not consume."[7] All entered into "fervent prayer, warmed by the fire of that burning tree."[8]

It is important to notice that while the HB (OT) prohibits the use of a sacred tree in the Moses' narrative, there is a type of sacred pole representing God's power and connecting earth to heaven. The sacred tree or pole is Moses' staff; it gives Moses power from God to perform signs (Exod 4:17). The staff, identified as belonging to God (Exod 4:20), becomes a snake and a staff again (Exod 4:3-4; 7:8-13); it turns the water in the Nile River into blood (Exod 7:17, 20); it causes frogs to come up on the land of Egypt (Exod 8:5); it turns dust into gnats (Exod 8:16-17); it brings down hail and fire (Exod 9:23-24); it brings locusts (Exod 10:13); it divides the sea (Exod 14:16); it brings water from rock (Exod 17:5); and it enables Joshua to beat Amalek (Exod 17:8-13). The staff of God is a type of world, universal, or cosmic tree, which serves as a portal for God to work wondrous deeds through Moses on the earth.

The Quran considers the burning bush in Exodus to be a tree as do the two tales about the Baal Shem Tov above. As the story in *The Quran* is narrated, Moses is "journeying with his family [when] he noticed a fire on the side of the mountain" (*Quran* 28:30). He goes to investigate the fire. "When he drew near, a voice called out to him from the tree on the blessed spot on

---

5. Schwartz, *Gabriel's Palace*, 193.
6. Ibid.
7. Ibid., 195.
8. Ibid.

the right side of the valley: 'O Moses, I am verily God, the Lord of all the worlds'" (*Quran* 28:30). Later, in narrating a number of things that he has done that people may believe in him, Allah echoes 28:30, asking, "Who gave you fire from a green tree, with which you ignite the flame"? (*Quran* 36:80)

Muhammad, who received *The Quran* from God through the angel Gabriel, flees from Mecca to Medina in 622 CE. Known as the Hejira (Hegira), it is Muhammad's escape from his enemies. A legend says that on the first night of the journey, the prophet took refuge in a cave, and, after he had entered, "a spider wove its web across the entrance and a pigeon laid its eggs there, while a thorn bush sprang up and concealed the opening."[9] While the thorn bush does not provide any divine revelation, it does, nevertheless, protect Muhammad from his enemies.

Moses' enlightenment near the burning bush is similar to that of the Buddha "beneath a fig tree which has since come to be known popularly as the bo tree (short for bodhi or enlightenment)."[10] While more will be said about the fig tree later, suffice it to be written here that "the Buddha, sensing that he was on the brink of enlightenment, seated himself that epoch-making evening with the vow not to rise until illumination was his."[11] According to Smith's narration,

> the bo tree rained red blossoms—giving it the image of a burning bush—as the Buddha's meditation deepened through watch after watch until, as the morning star glittered in the transparent skies of east, his mind pierced at least the bubble of the universe and shattered it to naught only, wonder of wonders, to find it miraculously restored with the effulgence of true being.[12]

While Moses was sent immediately on his mission, once the Buddha experienced enlightenment under the bo tree, he remained rooted there for forty-nine days.[13]

One of the legends surrounding Gilgamesh, "the fifth king of Uruk,"[14] does not feature a burning bush, a thorn bush, or a tree of enlightenment with red blossoms. It does, however, feature an orchard. Once Gilgamesh's mother gives birth to him, "her guards, fearing the king's rage [because the king was told that his daughter's son would seize the kingdom from him, and so he had her shut in a citadel and closely guarded], threw the baby off

---

9. Cavendish, *Legends*, 119.
10. Smith, *Religions*, 126.
11. Ibid.
12. Ibid., 127.
13. Ibid., 128.
14. Cavendish, *Legends*, 91.

the walls of the citadel, to kill him, but as he fell he was saved by an eagle, which caught him on its back and put him gently down in an orchard."[15] Since an orchard by definition is an area of land on which fruit or nut trees grow, Gilgamesh grows up to become a great, enlightened leader all because "[t]he keeper of the orchard, seeing the child's beauty, loved him and brought him up."[16]

Thus, the burning bush signifies the presence of the Divine's holiness, glory, enlightenment, and being. While it cannot be a tree in the HB (OT), it can in *The Quran*. There it becomes the source of God's gift of fire. As a bush, it also protects the prophet Muhammad during his escape from his enemies. As it rains red blossoms on the Buddha, it not only imitates the image of Moses' burning bush, but it fills the man sitting under it with enlightenment. Thus, the burning bush in its multiple varieties in sacred literatures is a sacred tree.

Journal/Meditation: In what ways can a bush in bloom with red flowers be a burning bush for you representing God's holiness, glory, and enlightenment? What tree is a type of burning bush for you?

Prayer: LORD, to your servant Moses you revealed yourself as I AM WHO I AM. As the cause of all that exists, you have enlightened countless leaders through the ages with insight into the very nature of your being. Enlighten me through the word of your Son, and inspire me with your Holy Spirit. You are one God forever and ever. Amen.

---

15. Ibid.
16. Ibid.

Cross

Text: "... Lord, holy Father, almighty and eternal God, ... you placed the salvation of the human race on the wood of the Cross, so that, where death arose, life might again spring forth and the evil one, who conquered on a tree, might likewise on a tree be conquered, through Christ our Lord."[1]

Reflection: Titled "The victory of the glorious Cross," the Preface for The Exaltation of the Holy Cross on September 14 in *The Roman Missal* compares the tree of the knowledge of good and evil in Eden (see Introduction) to the tree of the cross. Since the HB (OT) Book of Genesis states that the tree of the knowledge of good and evil is the mythological origin of death (Gen 2:17; 3:3, 19), the preface declares that the tree of the cross is the mythological origin of resurrected life. In fact it is referred to as "the wood of [Christ's] life-giving cross" in *The Roman Missal*.[2] Jesus underwent "the cross to save the human race."[3] The one who conquered on the tree of knowledge of good and evil was conquered by the one who died "freely mounted [on] the tree of the cross."[4]

Furthermore, the chants proscribed for "The Adoration of the Holy Cross" on Good Friday emphasize the tree of the cross. One states that "because of the wood of a tree joy has come to the whole world."[5] Another

---

1. *Roman Missal*, "Proper of Saints: September 14: The Exaltation of the Holy Cross: Preface;" cf. "Votive Masses 4. The Mystery of the Holy Cross: Preface."

2. *Roman Missal*, "Votive Masses: 4. The Mystery of the Holy Cross: Prayer After Communion;" cf. "Proper of Saints: September 14: The Exaltation of the Holy Cross: Prayer After Communion."

3. Ibid., "Collect."

4. *Roman Pontifical: Dedication of a Church and an Altar*, chapter 4, par. 48.

5. *Roman Missal*, "Friday of the Passion of the Lord [Good Friday]," par. 20.

calls the cross a "noble tree beyond compare," and adds: "Never was there such a scion, / Never leaf or flower so rare. / Sweet the timber, sweet the iron, / Sweet the burden that they bear!"[6]

Cavendish records a legend of the cross which ties together the tree of the knowledge of good and evil and the tree of the cross.

> ... [W]hen Adam lay dying, he sent his son Seth to Eden. The angel who guarded the gate of the paradise garden gave Seth three seeds of the forbidden fruit from the tree of knowledge. Seth placed the seeds on Adam's tongue, and Adam died happy in the knowledge that [human]kind would be saved from the consequences of his sin in Eden. The three seeds grew into a great tree, from which the cross was fashioned. Christ was crucified on it at the center of the world, at the place where Adam had been created and where he lay buried.[7]

Underlying both the concept of the wood of the life-giving cross and the legend narrated above is Paul's comparison of the first Adam and the second Adam (Christ). In his letter to the Romans, he writes that just as sin came into the world through one man, and death came through sin (Rom 5:12) so have the grace of God and the free gift in the grace of the one man, Jesus Christ, abounded for the many (Rom 5:15). Paul adds, "If, because of the one man's trespass, death exercised dominion through that one, much more surely will those who receive the abundance of grace and the free gift of righteousness exercise dominion in life through the one man, Jesus Christ" (Rom 5:17). One of the hymns proscribed for "The Adoration of the Holy Cross" on Good Friday in *The Roman Missal* ties together the two trees in this way: "For when Adam first offended, / Eating that forbidden fruit, / Not all hopes of glory ended / With the serpent at the root: / Broken nature would be mended / By a second tree and shoot."[8]

In another story, known as the "Legend of the Dogwood," the dogwood, the state tree of Missouri, used to grow into a very large woody plant from which crosses were made. After Jesus' cross was made from one, he cursed it so that it would no longer grow large enough for crosses again. In another version of the legend, God twisted and gnarled the trunk and branches so that no straight beams could be made again from the tree. In the spring when the dogwood blossoms, the four-petal, white flower is presented in the form of a cross. On the outer edge of each petal is a small red

---

6. Ibid.

7. Cavendish, *Legends*, 212–13; cf. Baring-Gould, *Curious Myths of the Middle Ages*, 107–110.

8. *Roman Missal*, "Friday of the Passion of the Lord [Good Friday]," par. 20.

hole or indentation, representing the nails used to pin Jesus to the cross. In the middle is a yellow cluster representing the crown of thorns that was placed on Jesus' head.

The idea that the tree of death became a tree of life is found in the CB (NT) Acts of the Apostles. Standing before the high priest and the Sadducees, Peter and the apostles declare: "The God of our ancestors raised up Jesus, whom you had killed by hanging him on a tree. God exalted him at his right hand as Leader and Savior that he might give repentance to Israel and forgiveness of sins" (Acts 5:30–31). Likewise, when Peter addresses Cornelius and his household, he states that Jesus was put to death by hanging on a tree, but God raised him to life three days later (Acts 10:39–40). Even Paul on one of his missionary journeys in the Acts of Apostles narrates how Jesus was killed, taken down from the tree, and laid in a tomb (Acts 13:29). Paul adds that God raised him from the dead (Acts 13:30).

Not only does the selection from the preface above declare that Christ has conquered death with death, but that he has conquered the stigma attached to death by crucifixion. While Jesus was crucified by the Romans, the Israelites practiced some form of capital punishment referred to as hanging on a tree. The HB (OT) Book of Deuteronomy states: "When someone is convicted of a crime punishable by death and is executed, and you hang him on a tree, his corpse must not remain all night upon the tree; you shall bury him that same day, for anyone hung on a tree is under God's curse. You must not defile the land that the LORD your God is giving you for possession" (Deut 21:22–23). Leaving a hanged body on a tree would leave the land in a state of ritual impurity; it would be defiled. Joshua is very careful not to violate this prohibition. Thus, after conquering the city of Ai, Joshua hanged the king of Ai on a tree until evening. At sunset Joshua commanded his men to take down his body from the tree. They threw it down at the entrance of the gate of the city, and put a great heap of stones over it (Josh 8:29). Similarly, after capturing the five kings of Jerusalem, Hebron, Jarmuth, Lachish, and Eglon, Joshua struck them down, put them to death, and hung their bodies on five trees. They hung on the trees until sunset, when Joshua commanded that the bodies be taken down from the trees and place in a cave (Josh 10:26–27). Likewise, in the Third Book of Nephi in *The Book of Mormon* there is the story of the Nephites capturing the leader of a group of robbers named Zemnarihah, who "was taken and hanged upon a tree, yea, even upon the top thereof until he was dead" (3 Ne 4:28). After Zemnarihah died, the Nephites "felled the tree to the earth" (3 Ne 4:28).

In his letter to the Galatians, Paul explains how "Christ redeemed [all] from the curse of the law by becoming a cruse . . . —for it is written, 'Cursed is everyone who hangs on a tree'" (Gal 3:13). According to Paul, the curse of the law is the inability of any human being to do everything in the Torah. According to Hartin, a tendency had developed "among the people of Israel where stress was placed on carrying out faithfully all the stipulations of the law: the focus shifted toward a legalism and their own human effort."[9] Applying the understanding from the Book of Deuteronomy that anyone hanged on tree is cursed, Paul concludes that Jesus was cursed. However, according to Paul, it took the curse of crucifixion to break the curse of the law. Such was "the wondrous power of the cross"[10]

The kings of Ai, Jerusalem, Hebron, Jarmuth, Lachish, and Eglon, the robber Zemnarihah, and Jesus are not the only men to be hanged on a tree. Littleton records a story about the Norse god Odin, who "underwent great suffering to win the runes, the source of wisdom and magical lore."[11] According to Littleton, Odin "hung on a windswept tree identified as the World Tree, Yggdrasil, for nine full nights without food or water, slashed with a spear and sacrificed . . . until, screaming, he was able by virtue of his suffering to reach down and seize the magical runes."[12]

One of the hymns in *The Roman Missal* proscribed for "The Adoration of the Holy Cross" on Good Friday praises the tree of the cross this way: "Lofty timber, smooth your roughness, / Flex your boughs for blossoming; / Let your fibers lose their toughness, / Gently let your tendrils cling; / Lay aside your native gruffness, / Clasp the body of your King!"[13]

Another verse of the hymn declares the tree of the cross to be: "Noblest tree of all created, / Richly jeweled and embossed: / Post by Lamb's blood consecrated; / Spar that saves the tempest-tossed; / Scaffold-beam which, elevated, / Carries what the world has cost!"[14]

In *The Roman Pontifical: Dedication of a Church and an Altar*, the cross is often referred to as an altar. The introduction to chapter 4 explains the phrase "the altar of the cross."[15] "By instituting in the form of a sacrificial meal the memorial of the sacrifice he was about to offer the Father on the altar of the cross, Christ made holy the table where the community would

---

9. Hartin, *Window*, 54.
10. *Roman Missal*, "The Order of Mass," par. 43.
11. Littleton, *Mythology*, 289.
12. Ibid.
13. *Roman Missal*, "Friday of the Passion of the Lord [Good Friday]," par. 20.
14. Ibid.
15. *Roman Pontifical: Dedication of a Church and an Altar*, chapter 4, pars. 39, 48, 60; chapter 5, par. 21; chapter 6, par. 9; *Roman Missal*, "Votive Masses, 4. The Mystery of the Holy Cross, Prayer over the Offerings;" "Proper of Saints, September 14: The Exaltation of the Holy Cross, Prayer over the Offerings."

come to celebrate their Passover. Therefore the altar is the table for a sacrifice . . . ."[16] On the altar "the sacrifice of the cross is perpetuated in mystery."[17]

Thus, the cross is a life-giving tree that brought new life to the world. It reverses the death brought into the world by the tree of the knowledge of good and evil through the resurrection of the one who was nailed to it. Because being hanged on a tree was a sign of being cursed by God, Jesus, by being nailed to a tree, reversed that understanding as well. Furthermore, the tree of the cross has power to break the curse of the law. The sacrifice of Jesus made on the cross is renewed using bread and wine on the altar of the cross. Indeed, the tree of defeat has become the sacred tree of victory.

Journal/Meditation: How is the cross a sacred tree of defeat? How is the cross a sacred tree of victory? What tree do you think about when the cross is mentioned or you see one?

Prayer: Holy Father, almighty and eternal God, you placed the salvation of the human race on the wood of the cross, so that where death arose life might again spring forth and the evil one, who conquered on a tree, might likewise on a tree be conquered. Help me to understand the paradox of such a sacred tree. I ask this through Christ, my Lord. Amen.

---

16. *Roman Pontifical: Dedication of a Church and an Altar*, chapter 4, par. 3.
17. Ibid., par. 4.

Cypress

Text: "The Master said, 'Only when the year grows cold do we see that the pine and cypress are the last to fade.'"[1]

Reflection: The proverb quoted by Confucius above identifies the cypress tree as a deciduous conifer. Thus, when winter comes, it loses its flat-blade leaves. The tree can live for many years and reach a height of one hundred to one-hundred twenty feet. Its bark may be gray-brown to red-brown, and is thin and fibrous with a stringy texture. Its seed cones begin as green and turn to gray-brown when they mature; the cone then disintegrates in order to release the seeds. There are over twenty-five different kinds of cypress trees, some of which are evergreen.

McKenzie states that cypress "timber is hard and close grained and of excellent quality for building."[2] And that is exactly how the Bible presents the use of the tree. Before the great flood God tells Noah, "Make yourself an ark of cypress wood" (Gen 6:14a). Because the tree is tall—like a cypress on the heights of Hermon (Sir 24:13) or like a cypress towering in the clouds (Sir 50:10)—it is Solomon's chosen timber for building the first temple in Jerusalem. After Solomon requests wood to build a house for the name of the LORD (1 Kgs 5:5) from King Hiram of Tyre (2 Chr 2:8), the king replies, "'Blessed be the LORD today, who has given to David a wise son to be over this great people. I have heard the message that you have sent to me; I will fulfill all your needs in the matter of . . . cypress timber.' So Hiram supplied Solomon's every need for timber of . . . cypress" (1 Kgs 5:7–8, 10; cf. 9:11). According to the First Book of Kings, Solomon covered the floor of the house with boards of

---

1. *Analects*, 9:27.
2. McKenzie, *Dictionary*, 167.

cypress (1 Kgs 6:15c), made for the entrance to the same two doors of cypress wood (1 Kgs 6:34), and lined the nave with cypress (2 Chr 3:5) because the cypress was considered a glorious tree (Zech 11:2).

The cypress also represents restoration. The prophet Hosea depicts God restoring Israel and declaring, "I am like an evergreen cypress; your faithfulness comes from me" (Hos 14:8). In other words, God's chosen people bear fruit because they are like the cones on an evergreen cypress tree. In a similar vein, the prophet Isaiah portrays the LORD declaring that he will set in the desert the cypress (Isa 41:19b); instead of the thorn shall come up the cypress (Isa 55:13a); as in the days of Solomon, the cypress will be used to beautify the place of the LORD's sanctuary (Isa 60:13).

Cypress is the name of a boy beloved by Apollo in Greek mythology. Cyparissus or Kyparissos has a favorite companion of a tamed stag given to him by Apollo. Cyparissus accidentally kills the buck with his hunting javelin as it was sleeping in the woods. After realizing what he has done, Cyparissus begins to grieve, and his grief was such that it transformed him into a cypress tree, a sign of mourning. While there is no Greek hero cult devoted to Cyparissus, his story can be found in Hellenized Latin literature and frescoes from Pompeii. The tale represents the process of initiation into adult life with a type of death and transfiguration motif. In another version of the story, Cyparissus asks Apollo to let his tears fall forever for the pet that he has killed. Apollo turns him into a cypress tree, whose sap forms tear drops on the trunk.

In the tale of Eurydice, the wife of Orpheus, the poet follows her to the underworld after she is bitten by a snake and dies. While he emerges from the underworld, she does not. As a result, women no longer please Orpheus. According to Caldecott, "His most constant companion was the cypress, who itself had once been a boy who pleaded to mourn forever for the beautiful stag he had inadvertently slain, and was now the friend of all who mourned the loss of a loved one."[3] And in another Roman tradition, the woodland god Silvanus loves a boy named Cyparissus, who has a tamed fawn, which Silvanus unintentionally kills. The boy is consumed by sorrow, and Silvanus turns him into a cypress tree to carry as a consolation.

In "Twelfth Night" or "What You Will," written by William Shakespeare in 1600 CE, the gentleman named Curio begins a song, singing, "Come away, come away, death, / And in sad cypress let me be laid."[4] The phrase "sad cypress" refers to a coffin made of cypress wood. However, Shakespeare is also alluding to Cyparissus and his eternal mourning associated with death.

3. Caldecott, *Myths*, 89.
4. Harrison, *Shakespeare*, "Twelfth Night," act 2, scene 4, lines 52–53.

The cypress tree also appears in "The Legend of the Cross." Baring-Gould tells the tale about Adam and his son, Seth. After Adam reached a great age, he sent Seth to paradise to get a balsam which would save him from death. While he cannot get into the garden, a cherub tells him: "The time of pardon is not yet come. Four thousand years must roll away ere the Redeemer shall open the gate to Adam, closed by his disobedience. But as a token of future pardon, the wood whereon redemption shall be won shall grow from the tomb of [your] father."[5] The cherub gives Seth three seeds taken from the tree of life with the instructions, "When Adam is dead, place these three seeds in [your] father's mouth, and bury him."[6]

Seth took the seeds and went home; three days after his arrival, his father died. Seth buried Adam on Golgotha with the three seeds in his mouth. "In the course of time three trees grew from the seeds brought from paradise."[7] The reader should immediately note that the three trees signal divine intervention. One of the three trees is a cypress. The three trees "grew with prodigious force, thrusting their boughs to right and left. . . . After a while the three trees touched one another, then, began to incorporate and confound their several natures in a single trunk."[8] The tale goes on to narrate how Solomon used cypress timber to build the temple. Then it states: "When the time of the crucifixion of Christ drew nigh, . . . [t]he executioners, when seeking a suitable beam to serve for the cross, found it and made of it the instrument of the death of the Savior."[9] Caldicott notes that "the cypress is both a phallic symbol and a symbol of death. It represents the first tree Seth saw [growing from Adam's body]—the tree associated with Adam's concupiscence."[10]

Thus, even though there are many kinds of cypress trees, all of them are known for their longevity and their usefulness as timber. As such, they were used in the biblical tale of Noah's ark and served as one of the primary building materials for Solomon's temple. The cypress is a sign of restoration and transformation as well as death and mourning. Furthermore, according to legend, the cypress is one of the trees from which the cross is made. Jesus dies on the beams of the sacred cypress tree.

---

5. Baring-Gould, *Curious Myths*, 109.
6. Ibid.
7. Ibid.
8. Ibid., 109–10.
9. Ibid., 110.
10. Caldecott, *Myths*, 133.

Journal/Meditation: What tree represents the change of seasons for you? How? What tree represents longevity for you? How? What tree represents transformation for you? How?

Prayer: In order to honor you, Father, King Solomon built your sanctuary out of cypress wood. You have made this tree the sign of longevity and transformation for your people. Grant that upon death I may be changed from mortality to immortality and live with you, the Holy Spirit, and my Lord Jesus Christ forever and ever. Amen.

Dry (Bad) Tree / Green (Good) Tree

Text: "Thus says the Lord GOD: I dry up the green tree and make the dry tree flourish." (Ezek 17:22a, 24c)

Reflection: A dry or bad tree is often contrasted with a green or a good tree in sacred literatures. In the passage above, the prophet Ezekiel makes it very clear that God the creator—who out of the ground made to grow every tree that is pleasant to the sight and good for food (Gen 2:9)—is also God the destroyer. He can dry up the green tree, and he can make the dry tree flourish. In another passage which further emphasizes this point, Ezekiel records the Lord GOD saying to the forest in the desert, "I will kindle a fire in you, and it shall devour every green tree in you and every dry tree; the blazing flame shall not be quenched..." (Ezek 20:47). The prophet Jeremiah records similar words spoken by the Lord GOD: "My anger and my wrath shall be poured out... on the trees of the field and the fruit of the ground; it will burn and not be quenched" (Jer 7:20). Isaiah, too, describes "[t]he glory of his forest and his fruitful land the LORD will destroy.... The remnant of the trees of his forest will be so few that a child can write them down" (Isa 10:18–19). In writing about the deaths of Joseph Smith and Hyrum Smith, the Mormon *Book of Doctrine and Covenants* records a proverb which is similar to those found in Ezekiel and Jeremiah: "... [I]f the fire can scathe a green tree for the glory of God, how easy it will burn up the 'dry trees' to purify the vineyard of corruption" (*D&C* 113:6). The Smith brothers are the green trees who died martyrs's deaths, but their deaths were considered flames which brought salvation to a ruined world.

Reflecting on the dry tree/green tree comparison, Jesus says, "...[E]very good tree bears good fruit, but the bad tree bears bad fruit. A good tree cannot bear bad fruit, nor can a bad tree bear good fruit. Every tree that does not bear good fruit is cut down and thrown into the fire" (Matt 7:17–19; cf. 3 Ne 14:17–19). That passage above from Matthew's Gospel with a parallel found in the Third Book of Nephi in *The Book of Mormon* is located in Jesus' first of five discourses or sermons commonly known as the Sermon on the Mount. By observing the actions of others, Jesus' followers can determine false prophets from true prophets. A false prophet is like a bad tree that bears bad fruit; a true prophet is like a good tree that bears good fruit. A bad tree should be felled and used as firewood, according to the Matthean Jesus.

Jesus' words echo those of his precursor, John the Baptist, who, earlier in the story, announced, "Even now the ax is lying at the root of the trees; every tree therefore that does not bear good fruit is cut down and thrown into the fire" (Matt 3:10; cf. Al 5:52; *D&C* 94:2). Jesus reprises his words later in the narrative after healing a blind and mute demoniac and being accused of healing him with the power of evil by the Pharisees. He tells the Pharisees, "Either make the tree good, and its fruit good; or make the tree bad, and its fruit bad; for the tree is known by its fruit" (Matt 12:33). A few verses later Jesus makes an application of the good tree/bad tree statement, saying, "The good person brings good things out of a good treasure, and the evil person brings evil things out of an evil treasure" (Matt 12:35). Then, he adds that a person will be justified either by his or her words or condemned by them (Matt 12:37).

Because the author of Matthew's Gospel and the author of Luke's Gospel use a common source, known as Q (from the German word *Quelle*, meaning *source*), the Lukan John the Baptist states, "Even now the ax is lying at the root of the trees; every tree therefore that does not bear good fruit is cut down and thrown into the fire" (Luke 3:9; cf. Al 5:52). In his Sermon on the Plain, the Lukan Jesus echoes the Baptizer, stating, "No good tree bears bad fruit, nor again does a bad tree bear good fruit; for each tree is known by its own fruit" (Luke 6:43–44a; cf. 3 Ne 14:18, 20). The Lukan Jesus, like his Matthean counterpart, makes an application of the verse, stating, "The good person out of the good treasure of the heart produces good, and the evil person out of evil treasure produces evil; for it is out of the abundance of the heart that the mouth speaks" (Luke 6:45).

The Quran contains a similar contrast between evil acts and good acts: "Do you not see how God compares a noble act with a healthy tree whose roots are firm and branches in the sky, which yields, by the leave of its Lord, its fruits in all the seasons[?] . . . An evil act is like a rotten tree torn out of the earth with no (base or) firmness." (*Quran* 14:24–25a, 26).

While trees are considered good generally—the man and his wife hide themselves from the presence of the LORD God among the trees of the garden (Gen 3:8)—during the plagues on Egypt, the hail shatters every tree in the field (Exod 9:25), and the locusts devour whatever was left of every tree in the field after the hail (Exod 10:5) so that nothing green was left, no tree in all the land of Egypt (Exod 10:15). The prophet Joel compares another locust plague to a "fire [that] has devoured the pastures of the wilderness, and flames [that] have burned all the trees of the field" (Joel 1:19). Earlier, Joel had written: "The vine withers, the fig tree droops. Pomegranate, palm, and apple—all the trees of the field are dried up; surely joy withers away among the people" (Joel 1:12). Capturing the same sentiment in one of his many speeches, Job states that God has uprooted his hope like a tree (Job 19:10b). Similarly, Isaiah records a eunuch saying, "I am just a dry tree" (Isa 56:3). The OT (A) Book of Sirach states that a person who falls into the grip of passion will have his or her leaves devoured, his or her fruit destroyed, and he or she will be left like a withered tree (Sir 6:3).

The HB (OT) Book of Deuteronomy sets limits on the devastation of siege warfare by the Israelites. Moses tells the people:

> If you besiege a town for a long time, making war against it in order to take it, you must not destroy its trees by wielding an ax against them. Although you may take food from them, you must not cut them down. Are trees in the field human beings that they should come under siege from you? You may destroy only the trees that you know do not produce food; you may cut them down for use in building siege works against the town that makes war with you, until it falls." (Deut 20:19–20)

However, the prophet Elisha contradicts this prohibition when he tells three kings about to make war on Moab to fell every good tree (2 Kgs 3:19), which is exactly what they did (2 Kgs 3:25). Later in the Second Book of Kings, Elisha leads the company of prophets to the Jordan River where they make shelter by cutting down trees (2 Kgs 6:4).

The Bible is full of wisdom when it comes to fallen trees. For example, the HB (OT) Book of Ecclesiastes reminds its readers than some things are beyond their control, such as whether a tree falls to the south or to the north (Eccl 11:3). The Book of Job states that wickedness can be broken like a tree (Job 24:20b). In the OT (A) Book of Wisdom, the author reflects on idolatry, specifically the making of idols from wood. He writes: "A skilled woodcutter may saw down a tree easy to handle and skillfully strip off all its bark, and then with pleasing workmanship make a useful vessel that serves life's needs, and burn the cast-off pieces of his work to prepare his food, and eat his fill" (Wis 13:11–12). The writer continues by reflecting on how it is from a piece of cast-off wood that the carver creates an idol and then worships it! Jeremiah alludes to this when he writes that "a tree from the forest is cut down, and worked with an ax by the hands of an artisan" (Jer 10:3), then people decorate it with silver and gold and worship it.

The destruction of Jerusalem by the Babylonians is imaged by Jeremiah as the cutting down of trees. Early in his book he records the LORD of hosts saying, "Cut down her trees" (Jer 6:6b). Shortly thereafter, Jeremiah records God saying that his anger and wrath shall be poured out "on the trees of the field . . . ; it will burn and not be quenched" (Jer 7:20). In words spoken against Egypt, but similar to those spoken against Jerusalem, Jeremiah writes that "her enemies march in force, and come against her with axes, like those who fell trees" (Jer 46:22).

The destruction of trees is also employed by *The Rig Veda*. Hymn 32 of book 1 compares Indra's slain water monster Vrtra to "trunks of trees" that "the ax has felled" (*RV* 1:32:5b; cf. 10:189:7). In another hymn Indra uses his lightning bolt to "crash down the trees, as when a craftsman fells, crashes them down as with an ax" (*RV* 1:130:4c). Likewise, Agni, the god of fire, is compared to an ax "[a]t whose close touch things solid shake, and what is stable yields like trees" (*RV* 1:127:3b).

The Dhammapada says that anyone who dwells upon what is pleasurable is "[l]ike the wind over a weak tree" (*Dhp* 1:7). Just like the wind blows off fruits and leaves, even destroying branches, unrestrained senses topple the person seeking enlightenment. However, restrained senses are "like the wind over a rocky crag" (*Dph* 1:8); they aide the person on the path to enlightenment. These sentiments are echoed later when the book records the teacher saying: "Cut down the forest! Not a tree / From the forest, fear arises. / Having cut down both forest and underbrush, / . . . be [you] without forests" (*Dhp* 20:283).

The teacher is not talking about a literal forest. As seen above, the teaching is about sensual defilements. Just as fears arise in a natural forest, so do fears arise on the path to enlightenment. Both large defilements and small ones need to be removed from the life of those who have recently gone forth; otherwise they are tethered to their sensual passions.

This line of thinking is continued later with these words: "As long as the roots are unharmed, firm, / A tree, though topped, grows yet again. / Just so, when the latent craving is not rooted out, / This suffering arises again and again" (*Dhp* 24:338).

In other words, if the sensual passions are not cut out of one's life all the way to the roots, they keep returning again and again, and they bring suffering. The HB (OT) Book of Job captures this concept is a positive way: "For there is hope for a tree, if it is cut down, that it will sprout again, and that its shoots will not cease" (Job 14:7). Likewise, the prophet Isaiah, hoping for a return of the Davidic monarchy, states, "A shoot shall come out from the stump of Jesse, and a branch shall grow out of his roots" (Isa 11:1).

The tension found between the dry (bad) tree and the green (good) tree is also found in the last book of the CB (NT): The Book of Revelation. Once the lamb opens the seventh seal, the first of seven angels blows his trumpet and brings a reprise of the plagues from Exodus. Fire and hail are hurled to the earth, where a third of the trees are burned (Rev 8:7). Later in the same book, there is a reprise of the locus plague when the fifth angel blows his trumpet. However, the locusts are told not to damage any tree (Rev 9:4).

The Book of Helaman in *The Book of Mormon* adds another dimension to the dry (bad) tree / green (good) tree discussion. Chapter 3 of Helaman narrates a migration of people forty-six years after the reign of the judges (He 3:3). They settled where they could find timber (He 3:5). As they continued to multiply and spread, "they did suffer whatsoever tree should spring up upon the face of the land that it should grow up, that in time they might have timber to build their houses, yea, their cities, and their temples, and their synagogues, and their sanctuaries and all manner of their buildings" (He 3:9). The story contains much more about shipping in timber to use for building, but the point is that green (good) trees are allowed to mature so that immigrants could fell them and use them for timber as building material.

Thus, God creates trees, and God can destroy them. He can dry up a green tree, and he can make a dry tree green. This is demonstrated by the locusts and the hail in the Book of Exodus and reprised in the Book of Revelation. Job says that God can uproot a person's hope just like he can fell a tree, whereas the OT (A) Book of Baruch states, "The woods and every fragrant tree have shaded Israel at God's command" (Bar 5:8). Jesus focuses on bad trees bearing bad fruit and good trees bearing good fruit to determine false prophets from true ones. Bad trees are felled; good trees are cultivated. Bad fruit and good fruit can be determined by observing a person's behavior. While limits were set on the destruction of trees in warfare, fallen trees serve as reminders that there are some things that are not under a person's control. Such is the case in the destruction of Jerusalem which begins with the felling of trees, representing God's wrath and anger. In *The Rig Veda*, the power of the Hindu gods is compared to the force needed to destroy a tree, whereas in *The Dhammapada* the passions are to be felled like a tree as part of the process of enlightenment. Finally, the OT (A) Book of Sirach reminds the reader of this important truth: "Like abundant leaves on a spreading tree that sheds some and puts forth others, so are the generations of flesh and blood; one dies and another is born" (Sir 14:18).

Journal/Meditation: When have you experienced yourself as being like a dry (bad) tree? When have you experienced yourself as being like a green (good) tree? What have you discovered about yourself?

Prayer: Creator, from the dry tree you can bring forth green leaves, and from the green tree you can bring forth destruction. Enlighten my mind with the wisdom of dryness, and fill my heart with the wisdom of growth. Keep me firmly planted in the garden of your grace. I ask this in the name of Jesus, who is Lord forever and ever. Amen.

Elder

Text: "Shortly after the gods [Odin, Vili, and Ve] had created the world they walked by the side of the sea, pleased with their new work, but found that it was still incomplete, for it was without human beings. . . . [T]hey made a woman out of an elder, and called . . . the woman Embla."[1]

Reflection: According to Norse mythology, the first woman is made from an elder tree. She receives life and soul, reason and motion, senses, expressive features, and speech from the gods.[2] Thus, the elder has a strong feminine association, such that elder trees are thought to be guarded by the Elder Mother. Before wood could be taken from an elder tree the Elder Mother would have to be asked. If a woodcutter failed to do so, bad luck was almost certain to befall him.

Because the elder tree was considered sacred, a variety of folk legends grew up around it. Because these are folk legends, they are impossible to document. However, they exist in a variety of forms. In the Christian legend, the cross upon which Jesus died was thought to have been made from elder wood. Likewise, the tree upon which the Matthean Judas uniquely hangs himself (Matt 27:5) was thought to be an elder. Of course, once the latter connection was made, the elder tree became synonymous with the devil. So, many people feared burning elder logs so as not to bring and release the devil in the house. Even crosses were made from elder twigs and put on barns to protect livestock, and growing an elder tree outside one's home kept witches away. Putting elder twigs in one's mouth was supposed to cure a toothache. An elder three was thought to be incapable of being hit

1. Bulfinch, *Mythology*, 329.
2. Herzberg, *Myth*, 265; Littleton, *Mythology*, 278.

by lightning. Elder was also associated with the fairy world in many oral traditions.

Other sources state that in Norse mythology the first woman was created by the gods from an elm tree.[3] The elm tree, which represents wisdom and strength of will and intuition, also connotes femininity. After finding the golden bough, a requirement that Aeneas had to meet before being able to travel to the underworld to visit his father, the hero experiences a black lake and gloomy forest. According to Caldecott, "At the center of this dark and terrifying place grew a giant elm tree, each leaf a false dream."[4] Aeneas quickly realizes that the leaves represent the empty lives of those who have died.

The bountifulness of the elder tree also adds to its association with femininity. Not only is the tree covered with edible fragrant blossoms in summer, but it bears juicy purple fruit in autumn from which people have made jams, jellies, syrups, and wines. Because its branches are hollow, it was often used to make pipes and bellows.

Thus, from the elder tree the first woman was made. This sets the stage in the Norse creation story to associate the elder with the feminine and the sacred. Once the tree is considered sacred, it cannot be cut without asking its guardian, the Elder Mother, and it becomes the source of all types of healing. However, it also becomes associated with evil—in the same way that Eve is in the HB (OT) creation story. Elder is the wood of the cross upon which Jesus is crucified, and from an elder tree Judas hangs himself. Even with those mythologies, however, the bountifulness of the elder overcomes such negative associations and brings it back to the status of the sacred and the abundance of the feminine.

Journal/Meditation: With what trees do you associate feminine characteristics? Why? With what trees do you associate masculine characteristics? Why? What do these sacred trees tell you about yourself?

Prayer: Almighty God, unlike the Norse gods who created woman from an elder tree, you created woman from a rib of the first man in order to show the unity of woman and man. Give me a greater appreciation for the feminine and the contribution of women everywhere to the betterment of the world. I ask this in the name of Jesus, the Lord. Amen.

---

3. Littleton, *Mythology*, 278.
4. Caldecott, *Myths*, 105.

Fig

Text: [O Vayu,] "Ride hither to the offering of the pleasant juice, the holy fig tree which victorious priests surround; victorious be they still for us." (*RV* 1:135:8)

Reflection: In Hinduism, Vayu is the lord of the winds. In hymn 135 of book 1 of *The Rig Veda*, Vayu is invited to come and drink the sacred soma juice from a bowl made from the holy fig tree which is offered by the priests surrounding it. In hymn 97 of book 10, the fig tree is again referred to as holy (*RV* 10:97:5). The holy or sacred fig tree is known by a variety of names. Principal among those names is bo or bodhi, peepal or pipal, and *ficus religiosa* or *ashwattha*. While the fig tree is primarily associated with the enlightenment of Siddhartha Gautama, better known as the Buddha, it appears in various sacred texts as food, sweetness, tranquility, prosperity, as a sign of watchfulness for the coming of the Son of Man, and a sign of Jerusalem and the temple.

According to Cavendish, on the day that Siddhartha Gautama was born in 566 BCE, there "was born the tree beneath which he would attain enlightenment."[1] It was under a peepal or pipal tree that the Buddha sat. It is also known as the bo or bodhi tree because bodhi means *enlightenment*, and the place where this occurred is Bodh Gaya (Bodhgaya).[2] Kaur adds, "In Hinduism it is believed that [the] roots of [the] peepal tree are Brahma, the trunk is Vishnu, and the leaves are Shiva."[3] Thus, this tree, signifying enlightenment and wisdom, often represents the Buddha in art and literature.

1. Cavendish, *Legends*, 29.
2. Witcombe, "Trees and the Sacred."
3. Kaur, "Sacred Trees Worship in India."

This fig tree can grow up to ninety-eight feet tall and sport a trunk almost nine feet in diameter. Its fruits begin growing green in color after it blossoms in the spring and ripen to purple in the summer. While the original fig tree at Bodh Gaya was destroyed, a branch of the original tree survived, and a bodhi tree must be able to trace its parent to another bodhi tree, and the line goes on until the first bodhi under whose branches sat the Buddha.[4] Although little is known about it, a fig tree which was sacred to Romulus grew near the Forum in ancient Rome.[5]

The fruit of the fig tree, namely figs, is considered to be food (Num 13:23). "Anyone who tends a fig tree will eat its fruit," states the HB (OT) Book of Proverbs (Prov 27:18). Hosea echoes this saying when he portrays God declaring to Israel, "Like the first fruit on the fig tree in its first season, I saw your ancestors" (Hos 9:10b). Isaiah, too, uses this image, but in a negative way. He compares Ephraim's (Israel's) leaders to a fading flower which "will be like a first-ripe fig before the summer; whoever sees it, eats it up as soon as it comes to hand" (Isa 28:4). The prophet Micah employs the same image when he writes: "Woe is [I]! For I have become like one who, after the summer fruit has been gathered, finds . . . no first-ripe fig for which I hunger" (Mic 7:1). The prophet Nahum uses the same image to describe Nineveh's fate, writing, "All your fortresses are like fig trees with first-ripe figs—if shaken they fall into the mouth of the eater" (Nah 3:12).

Figs are sweet and delicious (Judg 9:11). *The Rig Veda* attests to this fact, stating that one of two birds "eats the sweet fig tree's fruitage" (*RV* 1:164:20). "Upon its top . . . the fig is luscious" (*RV* 1:164:22b). In order to get the figs out of the tree, the tree had to be shaken. The CB (NT) Book of Revelation employs the image of a shaken tree to his vision of the stars falling out the sky "as the fig tree drops its winter fruit when shaken by a gale" (Rev. 6:13; cf. *D&C* 85:24). Sweet figs are used to make fig cakes (1 Sam 25:18; 30:12; 1 Chr 12:40) and dried fig cakes (Jdt 10:5). They also provide a sweet fragrance (Song 2:13). They are not gathered from thistles (Matt 7:16; 3 Ne 14:16), thorns (Luke 6:44), or a grapevine (Jas 3:12). And fig leaves can be sewn together to make clothing (Gen 3:7).

In much of biblical literature the fig tree represents tranquility. Sitting under one's fig tree (1 Kgs 4:25; Mic 4:4; Zech 3:10; 1 Mac 14:12; John 1:48–50) is a common way of expressing peace and serenity. The abundance of fig trees, each giving its full yield (Joel 2:22), also represents prosperity. The promised land is described as a land of fig trees (Deut 8:8). The Rabshakeh, the representative of the King of Assyria, tells the people of Jerusalem not

---

4. Caldecott, *Myths*, 40.
5. Witcombe, "Trees and the Sacred."

to let their king, Hezekiah, deceive them, but to make their peace with him. Then every one of them will eat from his or her own fig tree (2 Kgs 18:31; Isa 36:16). Through the prophet Haggai, the LORD, using the fig tree's yield, promises blessings (Hag 2:19).

The absence of fig trees represents chaos, war, and insecurity. Once the Israelites escape Egypt and get to the wilderness, a wretched place, where there are no figs (Num 20:5), they complain to Moses. However, while some of the people want to go back to Egypt, Psalm 105 reminds them that the LORD "struck their ... fig trees, and shattered the trees of their country" with hail (Ps 105:33). Similarly, Isaiah describes the LORD's destruction of the nations to be like fruit withering on a fig tree (Isa 34:4b). Jeremiah describes the invaders of Jerusalem as those who eat up fig trees (Jer 5:17d); God had wanted to gather his people, but there were no "figs on the fig tree; even the leaves [were] withered" (Jer 8:13). In the prophet Hosea, God declares that he will lay waste Israel's fig trees (Hos 2:12a). Similarly, Joel describes a locust plague as splintering fig trees, stripping off their bark, and throwing them down, leaving their branches white (Joel 1:7). Later, Joel declares that the fig tree droops (Joel 1:12a). The prophet Amos, too, recounts how locust devoured Samaria's fig trees (Amos 4:9). However, the prophet Habakkuk states that even "though the fig tree does not blossom" (Hab 3:17a), he will continue to rejoice in the LORD, the God who saves him.

The blossoms of the fig tree herald spring. According to Jesus in Mark's Gospel, the blossoms teach a lesson about the imminent coming of the Son of Man: "From the fig tree learn its lesson: as soon as its branch becomes tender and puts forth its leaves, you know that summer is near" (Mark 13:28; cf. Matt 24:32). The author of Luke's Gospel turns the verse into a parable, narrating, "Then [Jesus] told [his listeners] a parable: 'Look at the fig tree and all the trees; as soon as they sprout leaves you can see for yourselves and know that summer is already near. So also, when you see [the Son of man coming] . . . , know that the kingdom of God is near" (Luke 21:29–31; cf. D&C 34:4; 45:5). Earlier in the gospel, Luke portrayed Jesus telling another parable about a fig tree:

> A man had a fig tree planted in his vineyard; and he came looking for fruit on it and found none. So he said to the gardener, "See here! For three years I have come looking for fruit on this fig tree, and still I find none. Cut it down! Why should it be wasting the soil?" He replied, "Sir, let it alone for one more year, until I dig around it and put manure on it. If it bears fruit next year, well and good; but if not, you can cut it down." (Luke 13:6–9)

The familiar image of the fig tree blossoming and producing fruit is used by the Lukan Jesus as a call to repentance; if no repenting is done and no fruit produced, then the fig tree will be cut down.

Repentance means a change in thinking must occur which will precipitate a change in behavior. In Mark's Gospel, the author portrays Jesus cursing Jerusalem and the temple for its failure to repent. Using a fig tree as the image of Jerusalem and of the temple, the narrator of Mark's Gospel writes: "Seeing in the distance a fig tree in leaf, [Jesus] went to see whether perhaps he would find anything on it. When he came to it, he found nothing but leaves, for it was not the season for figs. He said to it, 'May no one ever eat fruit from you again'" (Mark 11:13–14). Jesus enters the temple and drives out all those engaged in commerce. "In the morning as [Jesus and his disciples] passed by, they saw the fig tree, withered away to its roots. Then Peter remembered and said to him, 'Rabbi, look! The fig tree that you cursed has withered.' Jesus answered them, 'Have faith in God'" (Mark 11:20–22).

The author of Matthew's Gospel takes the two parts of the cursing of the fig tree and merges them together to form an instantaneous miracle story that takes place on the day after Jesus solemnly enters Jerusalem and drives from the temple those engaged in commerce.

> In the morning, when [Jesus] returned to the city, he was hungry. And seeing a fig tree by the side of the road, he went to it and found nothing at all on it but leaves. Then he said to it, "May no fruit ever come from you again!" And the fig tree withered at once. When the disciples saw it, they were amazed, saying, "How did the fig tree wither at once?" Jesus answer them, "Truly I tell you, if you have faith and do not doubt, not only will you do what has been done to the fig tree, but . . . whatever you ask for in prayer with faith, you will receive." (Matt 21:18–22)

Just as the Matthean fig tree serves as a witness to Jesus' faith, in *The Quran* Allah calls "to witness the fig" that he "created man of finest possibilities" (*Quran* 95:1, 4).

A parable similar to the cursing of the fig tree story found in Mark's Gospel and rewritten by Matthew is found in the prophet Jeremiah. King Nebuchadrezzar of Babylon had invaded Jerusalem, taken King Jehoiachin into captivity, and installed his uncle, Zedekiah, as a client king in his place. Jeremiah has a vision:

> The LORD showed me two baskets of figs placed before the temple of the LORD. One basket had very good figs, like first-ripe figs, but the other basket had very bad figs, so bad that they could not be eaten. And the LORD said to me, "What do you see,

Jeremiah?" I said, "Figs, the good figs very good, and the bad figs very bad, so bad that they cannot be eaten." (Jer 24:1a, 2–3)

After the vision, the LORD interprets it for the prophet. The good figs represent the Jewish exiles in Babylon (Jer 24:4–5). God states: "I will set my eyes upon them for good, and I will bring them back to this land. I will build them up, and not tear them down; I will plant them, and not pluck them up" (Jer 24:6). The bad figs represent King Zedekiah, his officials, and all those remaining in Jerusalem. God states: "I will make them a horror, an evil thing, to all the kingdoms of the earth—a disgrace, a byword, a taunt, and a curse in all the places where I shall drive them" (Jer 24:9). Thus, just as the LORD promises that he will utterly destroy his people, Jesus curses the fig tree to indicate that Jerusalem and the temple will be destroyed by the Romans (which had already occurred in 70 CE, when Mark's Gospel was written, and by 80 CE, when Matthew's Gospel was written).

Just as Buddha was enlightened under a fig tree, the Bible portrays sitting under a fig tree as a time of tranquility, prosperity, and blessing. Sweet, ripe, summer figs not only are food, but their preceding spring blossoms are a sign of the coming of the Son of Man. In the CB (NT) the cursed and withered fig tree represents Jerusalem and the temple; what ought to be sacred has been turned into chaos, war, and insecurity. That is no place for the sacred fig tree or its fruit.

Journal/Meditation: In what specific way is the sacred fig tree a sign of enlightenment for you? In your culture, what would be an equivalent expression or phrase that would capture the meaning of the biblical phrase about sitting under one's fig tree?

Prayer: LORD God, you brought your people out of Egyptian slavery and into the promised land so they could sit under their fig trees and enjoy a time of prosperity and blessing. Grant that I might learn the lesson of the fig tree's blossoms and be found keeping watch for the Son of Man, who lives and reigns with you and the Holy Spirit, one God, forever and ever. Amen.

Fir

Text: "In [the trees of the LORD] the birds build their nests; the stork has its home in the fir trees." (Ps 104:17)

Reflection: In the HB (OT) Book of Psalms, Psalm 104 is a song of praise. The psalm mentions the fir tree in which the stork has its home. After comparing the city of Tyre to a well-built ship, the prophet Ezekiel states that her builders make all her planks of fir trees (Ezek 27:5a). Later, when he compares Pharaoh to a cedar, Ezekiel states that the fir trees could not equal its boughs (Ezek 31:8a). Those three mentions of the fir tree exhaust its biblical references.

The Mormon *Book of Doctrine and Covenants* contains one reference to the fir tree. In a revelation to Joseph Smith on January 19, 1841, God invites all his saints to come with precious metals and "the fir tree" to build a house to his name (*D&C* 107:10). Another reference is found in the Second Book of Nephi in *The Book of Mormon*: "Yea, the fir trees rejoice at [the LORD]" (2 Ne 24:8); he has broken the staff of the wicked and brought the whole earth to a state of rest.

And this could be the end of the chapter on the fir tree except for the fact that in the sixteenth century, according to legend, Martin Luther suggested that lights be "placed upon a fir tree to brighten the Christmas of his son."[1] There is a mention in 1605 of people setting up fir trees in the rooms of their home,[2] and another mention of the fir tree being used in Strasburg, Austria, in the 1740s as a Christmas tree which was erected in people's

---

1. Count, *4000 Years*, 83.
2. Ibid., 87.

homes.³ Count speculates on the origin of this custom: "Briefly and simply, the Christmas tree seems to have sprung from the devil-defying green with which longstanding tradition of the Northland had decorated house and barn at New Year's."⁴ Count also records a custom in Wittenberg of a little fir tree being set up for each person in a house and gifts placed below it.⁵ Thus, according to Count, the lighted and garnished Christmas tree came into being with the fir.⁶

"The Fir Tree" by Hans Christian Anderson not only made the fir tree famous, but the tale also attached a moral to the story. The narrative begins with these words: "In a clearing in the middle of a dark wood stood a young fir tree."⁷ However, the young fir tree was not happy because he was small. "I want to stretch my branches far around. I want the birds to build their nests in my branches," he told a very old tree.⁸ He bemoaned the fact that when woodcutters came to the forest, they only felled the older trees. The sun exhorted the fir tree to be happy where he was, but he still complained.

Before Christmas the woodcutters came into the forest again, and this time they cut some of the smaller trees. The sparrow explained to the little fir tree that the trees were "taken into houses in the town . . . [and] decorated with golden balls and colored ribbons."⁹ The little tree resolved to be taken the next year. However, the wind advised him to be happy where he was.

"When the woodcutters went into the wood one year later, the little fir tree had grown into a beautiful shape, and he was the first to be cut down."¹⁰ He felt sad to leave the forest, but began to feel better after he was carried into the town. Finding himself in the royal palace and planted in a tub of sand, he was decorated with colored balls, baskets filled with sweets, and candles by the ladies in the palace. On his top they placed a large star. During a party that night in the palace, his candles were lit. Once the candles burned out, the children in the palace were permitted to take his decorations. As the evening drew on, the little fir tree began to wonder what might be hung on his branches the next day.

However, the next morning he was taken to the loft of the palace by the servants. There he was without light or fresh air and very lonely. The only

3. Ibid., 85.
4. Ibid., 87.
5. Ibid., 91.
6. Ibid.
7. Apsley, *Tales*, 28.
8. Ibid.
9. Ibid., 29.
10. Ibid.

conversation he had for many months was with a mouse. However, "one day the door of the loft opened and he was dragged down the stairs."[11] He was tossed into a corner of the stable yard, but because he had dried out, he could not spread his branches. He saw a servant coming toward him with a saw, and he knew that he was going to be cut into firewood. He thought to himself, "O, how I wish I had enjoyed myself when I could. I should have been happy where I was."[12] Thus, the moral of the story is to be happy wherever one finds himself or herself.

The fir tree's branches and boughs are a home for the stork; the planks made from its trunk are used to build ships, and its large boughs could be cut and hung in homes. The fir became the Christmas tree because it was thought to be eternal due to the fact that it was green all year long. Anderson made the fir tree famous with his tale about being happy where one is. The sight of a lit and decorated tree at Christmastime is a suitable reminder that a person should be happy wherever he or she finds himself or herself.

Journal/Meditation: Are you happy where you are? If so, how does your happiness contribute to your quality of life? If not, what do you need to do to become happy? What tree do you associate with happiness?

Prayer: All praise be to you, Father, creator of all the trees, but especially of the fir in which the stork makes a home. Awaken me to your eternity when I see the evergreen fir. Awaken me to the happiness that I enjoy in being in your presence. Hear this prayer in the name of your Son, Jesus Christ, my Lord. Amen.

---

11. Ibid., 31.
12. Ibid.

Fruit

Text: ". . . God said, 'Let the earth put forth . . . fruit trees of every kind on earth that bear fruit with the seed in it.' And it was so. The earth brought forth . . . trees of every kind bearing fruit with the seed in it. And God saw that it was good." (Gen 1:11–12)

Reflection: While the Bible names a variety of trees, it also often refers to fruit trees or the fruit of trees in a generic manner. Such is the case on the third day of creation. God decrees that fruit trees should spring forth from the earth, and they do. On the sixth day, after creating humankind, God gives every tree with seed in its fruit for food (Gen 1:29). Like the first story of creation, the second also emphasizes that "the LORD God made to grow every tree that is pleasant to the sight and good for food" (Gen 2:9) and told the man that he could "freely eat of every tree of the garden" (Gen 2:16) except the tree of the knowledge of good and evil. After woman is created, she repeats the fact that she and the man may eat of the fruit of the trees in the garden (Gen 3:2). Furthermore, in the HB (OT) Book of Leviticus, God says to his people, "If you follow my statues and keep my commandments and observe them faithfully, I will give you your rains in their season, . . . and the trees of the field shall yield their fruit" (Lev 26:4). In recounting Jewish history, Nehemiah reminds the returned exiles that their ancestors found fruit trees in abundance (Neh 9:25) when they entered the promised land. Once the Maccabees drive out their Greek rulers, the First Book of Maccabees records that the trees of the plains gave their fruit (1 Macc 14:8).

According to the HB (OT) Book of Ecclesiastes, one aspect of pleasure is making "gardens and parks, and plant[ing] in them all kinds of fruit trees" (Eccl 2:5). When describing the results of putting a new shepherd in charge of his people, the LORD speaks through Ezekiel, stating, "The trees of the field shall yield their fruit" (Ezek 34:27), and "I will make the fruit of the tree . . . abundant" (Ezek 36:30). The prophet Joel echoes Ezekiel, as God states that the tree bears its fruit (Joel 2:22b). Likewise, the OT (A) Book of Sirach states, "Its fruit discloses the cultivation of a tree" (Sir 27:6a).

The Quran records how "God compares a noble act with a healthy tree whose roots are firm and branches in the sky, which yields, by the leave of its Lord, its fruits in all the seasons" (*Quran* 14:24–25). Likewise, God states that he grows orchards "which yield fruits in abundance" that people eat (*Quran* 23:19). *The Rig Veda*, too, mentions "a tree's ripe fruit" (*RV* 9:97:53).

The extravagance of God's re-creation of Jerusalem and the temple is mirrored in Ezekiel's vision of water flowing from the temple. It begins as a small stream and turns into a river. "On the banks, on both sides of the river, there will grow all kinds of trees for food. Their leaves will not wither nor their fruit fail, but they will bear fresh fruit every month, because the water for them flows from the sanctuary. Their fruit will be for food, and their leaves for healing" (Ezek 47:12). The author of the CB (NT) Book of Revelation used Ezekiel's description of fruit trees in his description of the river flowing from the throne of God and the Lamb. The basic difference is that in Revelation there is only the tree of life (Gen 2:10), which produces twelve kinds of fruit. John of Patmos records his vision: "On either side of the river is the tree of life with its twelve kinds of fruit, producing its fruit each month; and the leaves of the tree are for the healing of the nations" (Rev 22:2). The fruit tree in its abundance praises the LORD (Ps 148:9).

In the HB (OT) Book of Leviticus, God explains to his people that once they "come into the land and plant all kinds of trees for food, then [they] shall regard their fruit as forbidden [for] three years . . . [and] must not be eaten" (Lev 19:23). In the fourth year, the fruit of the trees is to be set aside as a first-fruits offering to God (Lev 19:24). Only in the fifth year may the people "eat of their fruit, that their yield may be increased" (Lev 19:25). It is important to note the significance of the number three, because it refers to God, and the number four, which represents the earth. Only after the earth has produced fruit for four years can it be offered to the LORD. Furthermore, according to Faley it took five years before the fruit had a good taste: "Not before the fourth year, when the fruit was truly well developed and worth eating, could it be offered to the Lord as a token of thanks. Hence, the people were forbidden to eat the fruit any time prior to the fifth year."[1] If the people fail to keep God's commandments, then, according to Leviticus, the trees of the land shall not yield their fruit (Lev 26:20).

---

1. Faley, "Leviticus," 74.

As indicated above, all the fruit of the trees "shall be set apart for rejoicing in the LORD" (Lev 19:24). This is another way of saying that a tithe of the fruit belongs to God. A tithe is a one-tenth portion of the fruit offered to God for use by the priests, Levites, the donor, aliens, orphans, and widows. Leviticus states that "all tithes from . . . the fruit from the tree are the LORD's" (Lev 27:30). Once the Jews return to Jerusalem from Babylonian captivity, they enter into solemn agreement with God to "bring the first fruits of all fruit of every tree, year by year, to the house of the LORD" (Neh 10:35). The First Book of Maccabees records a political move by a high priest named Jonathan which caused a king to cancel the half of the fruit of the trees that he was supposed to receive (1 Macc 10:30; cf. 11:34).

Sacred fruit trees were often the object of pestilence. The narrator of the HB (OT) Book of Exodus records that locusts ate "all the fruit of the trees that the [previous plague of] hail had left" (Exod 10:15). Among the curses that God will bring on the land for people's disobedience is the cicada, which will take over all their trees (Deut 28:42). Likewise, in the prophet Jeremiah, God promises to pour out his anger on all Jerusalem and its inhabitants and on the trees of the field (Jer 7:20). In describing the attack of his enemies, Jeremiah likens himself to a destroyed tree with its fruit (Jer 11:9); this is similar to the destruction of leaves and fruit described by Sirach (Sir 6:3). Isaiah employs the image of gleanings after a harvest when only "four or five" pieces of fruit are left "on the [highest] branches of a fruit tree" (Isa 17:6c) to describe destruction. And the CB (NT) Letter of Jude uses a similar image of "autumn trees without fruit" (Jude 1:12). The *Book of Doctrine and Covenants* states that "every tree that brings not forth good fruit shall be hewn down and cast into the fire" (D&C 94:2).

The Book of Alma in *The Book of Mormon* uses the fruit tree as an image of faith.

> . . . [A]s the tree begins to grow, you will say: Let us nourish it with great care, that it may get root, that it may grow up, and [that it may] bring forth fruit unto us. And now, behold, if you nourish it with much care, it will get root, and grow up, and bring forth fruit. But if you neglect the tree, and take no thought for its nourishment, behold, it will not get any root; and when the heat of the sun comes and scorches it, because it has no root it withers away, and you pluck it up and cast it out. (Al 32:37–38)

Alma's image is like that of Psalm 1: Those who delight in the LORD's Torah "are like trees planted by streams of water, which yield their fruit in its season, and their leaves do not wither" (Ps 1:3).

Thus, the generic fruit trees, fruit of trees, or fruit of the trees of the field are created by God for people, who take pleasure in planting them and glory in their abundant yield. Healthy trees bring forth much, ripe fruit which can be measured in the extravagance of fresh fruit every month or fresh fruit every month from the same tree! Fruit is a blessing, which can be used for tithes, whereas pestilence is a curse. The way a person plants and grows a tree so that it produces fruit is the same way he or she should plant and grow faith so that it produces abundantly.

Journal/Meditation: In what ways are you like a fruit tree? How well are you rooted? At what stage of growth are you? What fruit have you produced?

Prayer: Creator God, on the third day of your work, you commanded the earth to put forth fruit trees of every kind. After seeing that they were good, you gave them to the first man and woman as food. Pour your fertilizing grace on me that I may yield an abundance of good words and deeds in your sight. Hear me in the name of your Son, Jesus Christ, my Lord. Amen.

Glastonbury Hawthorn

Text: "Joseph [of Arimathea] . . . had learned a great deal about the druids, the Celtic priesthood. . . . [The apostle] Philip had suggested that he should go to [Britain] and establish a bridgehead for the Christ there, taking with him eleven companions. . . . At last they came to a place—a hilly island rising from the surrounding marshes like a beacon, green and forested, an island that was sacred to the druids, who believed it was the entrance to the otherworld where the dead went to await rebirth.

'This is the place,' said Joseph of Arimathea, and he plunged his staff into the rich, soft soil. . . . They made camp where they had stopped, prayed, and settled down for the night. In the morning the staff that Joseph had placed in the earth was rooted and flowering. . . .

From a nearby well sacred to the ancient earth goddess, Joseph drew water in the chalice he had brought from Jerusalem—the chalice from which the Christ had drunk at his last meal on earth, the chalice they had raised to catch his blood as he hung on the cross. With this water, poured from this chalice, he purified the land where they were to build their church . . . .

On the rough stone altar of this early church, Joseph laid a cross fashioned from a branch of his flowering thorn tree—for it was the miracle of this tree that brought most of his Celtic converts to him."[1]

Reflection: After narrating the tale of "The Glastonbury Thorn," Caldecott presents five pages of comments on the story. "That Joseph of Arimathea, supposed to be the uncle of Jesus of Nazareth, came to Glastonbury in Somerset and founded the first Christian church in Britain is a most persistent legend,"

---

1. Caldecott, *Myths*, 183–5; cf. Count, *4000 Years*, 89.

he writes.² According to Caldecott: "Glastonbury has always been a place of pilgrimage, from very ancient pagan times, when it was thought to be the entrance to the otherworld . . . ."³ In other words, the hawthorn marks the portal; the staff-turned-hawthorn tree connects the underworld to the earth and to the world above. Thus, it can be considered a sacred universal, world, or cosmic tree. Furthermore, "[t]he three thorn trees in Glastonbury are said to be the descendants of Joseph's original staff."⁴ It is important to note the significance of the number three, which represents the divine and signals the presence of God. Caldecott explains that the "hawthorn was a tree very sacred to the ancient Celts, and the fact that it was a hawthorn that burst into blossom must surely have influenced the Celtic acceptance of the miracle."⁵ She adds, "An interesting aspect of the Glastonbury thorn legend is that one of the relics listed in old records of the abbey was Aaron's rod."⁶ Like Joseph of Arimathea's staff, Aaron's staff burst into blossom (Num 17:8). "When Aaron's . . . and Joseph's . . . staffs bloom, the message is that they are men . . . so in tune with God that they are capable of using that force within them that was made in God's image," writes Caldecott. "They are therefore men . . . who can be trusted to bring us safely nearer to a relationship with the creative divinity."⁷ She concludes that Joseph's

> attunement with God through [his] conscious use of [his] deepest and most profound faculties of soul is what may have caused the [staff] to flower, creating an outward and visible sign that [he was] ready, and could be trusted, to deliver the message as accurately as it is possible for any human being to do so. It could have been God and humanity working together that caused the miracle.⁸

The hawthorn tree, the state flower of Missouri, is regarded as a sacred tree by many Christians. The Glastonbury Hawthorn tree is unique in that if flowers twice a year around Easter and Christmas. Of course, through the years cuttings were propagated from the original tree so that there is always original stock to replace trees that die.

In "Merlin and the Hawthorn Tree," Caldecott records a tale about Merlin as an old man. The handmaiden of the goddess who had given the sword Excalibur to Arthur was named Vivien; she was envious of Merlin's

2. Ibid., 185.
3. Ibid., 186.
4. Ibid.
5. Ibid.
6. Ibid., 188.
7. Ibid., 189.
8. Ibid., 190.

great powers. She followed him wherever he went. Her greatest desire was to know "how it was possible to imprison a man within a tree."[9] Caldecott writes: "Within seconds of obtaining knowledge of this spell she implemented it. The mighty Merlin, the wisest of all men, was confined forever within a cage of bark—a hawthorn tree."[10] In her comments on the tale, Caldecott notes that "the hawthorn tree . . . is associated with the magic and mystery of the pre-Christian religion."[11]

Thus, the hawthorn tree is sacred to many people. It stands as a sign of the unity of the world, and it serves as a portal for a three-storied universe. It is a miracle means of God's connection from the world above to the world below. The flowering staff of Joseph of Arimathea is a sign of both the tree's *axis mundi* role and its role as a portal to worlds unseen. This is why Merlin is trapped within a hawthorn tree and never dies; he is able to migrate from one world to another with the expectation that one day he may return to earth.

Journal/Meditation: How does the phrase "bloom where you are planted" refer to you? In other words, how are you like Joseph of Arimathea's staff planted in the ground and growing into a hawthorn tree?

Prayer: Heavenly Father, from the legend of Joseph of Arimathea and the hawthorn tree I have learned that it is through attunement with your will that I become rooted and flower. Pour on me the Holy Spirit that I may blossom in this life and await rebirth in the next. I ask this in the name of your crucified and risen Son, Jesus Christ, who lives and reigns with you and the Holy Spirit, one God, forever and ever. Amen.

---

9. Ibid., 178.
10. Ibid.
11. Ibid.

Hemlock

Text: "How oft beneath the burning sun / You've sought my cool refreshing shade! / How often, when sudden storms have come, / My arms for you a shelter made! / The great, the noble, and the wise, / Towards me would have but one desire: / A tree of such a noble size / They'd keep for others to admire. / A monument of bygone days, / I've kept the place where now I grow; / And, over all, my head did raise / Above a thousand years ago. / What mighty changes in that space! / What revolutions on the earth! / What strange events have taken place! / What wonders since I date my birth! / Of these I have laid up a store, / And at your service they shall be; / When you would think on days of yore / Come sit beneath the hemlock tree. / In every branch I have a tongue, / I have a voice in every breeze; / And when I speak to old or young, / My aim is to instruct and please."[1]

Reflection: *The Hemlock Tree and Its Legends*, from which the above text comes, was published in 1859. The author, Robert Bradbury, portrays an ancient hemlock tree narrating some of the events that it had seen in its long life. The one-hundred fourteen-page text, written in rhyme, tells the story of Indian (Native American) tribal wars. The Oneida capture the great warrior Conshomon from the Lenape or Wappanaohi. Conshomon is compared to other great warriors, such as an Egyptian pharaoh, a Babylonian king, the Persian Cyrus, Alexander the Great, and the Roman Caesars. His captors decide to make him run a gauntlet to save his life, but when he succeeds, they decide to burn him at the stake. At that moment a squaw named Pearly Dew comes forward and promises to marry him in order to save his life, but he tells her that he already has a wife with the Lenape. Just as the Oneida are

---

1. Bradbury, *Hemlock Tree*, 15–16.

getting ready to light the fire, Conshomon is saved by a brave from the Lenape, named Snake, who disguises himself as a Mohawk—who have joined the Oneida in their battle with the Lenape—and sneaks into their camp. After he rescues Conshomon, Snake marries Pearly Dew, the war ends, and peace is made.

It is important to distinguish between two different kinds of hemlock. Most people think of the extremely poisonous, biennial, herbaceous plant which grows only three to five feet tall. The plant is noted for its deep or dark red mottling on the lower half of its stem. In folklore, it is associated with European witchcraft. This extremely toxic plant is not related to the hemlock tree, which gets its name from its needles, which, when crushed, give off a similar smell to the toxic hemlock shrub. The most famous poisoning by hemlock is, of course, the Greek philosopher Socrates, who, after making speeches about his humanistic and democratic principles, was sentenced to death and chose willingly to consume the hemlock drink. It seems that in Athens hemlock poison was the traditional method of death for criminals. There is also a Christian myth which explains how the hemlock became toxic, namely, during Jesus' crucifixion, his blood touched the plant growing on the hillside where his cross was placed and turned it toxic.

The hemlock tree is an evergreen, ranging from thirty-three to one hundred feet tall, with a trunk of a diameter of five or more feet. It features a conical to irregular crown, and the leading shoots generally droop. It displays scaly bark, often deeply furrowed with age, the color ranging from gray to brown. As indicated in the text above, the tree is also known for its longevity, often living for hundreds of years. Its horizontal-from-the-trunk branches display flattened leaves, often referred to as needles, with very small yellowish-white to pale-purple oblong seed cones on year-old twigs. Once the seeds mature, the cones are shed. Hemlock trees prefer cool, wet, dark forests, being very shade tolerant. Their flexible branches and feathery needles embrace snow and bend and bow under its weight without breaking. This conifer, unlike the plant identified above, is not toxic. The needles, which usually spend three years on the tree before falling off, can be brewed to make tea. The wood, a soft-course-grained light-buff in color, can be used in general construction projects, but especially to make shipping crates, railroad ties, and pulp in paper manufacturing.

As mentioned above, hemlock needles can be used to make tea. The Native American Seneca legend titled "Hotho," features the cold's (Hotho's) attempt to conquer a man who had been hunting.

> They had a long discussion and at last agreed that when night came, they would have a trial of strength. The man went home,

carried in wood enough to burn till morning, built a huge fire and made a kettle full of hemlock tea. He stood in front of the fire all night, turning first one side then the other toward the heat, often drinking a cup of hot tea. It was terribly cold and grew colder and colder till near morning. Just at daybreak, Hotho ... came into the house. "You have beaten me," said he, and that minute it began to grow warm and thaw. This shows that man can conquer Hotho" with hemlock tea.[2]

As can be concluded from *The Hemlock Tree and Its Legends*, this woody plant is considered to be sacred by Native Americans. Reed College presents the mythology that explains the small cones borne by the tree in a story featuring Harry Hemlock:

> Harry was playing with his friends one day, and he didn't hear his teacher call him to select a cone. Cindy Cedar heard the call and ran up to get a good cone. Doug Fir heard the call and ran to get a good cone. But, by the time Harry looked up and saw what was happening, it was too late. All the good cones were gone and poor Harry was stuck with tiny little cones, and he could only hang his head in shame. Ever since then, hemlocks have been easy to recognize by their tiny cones and the tops that hang over to the side.[3]

According to Bradbury's book, the tree is sacred because it protects those who take refuge under it. The Native Americans decide to hold a council, and the tree states: "Then from each little band a few. / In council wise, in courage true. / For stern deliberation here / Beneath my ample shade appear; / And taking seats upon the ground / Await in silence most profound / The movement of some ancient sage ...."[4] In "Okteondo and His Uncle, the Planter, or, Winter Delaying Spring," a lengthy Seneca legend, Okteondo, who lived in the woods,

> said to his friends, "We will camp on the ice ...." And getting a handful of dry leaves and hemlock boughs he said to the men, "Follow in my steps, and be sure to put your feet in my tracks." ... He put down his handful of boughs and leaves and it became a great pile. He said, "I want a fire!" And there was a fire. He scattered a handful of hemlock boughs on the other side of the fire, and said, "Here will be our house and beds." And straightway a

---

2. "Hotho."
3. "Hemlocks."
4. Bradbury, *Hemlock Tree*, 41.

> house of hemlock boughs covered their fire, and in the house was a place for each one of the four men to sleep.[5]

Of course only the part of the narrative featuring the hemlock is quoted above in order to display its protecting characteristic.

Another lengthy Seneca legend, titled "A Little Boy and His Dog, Beautiful Ears," also features the hemlock serving a protective role. "A man and his wife went into the woods to hunt. They built a house of hemlock boughs, and lived happily," the legend begins. "After a while, a boy was born to them. . . . Another child was born to them, a girl." The woman figures out that the man is abusing their son.

> . . . [S]he caught up a club and struck her husband till he was helpless. Then, leaving him on the ground, she ran home, put her children outside, and set fire to the cabin. The hemlock boughs blazed up quickly, and soon the cabin was in ashes. Then she said to her children, "You must stay here. Everything will be all right." And taking up a handful of ashes, she threw the ashes into the air and said, "Let there be a snowstorm, and let the snow be as high as these trees." When snow began to fall, the mother said to the little boy, "Here is your dog; keep him with you and take care of your sister." Then she started off. Snow fell fast and soon the boy and girl were covered up, but they felt as warm and comfortable as if in a house. After a time the father dragged himself toward home. . . . He searched for his children and at last found them; then he set about building a house of boughs.[6]

While there is much more to the legend, the two houses constructed out of hemlock boughs protect the family.

In "The Dream Fast," a boy named Opichi goes on a vision quest at the urging of his father. He and his father go into the forest, and on the top of a hill "Opichi made a small lean-to of saplings, covering it with hemlock boughs." Even though the father checks on his son every day and the son reports his vision from the night before, the father keeps telling him to wait for a more powerful dream. Finally, on the morning of the seventh day, Opichi's mother states that it is time to bring home their son. When they looked

> into the small lean-to of hemlock boughs and saplings, . . . a bird came flying out. . . . It sang as it perched on a branch above them. "My parents," said the bird, "you see me as I am now. The one who was your son is gone. You sent him out too early and asked

---

5. "Okteondo."
6. "A Little Boy."

him to wait for power too long. Now I will return each spring . . . . My song will let people know it is the time for a boy to go on his dream fast. . . ." Then, . . . the robin flew off into the forest.[7]

Another Native American legend explains the line from the above text, which stated: "In every branch I have a tongue, / I have a voice in every breeze." In a Seneca legend, titled "How the Conifers Show the Promise of Spring," a long time ago "the trees had tongues, and they talked."[8] Winter and Spring are fighting.

> "I am the friend of Spring," spoke up White Pine. "That may be," answered Winter, "but when I give the order, away will go your green leaves, and I shall cover them with snow." . . . White Pine called a council of all his tribe. . . . "Who will stand with me as Winter comes?" called out Pine. "Who will defy Winter and stand his blasts? Who, as a friend of Spring, will stand as an eternal promise that Spring will return?" . . . "I will," said Hemlock [, among others]. . . . The gods of Winter ruled long and harshly, holding the Earth in a cold embrace. But they could not overcome Pine and his friends. . . . And so, forever afterward, the kinsmen of Pine hold forth the promise of Spring's return, and their green robes are the despair of Winter and all his furious hosts.[9]

For Native American Haida and Aleut the hemlock represents transformation. In "How Raven Brought Light to the World," the legend begins with raven, a trickster character, bumping into things in the dark and vowing to steal the light. He stumbled upon an old man who had all the light of the universe contained in a tiny box. Here was his plan:

> He waited until the old man's daughter came to the river to gather water. Then the raven changed himself into a single hemlock needle and dropped himself into the river, just as the girl was dipping her water-basket into the river. As she drank from the basket, she swallowed the needle. It slipped and slithered down into her warm belly, where the raven transformed himself again, this time into a tiny human. After sleeping and growing there for a very long time at last the raven emerged into the world once more, this time as a human infant.[10]

---

7. "Dream Fast."
8. "How the Confers Show the Promise of Spring."
9. Ibid.
10. "How Raven Brought Light."

After begging his grandfather to let him hold the box of light, his grandfather granted him permission to do so.

> As the light was moving toward him, the human child transformed into a gigantic black shadowy bird-form, wings spread ready for flight, and beak open in anticipation. As the beautiful ball of light reached him, the raven captured it in his beak! Moving his powerful wings, he burst through the smoke-hole in the roof of the house, and escaped into the darkness with his stolen treasure. And that is how light came into the universe.[11]

In "Princess Raven," a princess is transformed into a raven. In this Aleut legend, the chief

> did not like raven because he could transform himself into various things. . . . "I will fly into the air above the river and turn myself into a hemlock needle. When it floats down to you, pick it up and swallow it" [, he said to the princess. The] princess nodded and wondered what was going to happen as raven flew into the air. In an instant he was gone. A small hemlock needle slowly fell towards the water. When it floated down to her, [the] princess picked it up and swallowed it. She waited, but nothing happened. Then she felt a jerk in her back. The princess reached back to see what the pain was, and to her surprise she felt feathers; a wing grew out of her back and wrapped around her. It was so warm. The princess felt a love like never before. . . . Raven and the princess were joined together throughout all time.[12]

In a long Micmac legend, titled "The Adventures of the Great Hero Pulowech, or the Partridge," Pulowech encounters two evil magicians who attempt to roast him to death in a cavern. He enters the cavern and seats himself before them. The

> woman was of the Porcupines, who are never long without raising their quills, and they are fond of heat. Now there was in the cave much hemlock bark, and this she began to heap on the fire. Then it blazed, it crackled and roared; but Pulowech sat still, and said naught, neither did his eyes change. And he called unto himself all his might, the might of his magic did he awaken, and the spirit came unto him very terribly, so that all [the wicked wizards] with their vile black witchcraft were but as worms before him . . . . And when the fire had burned low, he brought in by his will a great store of bark, so that the whole cave was filled,

11. Ibid.
12. "Princess Raven."

and closing the door he lighted the fuel. Then the Porcupines, who were those who had slain his wife and friend, howled for mercy, but he was deaf as a stone to their cries. Then the roof and sides of the cavern cracked with the heat, the red-hot stones fell in heavy blocks, the red flames rose in the thickest smoke, but Pulowech sat and sang his song until the witch and wizard were burned to cinders.[13]

Thus, Pulowech, using hemlock, transformed evil magicians into ash.

The hemlock tree serves as an *axis mundi* and a means of escape in several Native American legends. For example, in the very long-titled and very long Micmac story—"Of the Surprising and Singular Adventures of Two Water Fairies Who Were Also Weasels, and How They Each Became the Bride of a Star, Including the Mysterious and Wonderful Works of Lox, the Great Indian Devil, Who Rose from the Dead"—two sisters, who travel to the stars, return to earth only to discover that they are

> in the summit of a tall spreading hemlock tree, and that in such a manner that they could not descend without assistance. . . . And as they sat there and day dawned, men of the different Indian families went by, and unto all of these they cried for help. It is true that their star husbands had made for them in the tree a bed of moss, but they cared not to rest in the hemlock. . . .[14]

The hemlock tree connects the realm of the stars to the realm of earth.

In the Seneca legend titled "A Raccoon Story," the hemlock serves a similar purpose. A young man, who can control the elements, is attacked by a huge bat.

> The young man took a hemlock leaf from his pocket and dropping it over the rocks, sang, "A tree must grow from this hemlock leaf. A tree must grow from this hemlock leaf." Soon a tree came in sight. Then the man talked to the tree [saying], "Come near and have many limbs." As the tree came to a level with the place on the rocks where the young man was sitting, it stopped growing. He had seen that along the narrow shelf of rocks there were many men. He called to the nearest one to tell all to come and they could escape. The men crept up, one after another, [and] went down on the tree.[15]

The hemlock tree, grown through magical means, becomes a means of escape.

13. "Adventures."
14. "Of the Surprising and Singular Adventures of Two Water Fairies."
15. "Raccoon Story."

Likewise, in another Seneca legend titled "Mink and His Uncle," the hemlock serves as a ladder for Mink, who is trapped on a rock. The tale is long, but the point of interest here concerns the magic hemlock tree.

> He leaned over the cliff, ran his fingers down his throat, and, trying very hard, vomited a little. Then he began to sing, "Let a great hemlock tree grow from that. Let a great hemlock tree grow from that." As he sang, a tree began to grow, and it grew till its boughs were far above the cliff. . . . As he went down, the tree decreased. When he reached the ground, it disappeared.[16]

"Uncle and Nephew" is a third Seneca legend featuring a magic hemlock tree that serves as an *axis mundi* and a means of escape. The boy, who is trapped in a ravine, has a dream about getting out; a woman appears to him and tells him what he needs to do.

> Just at sunrise the next morning, the boy vomited as the woman of the dream had said he would, and he found a little hemlock leaf. He stuck the leaf in the ground near the wall of the ravine and began to sing. The leaf became a tree, and, as the boy sang, the tree grew higher and higher. . . . The limbs of the tree were near together, like a ladder, and the [boy] climbed easily.[17]

Waite narrates the history of Hemlock Lake and the three-mile Hemlock Valley in which it is located in western New York, noting that "it was probably so named [by the Seneca, who made it one of their great fishing grounds,] from the hemlock forest, lying along its western shore."[18] Referring to the biblical Adam, he states that "if Adam's early education [were] not neglected, he might have made the tour of America and taken in the Hemlock on his way."[19] Waite also narrates the legend of the tribal war between the Munsees and Mengwees. The Mengwees defeat and kill all the Munsees, except for Onnolee, a maiden, who "was taken, bound, to the red belt of a famous leader, called Mickinac, and compelled to follow him, but at noon they rested for dinner beneath the branches of a spreading oak." She with

> stealthiness of hand saw and grasped from his belt, and, with one mighty thrust, buried his belt-knife deep into the side of her captor. . . . [S]he fled while arrows went whizzing by her in all directions. She gained at last a crag that beetled over . . . the Hemlock. [In] a low, mournful death hymn [she] sang. [Then]

16. "Mink."
17. "Uncle and Nephew."
18. Waite, "Up and Down the Hemlock."
19. Ibid.

on hill and forest looked her last, one glance upon the water cast, and from that high rock she sprang.[20]

According to the legend, for over three hundred years Onnolee could be seen rising from the waters and vanishing during the summer. Thus, in some ways Hemlock Lake, surrounded by hemlock trees, shares in the same magic legends narrated above.

Thus, the non-poisonous hemlock tree is known by its small cones, its longevity, and the tea that can be made from its leaf-needles to conquer the cold. As seen in multiple legends featuring the hemlock, it is a sign of protection, especially when used in construction of shelters. As an evergreen, it is a sign of spring, transformation, and a means of escape. Most importantly, this sacred tree is an *axis mundi* connecting different levels of the world.

Since this entry began with verses from *The Hemlock Tree and Its Legends*, it seems only fitting that it should end that way. So, after Conshomon is reunited with his wife and Snake marries Pearly Dew, the hemlock tree narrates: "How oft beneath my shade they sat / And filled the air with lively chat. / While Conshomon and his loved wife / Would often to the scene add life; / And often to their wives they told / Adventures wild and exploits bold. / While pledges of their loves would stray / Around, or wildly skip and play. / And happier couples than the two, / I ne'er expect again to view. / Here ends my tale; should you incline / Some more to hear, another time, / Come sit beneath the hemlock tree / Again, and listen unto me, / And many a legend, yet untold, / With pleasure, I'll to you unfold."[21]

Journal/Meditation: What specific characteristic of the sacred hemlock tree—a sign of longevity, protection, spring, transformation, escape—captures your imagination? How do you find this characteristic manifested in your life? If the hemlock tree could talk, what would it say to you?

Prayer: Ever-living God, Father of all peoples, you entrust the care of your creation to those you have endowed with reason. Give me a great respect for all that you have made. Grant me the grace to hear your voice in the wind whispering through the hemlock trees. I ask this in the name of your Son, Jesus Christ, who lives and reigns with you and the Holy Spirit, one God, forever and ever. Amen.

---

20. Ibid.
21. Bradbury, *Hemlock Tree*, 113–4.

Holm

Text: "The carpenter stretches a line, marks [the idol] out with a stylus, fashions it with planes, and marks it with a compass; he makes it in human form, with human beauty, to be set up in a shrine. He cuts down cedars or chooses a holm tree or an oak and lets it grow strong among the trees of the forest. Then he makes a god and worships it, makes it a carved image and bows down before it." (Isa 44:13–14a, 15c)

Reflection: In all of sacred literature there is only one mention of the holm tree, also known as the holm oak, the holly oak, and the evergreen oak. That one notation occurs in the passage above from the prophet Isaiah. In a much longer section (Isa 44:9–20), the prophet explains how people make idols out of this high-grade durable wood. In his reproof of idolatry, the prophet explains that since human beings make idols, they are false gods; people cannot create gods!

The holm tree is known as a holm oak because its fruit is an acorn, and its wood is hard and durable like any oak tree. Since the prophet Isaiah is referring to the idols made from it, he has in mind its toughness and use since ancient times for pillars, tools, wagons, and, obviously, idols. The holm tree is called a holly oak because of its leaves. It grows leathery toothed leaves with a dark green upper surface and fine whitish-gray hairs on the lower surface; the spiny leaves look just like holly leaves. The holm tree is also known as the evergreen oak because, unlike other types of oak, it does not lose its leaves in the winter. There is a reference to this tree which grows in the garden of Joakim in Susanna 1:58 (Dan 13:58) (see Oak). No matter by what name it is known, it grows throughout the Mediterranean basin.

In narrating the story of "Aeneas and the Golden Bough," Caldecott mentions the holm oak. Aeneas, the son of Anchises and Venus, asks the Cumean sibyl if he can visit his father in the world of the dead. She tells him that he can if he can find the golden bough of Juno which is hidden in a dark forest and pluck it for Persephone, queen of the underworld. As a great hero of the Trojan War, he prays that the bough will reveal itself to him. Two doves appear and lead "him to a gigantic holm oak deep in the darkest and most inaccessible part of the forest."[1] Peering through the branches, he sees the gleam of gold, and, reaching up, Aeneas takes hold of it and breaks it off in order to bring it to the Cumaen sibyl.

Since the oak tree will be covered in depth in the chapter dedicated to the oak, here the focus is on the "Legend of the Holly," since the holly oak's leaves look like holly leaves. According to the version found in McGinley, the red holly berry was once white, blooming "on its tree by a stable door." After Jesus is born, one of the villagers who came to see the child "has nothing of note, so he fetches a branch of the holly tree" and the newborn pricks "his finger upon a thorn," leaving "his blood on the spiny leaves." Because the holly is heavy-hearted, it grieves and sees in a vision "how a crown of holly shall bind his brow when [the] child is [a] man."[2] Once the holly has the vision, it blushes and its berries turn red. Thus, to this day the fruit of the holly is red.

According to Count, "[t]he spines of the holly leaves" were used at Christmastime because they became "thickets to catch and hold the hags."[3] Furthermore, because holly is a type of evergreen, buildings were decked with holly. "Green belongs in the realm of summer and life," states Count; "winter kills most of summer's train, but the greens remain steadfast."[4] The understanding was simple: "Where the greens are, it is not winter. They are the enemies of winter's white death."[5]

Thus, the sacred holm tree has many names, and each name has a different connotation. It was used to make idols and to drive away demons. As an evergreen, it is an enemy of winter. It is like an oak because its wood is hard and its fruit is an acorn. It is like a holly because it leaves look like spiny holly leaves. As legends grew around it, its once-white berries became red with the blood of the child Jesus. Furthermore, it became the crown of thorns he wore to his death on a cross. Because it once blushed, the berries turned red to remind those who decorate with it at Christmas that this sacred tree's fruit is the color of blood shed on the cross.

1. Caldecott, *Myths*, 104.
2. McGinley, *Wreath*, 61.
3. Count, *4000 Years*, 75.
4. Ibid., 77–8.
5. Ibid., 78.

Journal/Meditation: Figuratively, what idol have you carved recently? Is it a career, spouse, sport, etc.? What fruit did your idol produce?

Prayer: LORD God, at one time in history your chosen people carved idols from the holm tree even though you had revealed yourself to them as an unimaginable deity. Grant me the grace to recognize the idols I create and the One who saved me from them with his blood on the cross: Jesus Christ, who is Lord forever and ever. Amen.

Incense (Myrrh, Aloes)

Text: "Your channel is an orchard . . . with all trees of frankincense, myrrh, and aloes . . . ." (Song 4:14).

Reflection: In the HB (OT) Song of Songs or Song of Solomon, the unnamed man praises the beauty of the unnamed woman by comparing her channel, an intimate part of her body, to a garden or a park with an orchard of trees that provide exotic, fragrant, desirable ointments and spices—all known for their sweet scents. "The wide variety of precious and fragrant growth cannot be found in any one place," states Murphy.[1] "Botany yields to an imagination that strives to capture female charms."[2] While not mentioning the specific trees indicated above, the OT (A) Book of Baruch declares, "The woods and every fragrant tree have shaded Israel at God's command" (Bar 5:8).

Incense

While the author of Song of Songs may have been focused on communicating the fragrance of his lover's body, there is no such thing as an incense tree. More specifically, the product is known as frankincense, "a fragrant gum-resin occurring in the form of large tears light yellowish-brown in color."[3] According to McKenzie, "The gum is yielded by Boswellia trees native to

---

1. Murphy, "Canticle," 464.
2. Ibid.
3. McKenzie, *Dictionary*, 386.

Somaliland and Southern Arabia."[4] Jeremiah mentions "frankincense that comes from Sheba" (Jer 6:20) in Southern Arabia, modern-day Yemen, as does Isaiah (Isa 60:6).

Frankincense to be burned before the LORD is made from "sweet spices, stacte, and onycha, and galbanum, sweet spices with pure frankincense (an equal part of each)" (Exod 30:34; cf. Sir 24:15). It is "blended as by the perfumer, seasoned with salt, pure and holy" and beaten "into powder" (Exod 30:35–36; cf. Sir 49:1). This incense is not made for people; it is holy to the LORD (Exod 30:37). It is used with grain offerings (Lev 2:1–2, 15–16; 6:15; Jer 17:26), the twelve loaves of bread set out weekly on the Sabbath (Lev. 24:7), and a memorial offering (Isa 66:3). Only the author of Matthew's Gospel narrates the story of the magi bringing the gift of frankincense to the newly-born Jesus (Matt 2:11), and the Book of Revelation mentions it as one of the lost-wealth products mourned by the merchants after Babylon falls (Rev 18:13).

As McKenzie states, "Other aromatic substances were burned as perfume."[5] Generally, the Bible refers to these as "fragrant incense" (Exod 25:6; 31:11; 35:8, 28; 37:29; 39:38; 40:27; Num 4:16; 2 Chr 2:4; 13:11) which is placed in dishes (Exod 25:29; 37:16; Num 4:7; 1 Kgs 7:50; 2 Kgs 25:14)—made out of gold (Num 7:14, 20, 26, 32, 38, 44, 50, 56, 62, 68, 74, 80, 86)—and offered to God on an altar (Exod 30:1, 7–9, 27; 31:8; 35:15; 37:25; 40:5; Lev 4:7; 1 Sam 2:28; 1 Kgs 9:25; 1 Chr 6:49; 28:18; 2 Chr 34:7; 1 Macc 4:49–50; 2 Macc 2:5; Heb 9:4). While it is not described, the HB (OT) Book of Leviticus mentions a censer full of coals of fire upon which two handfuls of crushed sweet incense are placed and presented to the LORD (Lev 16:12; Num 16:7, 17, 18, 46, 47; 2 Chr 26:19; Sir 50:9; Ezek 8:11). This seems to be some kind of pot with fire or a pot with fire attached to a chain or chains into which incense is placed.

The wisdom literature of the Bible assigns various meanings to the incense. Psalm 141 compares it to prayer (Ps 141:2), as does the CB (NT) Book of Revelation, which mentions "golden bowls full of incense, which are the prayers of the saints" (Rev. 5:8; cf. 8:3–4). The Book of Proverbs states that it makes the heart glad (Prov 27:9). The OT (A) Book of Wisdom says it atones for sins (Wis 18:21; Sir 45:16). Ryken states that "incense indicates one's reverent allegiance and dependence upon God."[6]

---

4. Ibid.

5. Ibid.

6. Ryken, *Dictionary*, 419.

Myrrh

Unlike incense that is not the name of a tree, myrrh trees do exist, as named above in the text from Song of Songs. Furthermore, Segal states that Adonis's mother, Smyrna, was "turned . . . into a myrrh tree"[7] after she prayed to the gods to rescue her from her father. Witcombe also records that "the terraces of the Funerary Temple of Hatshepsut . . . were planted with myrrh trees."[8] The trees grew at the southern end of the Red Sea. McKenzie identifies myrrh as "a spice produced from the gum resin of a large bush or small tree . . . ."[9] He explains: "The aromatic gum appears when the thin bark is pierced; it hardens and turns red when exposed to the air."[10] Dharmananda further explains this collection process: "Most resin is obtained by tapping: making deliberate incisions with a specially designed tool or ordinary ax, about two inches long, into the bark of the tree. The milky liquid that exudes hardens on exposure to air into droplets or 'tears,' which are then easily detached by the collector about two weeks later."[11]

In the Bible, myrrh appears primarily in liquid form. It is a primary ingredient in making a sacred anointing oil (Exod 30:23) used to anoint the tent of meeting, the ark of the covenant, the lampstand, the altar of incense, Aaron and his sons, and more (Exod 30:22–33). Whatever the holy anointing oil (Exod 30:23) touches becomes consecrated or holy to the LORD (Exod 30:29).

Besides being used to anoint objects as the primary ingredient in the sacred anointing oil, myrrh is considered to be an essential oil used as a perfume with intoxicating qualities. Psalm 45, a royal hymn praising the king, declares that his "robes are all fragrant with myrrh" (Ps 45:8). The HB (OT) Book of Proverbs narrates a tale of adultery; the married woman seduces a young man after having "perfumed [her] bed with myrrh" (Prov 7:17). And in the CB (NT) Book of Revelation, the merchants of Babylon weep because of their lost wealth; no one buys their myrrh any more (Rev 18:13).

In addition to the reference above, the Song of Songs mentions myrrh six more times. Using erotic language, the woman declares that her lover is to her "a bag of myrrh that lies between [her] breasts" (Song 1:13); in other words, he smells as good as the rare perfume she spreads between her cleavage! Later, she compares him to "a column of smoke, perfumed with myrrh" (Song 3:6)

---

7. Segal, *Myth*, 6.
8. Witcombe, "Trees and the Sacred."
9. McKenzie, *Dictionary*, 595.
10. Ibid.
11. Dharmananda, "Myrrh and Frankincense."

coming from the wilderness. He refers to her breasts as a "mountain of myrrh" (Song 4:6b) which he gathers or touches (Song 5:1). Using even more erotic language, she declares, "I arose to open to my beloved, and my hands dripped with myrrh, my fingers with liquid myrrh" (Song 5:5). Later, she describes his lips as being like lilies, "distilling liquid myrrh" (Song 5:13b). Likewise, the OT (A) Book of Sirach describes lady wisdom using sexually charged language; she states that like choice myrrh she spread her fragrance (Sir 24:15a). The HB (OT) Book of Esther indicates that myrrh was used as a cosmetic treatment to prepare Esther to meet King Ahasuerus; for six months she was treated with oil of myrrh (Esth 2:12) in order to make her appealing to the king. Ahasuerus fell in love with Esther, who won his favor and devotion; upon her head he placed the queen's crown (Esth 2:17).

In Egypt, myrrh was used for embalming the bodies of pharaohs and other important officials. This is why the author of Matthew's Gospel in the CB (NT) uniquely portrays magi bringing the gift of myrrh to Jesus (Matt 2:11). Along with their other funerary gifts of gold and frankincense myrrh indicates to the reader of the story that by its end the child will be dead. This use of myrrh is further confirmed in John's Gospel when the unique character Nicodemus brings "a mixture of myrrh and aloes, weighing about a hundred pounds" (John 19:39) to place within the linen cloths that wrapped the body of Jesus before he was placed in the tomb; the myrrh was used to reduce the smell of decay.

Only Mark's Gospel mentions that the soldiers who crucified Jesus "offered him wine mixed with myrrh, but he did not take it" (Mark 15:23). Myrrh added to wine creates a sedative which brings the person who takes it to a state of calm, much like a modern anesthetic works today.

Aloes

The final item mentioned in the Song of Songs is aloes, another "aromatic oil derived from a tree . . . from which both the product and the name are probably derived."[12] The prophet Balaam states that the camp of the Israelites is like aloes that the LORD has planted (Num 24:6b); thus, he indicates that there is a tree named aloes. The royal hymn in honor of the king declares that his robes are all fragrant with aloes (Ps 45:8). Like myrrh, aloes was a milky sap extracted from a tree that hardened into a costly fragrant resin. According to the Book of Proverbs, it was used to perfume one's bed (Prov 7:17), and it is usually mentioned in biblical texts with myrrh, as it is in John 19:39. As already noted, the author of the Fourth Gospel uniquely narrates

12. McKenzie, *Dictionary*, 21.

that Nicodemus brings a mixture of myrrh and aloes (John 19:39) to use in preparing the body of Jesus for entombment. As noted above, with myrrh aloes were used by the Egyptians to embalm dead bodies.

Thus, sacred trees produce fragrant resins which are used to make (frank)incense, myrrh, and aloes. Frankincense is holy to the LORD; it is added to offerings. Its holy smoke represents the offerings and prayers rising to God; in a three-story universe where God lives above the dome of the sky and people live on the earth, the rising smoke of the burned offerings and spices—from which frankincense is made—rises up to God. Likewise sacred to God is myrrh, used in making sacred anointing oil, but also used as a costly perfume for clothes and beds. In the Song of Songs myrrh becomes the metaphor for lots of erotic images of lovers. It is also used for embalming and burials to reduce the stench of a decaying body. Like myrrh, aloes was also used in embalming and burials. As an expensive perfume, it was used for clothes and beds. All these fragrant resin-based spices come from sacred trees.

Journal/Meditation: What oils or spices that come from trees do you have in your house? Check the labels on items in your medicine cabinet, cosmetic case, and spice rack to determine from which sacred tree those items come.

Prayer: As frankincense rises to you, O God, let my prayer come before you. Anoint me with the fragrant myrrh of the Holy Spirit and perfume me with the aloes of your dead and resurrected Son, Jesus Christ. Raise me to new life with him; he is Lord forever and ever. Amen.

Joshua

Text: "... [T]he LORD said to Joshua, 'Stretch out the sword that is in your hand toward Ai; for I will give it into your hand.' And Joshua stretched out the sword that was in his hand toward the city. . . . Joshua did not draw back his hand, with which he stretched out the sword, until he had utterly destroyed all the inhabitants of Ai." (Joshua 8:18, 26)

Reflection: The Bible does not contain a reference to the Joshua tree, which is native to the arid southwestern area of the United States in California, Arizona, Utah, and Nevada, and is found mostly in the Mojave Desert. According to legend, the name of the tree was given by Mormon pioneers and settlers who crossed the desert in the nineteenth century.[1] They saw the unique shape of the tree, and it reminded them of the story of Joshua holding his hand outstretched toward the city of Ai. The Mormons interpreted Joshua's action as prayer. Thus, seeing the gnarled branches of the tree reaching up to the sky, the Mormons named it Joshua in honor of Moses' successor as leader of the Israelites. Just as Joshua's raised hand pointed the way for his army to defeat Ai, so the Joshua tree pointed the way for the Mormons.

    Joshua's action of holding his hand with the sword toward Ai until the city was destroyed is meant to echo the account of Moses doing something similar. When Joshua engaged Amalek in battle, Joshua was assisted by Moses, who stood on the top of a hill with the staff of God in his hand (Exod 17:9). The narrator states: "Whenever Moses held up his hand, Israel prevailed; and whenever he lowered his hand, Amalek prevailed" (Exod 17:11). Ultimately, Moses' hands grow weary, and Aaron and Hur seat Moses on a rock and stand on either side of him, holding up his hands until Joshua wins

---

1. Clarke, "Joshua Tree."

the battle (Exod 17:12–13). Just as Moses' held up hands in a type of prayer gave success to the Israelites in battle, Joshua, who is biblically modeled on Moses, held up his hands to give the Israelites success in battle.

Joshua, whose name means *Yahweh is salvation*,[2] is commissioned by Moses to be his successor as leader of the Israelites. The LORD tells Moses, "Take Joshua son of Nun, a man in whom is the spirit, and lay your hand upon him" (Num 27:18). Thus, the divine spirit that God gave to Moses is transferred to Joshua. The Book of Deuteronomy makes this clear: "Joshua son of Nun was full of the spirit of wisdom, because Moses had laid his hands on him; and the Israelites obeyed him, doing as the LORD had commanded Moses" (Deut 34:9). However, earlier, the Book of Deuteronomy states that "the LORD commissioned Joshua son of Nun and said, 'Be strong and bold, for you shall bring the Israelites into the land that I promised them; I will be with you'" (Deut 31:23). In either story of commissioning Joshua is given God's spirit which will enable him to save the Israelites by leading them into battle and into the promised land. Likewise, Mormon pioneers saw the Joshua tree as the way to their salvation as they headed west.

Because Mormon settlers possessed a biblical paradigm, they considered themselves going to their promised land through the desert just like Moses and Joshua led the Israelites through the desert to the promised land; therefore, it was a logical next step that they would name a tree after the Israelite leader who guided them through the desert. Furthermore, the long life of the Joshua tree, not to mention its survival rate in the desert, adds to its association with Joshua and his ability to survive by defeating the occupants of the promised land. Likewise, the palm-like leaves of the Joshua tree, sometimes called the yucca palm, gave it an association with the palm trees that grew in the promised land.

The name Joshua is Hebrew and was very common at the beginning of the first century CE. In Greek Joshua is rendered *Jesus*. Its meaning is alluded to by the angel who appears to Joseph in Matthew's Gospel. Joseph is told to name the child born of Mary "Jesus, for he will save his people from their sins" (Matt 1:21); literally, the name means *the Lord saves*, *he saves*, or *Yahweh helps*, basically the same meaning of Joshua given above. Jesus' role is that of leader to the new promised land, the kingdom of God.

Thus, the name given to the tree now known as Joshua not only bears the name of a well-known biblical leader, but it identifies the tree as sacred. It associates the tree with the HB (OT) successor to Moses—Joshua—and it associates it with the CB (NT) savior—Jesus. The Joshua tree marked the way for the Mormon pioneers and settlers through the desert as they headed to the

---

2. McKenzie, *Dictionary*, 457.

new promised land. It reminded them to pray and to follow their leader. And, as a sacred tree, more importantly, it reminded them that God saves.

Journal/Meditation: What tree reminds you to pray? What tree reminds you of your need for a leader or your commission to lead? What tree reminds you that God saves?

Prayer: LORD, you told your servant Joshua to be strong and bold, so that he could lead the Israelites into the land that you showed them. You promised to be with him and to save them from their enemies. In the person of Jesus, you came to save all people and lead them to your kingdom, where you live and reign with Christ and the Holy Spirit, one God, forever and ever. Amen.

Kadam

Text: "I saw the herdsman, him who never stumbles, approaching by his pathways and departing. He, clothed with gathered and diffusive splendor, within the worlds continually travels." (*RV* 1:164:31)

Reflection: The kadam, also known as the kadamb and kadamba, tree is an evergreen which, in Hindu mythology, was the favorite tree of Krishna, who is an incarnation of Vishnu. Some think that "the herdsman . . . who never stumbles" from verse 31 of hymn 164 in *The Rig Veda* refers to a story about Krishna as a cowherd who is often depicted playing his flute under a kadam tree. There are a number of versions of the story, but the basic theme is that he loved to play his flute for milk maids under a kadam tree. The milk maids found him charming and fell in love with him. One in particular named Radha fell madly in love with him and became immortal. In many images representing their immoral love she is depicted next to him under the kadam tree.

In another version of the story about the milk maids, Krishna is accused of stealing the clothes of the milk maids while they were bathing. He took the clothes to a kadam tree and spread them on the branches. Then, hiding behind some branches, he perched in the tree. When the milk maids noticed that their clothes were gone, they looked up into the branches and saw Krishna in the kadam tree and their clothes hung on the branches.

The kadam tree is also associated with the goddess Parvati, the wife of Shiva. Parvati is thought to dwell in a kadam forest, thus it is often called her tree. She is the Hindu mother goddess with over a hundred names, but mostly associated with fertility, love, devotion, divine strength, and power.

Those who pay homage to the kadam tree are supposed to ensure for themselves wealth and progeny.

These stories illustrate the Hindu concept of play for fun and enjoyment. Krishna played the flute and the milk maids came to the kadam tree to join him in singing and dancing. Play is also illustrated by the tale of Krishna stealing the milk maids's clothes while they were bathing in the river. The story presents a lightness to this Hindu god who sat under or in a sacred kadam tree. To honor both Krishna and Parvati, kadam flowers are offered at their various temples.

Journal/Meditation: What tree is sacred to you? How important is play in your life? Where do you engage in play? What is the most outrageous prank you have ever pulled?

Prayer: God of the forests, you have given the woods as playgrounds to your people. When I camp, hike, or walk among your trees, fill me with a greater appreciation for your splendor. Hear this prayer in the name of your Son, Jesus Christ, my Lord. Amen.

Laurel

Text: "Athletes exercise self-control in all things; they do it to receive a perishable wreath, but we an imperishable one." (1 Cor 9:25)

Reflection: In Paul's First Letter to the Corinthians, he employs an athletic metaphor to encourage his readers to use self-discipline in their lives as they engage in the race toward eternal life. In other words, those who engage in sports have to train, and part of training involves disciplining their desires. Likewise, those who follow Christ have to train, and the Christian life involves disciplining desires. The athlete who won the race in Paul's day received a perishable wreath, which was often made from the branches of the laurel tree. Christians were not racing for a laurel crown, which ultimately withers, but for the crown of eternal life which never perishes.[1]

Before Paul employed the athletic laurel wreath crown, the author of the Fourth Book of Maccabees used it. After recounting stories of fearless Jews who suffered death rather than apostatize before their Greek rulers, the author states, "Reverence for God was victor and gave the crown to its own athletes" (4 Macc 17:15). Steadfastness in the face of persecution for this author was like winning a game and receiving the laurel wreath of victory.

Bulfinch narrates the story of how the leaves of the laurel tree came to be placed on the head of those who won athletic contests, especially Greek and Roman games. Apollo, one of the great gods of Olympus, son of Jupiter and Latona, fell in love with the nymph Daphne, daughter of the river god Peneus. As Apollo pursued her, she asked her father to change her form. Bullfinch states:

---

1. Grundmann, "Stephanos," 629.

... [A] stiffness seized all her limbs; her bosom began to be enclosed in a tender bark; her hair became leaves; her arms became branches; her foot stuck fast in the ground, as a root; her face became a tree top, retaining nothing of its former self but its beauty. Apollo stood amazed. He touched the stem, and felt the flesh tremble under the new bark. He embraced the branches, and lavished kisses on the wood. The branches shrank from his lips. "Since you cannot be my wife," said he, "you shall assuredly be my tree. I will wear you for my crown; I will decorate with you my harp and my quiver; and when the great Roman conquerors lead up the triumphal pomp to the Capitol, you shall be woven into wreaths for their brows. And as eternal youth is mine, you also shall be always green, and your leaf know no decay." The nymph, now changed into a laurel tree, bowed its head in grateful acknowledgement.[2]

Before this event attributed to Apollo, Bulfinch narrates the story of Apollo killing the Python, an enormous serpent. As a result of Apollo's victory, the Pythian games were held, and the winners were crowned "with a wreath of beech leaves; for the laurel was not yet adopted by Apollo as his own tree."[3] Grundmann states, ". . . Apollo . . . took a crown of laurel berries after defeating the dragon Delphys."[4] Tresidder says, ". . . Apollo . . . purified himself with [laurel] in the groves of Tempe in Thessaly after slaying the Python at Delphi."[5] Caldecott states, "The laurel becomes the means by which Apollo can commune with the gods at Delphi."[6]

Apollo is not the only god to wear the laurel. Grundmann notes: "Zeus wears a crown of laurel . . . . Aphrodite is similarly crowned, and soldiers wear the laurel when receiving imperial bounty and at triumphs."[7] She adds, "The emperor Tiberius put on a laurel crown during thunder storms because the laurel was a protection against lightning."[8] Tresidder notes that Dionysus (Bacchus) Zeus (Jupiter), Hera (Juno) and Artemis (Diana) considered laurel "an emblem of truce or peace as well as of triumph."[9]

In another legend about the laurel tree—found in The Proto-Gospel of James—Anna, wife of Joachim, is lamenting her barrenness. In the middle

2. Bulfinch, *Mythology*, 22; cf. Caldecott, *Myths*, 71–2.
3. Ibid., 19.
4. Grundmann, "Stephanos," 617.
5. Tresidder, *Dictionary of Symbols*, 283.
6. Caldecott, *Myths*, 74.
7. Grundmann, "Stephanos," 617.
8. Ibid., 619; cf. Tresidder, *Dictionary of Symbols*, 284.
9. Tresidder, *Dictionary of Symbols*, 284.

of the afternoon she goes for a walk in her garden. "She saw a laurel tree and sat beneath it, and after resting a bit she prayed" to God, asking him to give her a child (Proto-Jas 2:4).[10] According to Cavendish's summary of this story: "... [S]he saw a nest of young sparrows in the branches. She burst into a lament, contrasting her barren state with the fecundity of the birds, and suddenly an angel appeared to her and told her that she would bear a child whose fame the whole world would acknowledge."[11] In the meantime, Joachim, too, receives a similar message from an angel. In due time, Anna gives birth to Mary, the mother of Jesus. Her victory over her barrenness occurs under a laurel tree.

Caldecott narrates a myth about two wish-granting laurel trees. A herder boy named Michael sleeps under a tree in the heat of the day for three consecutive days and dreams about a lady visiting him who gives him directions as to where to go to find a princess to marry. He gets a job working with the gardener of the castle where twelve princesses live. One night in his dream he sees the lady again. "This time she was holding two young laurel trees.... She told him to plant the two laurels in two large pots and to take great care of them.... When they were grown..., he could ask them for anything he wished."[12]

Caldecott continues: "When he woke he found the two laurel trees beside him. He planted them and took great care of them as the lady had charged him, and when they were grown he asked one of them to make him invisible. Instantly a white flower appeared on the tree and he put it in his buttonhole."[13] This enabled him to follow the princesses to a dance without being detected. Once they find out that he has spied on them, they plot to have him thrown into the dungeon. "Michael heard their plot and went to the second laurel tree and asked to be dressed like a prince. A pink flower appeared, which he placed in his lapel, and at once he was dressed like a prince."[14] He ended up marrying the youngest princess, who "cut down the laurel trees so that he would never again have such an advantage over her."[15]

Peck records a folk tale, titled "A Bunch of Laurel Blooms for a Present," about a man leaving his home on business and asking his three daughters what they want him to bring them when he returns. "The youngest girl

---

10. Ehrman, *Apocryphal Gospels*, 43.
11. Cavendish, *Legends*, 208.
12. Caldecott, *Myths*, 170.
13. Ibid.
14. Ibid., 170-1.
15. Ibid. 172.

wanted him to bring her a bunch of laurel blooms for a present."[16] The man waited until he was ready to head home to find the laurel blossoms so they would not wilt. He found some on the edge of the woods.

> After he picked the laurel blooms, an old witch came out of the laurel bushes and said they belonged to her, and she didn't aim to let nobody pick them. She said he had already picked some, and he would have to die. He told her the flower blooms were for a present to his youngest girl. Then the old witch said he could live if he would give his youngest girl to her.[17]

The witch permitted the father of the three daughters to return home. He gave the laurel blossoms to his youngest daughter, who received them with joy and put them in water to keep them fresh. After he told her that he had to go back to see the witch, the youngest daughter ran off in the night in his place. The witch gave her a nice little house in which to live. She discovers a toad frog in the house which, of course, turns into a handsome young man. "They lived there amongst the laurel blooms together in the nice little house with an upstairs [all because] the youngest sister [had] asked for nothing more than a bunch of laurel blooms."[18]

Thus, the laurel tree, according to mythology, became a sacred aromatic evergreen with green, long, broad glossy leaves which were used to weave wreaths to be placed on the heads of the winners of athletic games as early as the seventh to sixth century BCE. As a sign of victory, Apollo was depicted wearing a laurel wreath on his head, and Anna is depicted sitting under a laurel tree in order to achieve victory over her barrenness. Two laurel trees enable Michael, a herder, to become a prince victoriously and to marry a princess victoriously. Consequently, the laurel wreath was also awarded to those who won martial victories. The wreaths could be shaped like a horseshoe or like a ring to indicate power and glory. In Christian iconography, the laurel wreath became a symbol of eternal life.[19] For example, the image of Christ painted in the apse of St. Meinrad Archabbey Church in St. Meinrad, Indiana, depicts Jesus holding in his right hand the "the laurel wreath crown of victory."[20] The wreath from the sacred laurel tree represents that Christ has been raised from the dead; he has defeated death by being raised to new life by God.

16. Peck, *North American Folktales*, 311.
17. Ibid.
18. Ibid., 313.
19. Taylor, *How to Read a Church*, 206.
20. "Renewed Heart," 14.

Journal/Meditation: In the practice of your faith, how are you like an athlete running the Christian race and hoping to win the laurel wreath of eternal life? In athletic contests today, what is the modern adaption of the laurel crown?

Prayer: Father of the Lord Jesus Christ, after your Son slept in death you awakened him, raised him to new life, and placed the laurel wreath of victory on his head. Keep me faithful to my race of the Christian life, and grant that I may be awarded the laurel wreath of eternal life. Hear me in the name of the same Jesus Christ, who lives and reigns with you and the Holy Spirit, one God, forever and ever. Amen.

Mastic

Text: "... [Daniel] summoned one of [the elders] and said to him, 'You old relic of wicked days, your sins have now come home, which you have committed in the past, pronouncing unjust judgments, condemning the innocent and acquitting the guilty, though the Lord said, "You shall not put an innocent and righteous person to death." Now then, if you really saw this woman [Susanna], tell me this: Under what tree did you see [her and the young man] being intimate with each other?' He answered, 'Under a mastic tree.'" (Sus 1:52–54 [Dan 13:52–54])

Reflection: The mastic tree is mentioned only in the OT (A) Book of Susanna (Daniel). Furthermore, chapter 13 of Daniel appears only in the Septuagint (the Greek translation of the Hebrew Bible) and in the Vulgate (the Latin translation of the Hebrew Bible). Serving as a type of novella, the sixty-four verses, often referred to as Susanna, are meant to portray the vindication of a righteous woman, who is accused of adultery by two corrupted Jewish elders. The elders want to have sex with Susanna, who is married to Hilkiah, but she refuses them. They plot a trap for her that consists of them lying that they saw her in the garden with a young man. Just as she is about to be executed for adultery—in a patriarchal culture the elders's truth will trump a woman's truth—Daniel enters the picture. He interrogates each of the two elders separately by asking under which tree in the garden they saw Susanna and the young man. One answers the mastic tree, and the other answers the oak tree. This discrepancy in testimony leads to the understanding that both are lying, and Susanna is saved.

    A mastic is an evergreen tree which grows in dry and rocky areas around the Mediterranean basin. It sports deep green, leathery leaves, but it is the resin—also known as mastic—that is harvested from it and used. The branches receive small cuts in order to bleed the tree of its liquid sap, which hardens into tear-shaped drops or beads. Once it is collected, the aromatic, ivory-colored resin is washed and harvested as a spice. The meaning of its name *mastic—to chew* or *to gnash the teeth*—indicates one of its ancient uses as chewing gum or breath freshener. When it was chewed, the resin softened and turned into a bright white and opaque gum. As a spice, it was used to flavor a variety of drinks and foods. It was also used to make lacquer and varnish.

Some biblical scholars think that "the valley of Baca" mentioned in Psalm 84:6 is another reference to the mastic tree. Since the Hebrew word *baca* appears to be derived from the Hebrew word for crying or weeping and refers to the tears of resin secreted by the mastic tree, "the valley of Baca"—which may have been near Jerusalem—was probably covered in mastic trees. Also, in "the valley of Rephaim," mentioned in 2 Samuel 5:22 (cf. 1 Chr 14:9), David is told by the LORD to listen to "the sound of marching in the tops of the balsam trees" (2 Sam 5:24; cf. 1 Chr 14:15) as his signal to attack the Philistines. Since balsam trees are mentioned in the Bible only two times in 2 Samuel (5:23, 24) and two times in 1 Chronicles (14:14, 15)—which narrates the same story—some scholars conclude that the authors are really describing mastic (baca) trees or shrubs, and instead of *balsam* the word should be *mastic*.

In the Book of Daniel, the mastic tree represents the chewing of an innocent young woman named Susanna by two lustful elders. Because of their status and power in the community, the elders have convinced others of Susanna's adultery, and she is about to be chewed—executed—for a crime she did not commit. The two elders have been chewed by lust. However, Daniel prefers to chew on justice, which he extracts from the elders through separate interrogations. At the end of the novella, the elders were put to death (Sus 1:62 [Dan 13:62]) and innocent blood was spared. Furthermore, the Greek word for mastic is *schinon*, which means *to cut*. Daniel tells the elder who identifies the couple as being under a mastic tree, "This lie has cost you your head, for the angel of God has received the sentence from God and will immediately cut you in two" (Sus 1:55 [Dan 13:55]). The word play illustrates the connection between the meaning of the sacred tree's name in Greek and the fate of the elder who lied.

Journal/Meditation: What lie have you recently told? Do you need to chew on it and enact justice? How can you repair the damage done by your lie?

Prayer: LORD God, you spared the life of Susanna through the wisdom of your prophet Daniel. With the inspiration of the Holy Spirit, guide me in the way of justice and truth. I ask this in the name of your Son, Jesus Christ, my Lord. Amen.

Mulberry

Text: "Pyramus was the handsomest youth, and Thisbe the fairest maiden . . . . Their parents occupied adjoining houses; and neighborhood brought the young people together, and acquaintance ripened into love. They would gladly have married, but their parents forbade [it]. . . . In the wall that parted the two houses there was a crack, caused by some fault in the structure. No one had remarked it before, but the lovers discovered it. . . . It afforded a passage to the voice; and tender messages used to pass backward and forward through the gap. . . . [T]hey agreed that . . . when all was still, they would slip away from watchful eyes, leave their dwellings, and walk out into the fields; and to insure a meeting, repair to a well-known edifice . . . at the foot of a certain tree. It was a white mulberry tree, and stood near a cool spring.

Then cautiously Thisbe stole forth, unobserved by the family, [and] made her way to the monument and sat down under the tree. As she sat alone in the dim light of the evening, she [saw] a lioness, her jaws reeking with recent slaughter, approaching the fountain to slake her thirst. Thisbe fled at the sight, and sought refuge in the hollow of a rock. As she fled, she dropped her veil. The lioness after drinking at the spring turned to retreat to the woods, and seeing the veil on the ground, tossed and rent it with her bloody mouth.

Pyramus, having been delayed, now approached the place of meeting. He saw in the sand the footsteps of the lion . . . , [and] he found the veil all rent and bloody. He took up the veil, carried it with him to the appointed tree, and covered it with kisses and with tears. . . . [D]rawing his sword, [he] plunged it into his heart. The blood spurted from the wound, and tinged the white mulberries of the tree all red; and sinking into the earth reached the roots, so that the red color mounted through the trunk to the fruit.

By this time Thisbe, still trembling with fear, yet wishing not to disappoint her lover, stepped cautiously forth, looking anxiously for the youth, eager to tell him the danger she had escaped. When she came to the spot and saw the changed color of the mulberries, she doubted whether it was the same place. While she hesitated, she saw the form of one struggling in the agonies of death. She started back, [and] a shudder ran through her frame as a ripple on the face of the still water when a sudden breeze sweeps over it. But as soon as she recognized her lover, she screamed and beat her breast, embracing the lifeless body. . . . 'O Pyramus,' she cried. . . . Pyramus opened his eyes, then [he] closed them again. She saw her veil stained with blood and the scabbard empty of its sword. 'I will follow [you] in death, [she said,] for I have been the cause. . . . And [you], tree, retain the marks of slaughter. Let [your] berries still serve for memorials of our blood.' So saying she plunged the sword into her breast. . . . The two bodies were buried in one sepulcher, and the tree ever after brought forth purple berries, as it does to this day."[1]

Reflection: "Pyramus and Thisbe," the title of the above tale of two lovers, is a Babylonian myth—although it may have roots in Greek and Roman mythology—explaining why mulberry trees produce purple fruit. The story first appears in Ovid's *Metamorphoses* in 8 CE. In the fourteenth century, Chaucer translated the story into English in "The Legend of Good Women." Herzberg notes that Shakespeare used this story "in an amusing burlesque form" in *A Midsummer Night's Dream*.[2] And, of course, the reader cannot help but notice the parallels between the death of Pyramus and Thisbe and the two lovers, Romeo and Juliet, both Shakespeare's play and Arthur Brook's poem. The story is adapted by many different writers and appears in and is alluded to in many different tales, poems, and musical adaptations. However, the interest here is the mulberry tree under which the Roman lovers meet and the metamorphosis of the white fruit to purple. The tree's blood-stained white fruit turned purple serves as a landmark for the deaths of Pyramus and Thisbe because of their forbidden love.

According to McKenzie, the mulberry "is a large tree with green heart-shaped leaves and clusters of berries."[3] It is a deciduous tree, growing to fifty feet tall. There are many species of mulberry; thus, immature fruits can be white, green, or pale yellow. In most species the white fruits first turn pink, then red, then dark purple or black when ripe. When fully ripe, the fruit is sweet and edible.

1. Bulfinch, *Mythology*, 23–5; cf. Herzberg, *Myths*, 63–4.
2. Herzberg, *Myths*, 65; cf. Bulfinch, *Mythology*, 26.
3. McKenzie, *Dictionary*, 592.

MULBERRY

The Official King James Version of the Bible Online contains four references to mulberry trees. However, there are really only two mentions of mulberry trees, because the two in the Second Book of Samuel are repeated in the First Book of Chronicles. The two quotations appear in the narrative about King David defeating the Philistines in the valley of Rephaim. David seeks advice from the LORD as to what to do about the Philistines. According to the King James Version (KJV) of the Bible, the LORD says, "Thou shalt not go up, but fetch a compass behind them, and come upon them over against the mulberry trees" (2 Sam 5:23; 1 Chr 14:14, KJV). The New Revised Standard Version (NRSV) translates the verse this way: "You shall not go up; go around to their rear, and come upon them opposite the balsam trees" (2 Sam 5:23; 1 Chr 14:14, NRSV).

God continues giving directions to King David, stating, "When you hear the sound of marching in the tops of the balsam trees, then be on the alert; for then the LORD has gone out before you to strike down the army of the Philistines" (2 Sam 5:24; cf. 1 Chr 14:15, NRSV). The King James Version translates this latter verse this way: "'And let it be, when thou hearest the sound of a going in the tops of the mulberry trees, that then thou shalt bestir thyself; for then shall the LORD go out before thee, to smite the host of the Philistines" (2 Sam 5:24; cf. 1 Chr 14:15, KJV).

A variety of biblical scholars note that the leaves of mulberry trees do not make a rustling sound when the wind blows through them. Thus, the NRSV has a more accurate translation. They are popular trees, which do make the sound referred to. According to Masterman, "The sound of marching in the tops of the mulberry trees has been explained to refer to the quivering of the leaves of poplars, but there is not much to support this view. The translation 'mulberry trees' is, however, even more improbable, as this tree, though very plentiful today, had not been introduced into Palestine in Old Testament times."[4] Thus, the two (four) references to mulberry trees above should be translated, as can best be determined, as poplar trees.

This leaves three references to mulberry trees in the NRSV of the Bible. The prophet Isaiah mentions them in his taunt of idol-makers. "As a gift one chooses mulberry wood—wood that will not rot—then seeks out a skilled artisan to set up an image that will not topple" (Isa 40:20). While the footnote for this verse indicates that the Hebrew text is uncertain and Masterman's evaluation above would apply here as well, the meaning of the text—Israel's God created the tree and, therefore, the tree cannot be a god—nevertheless stands.

---

4. Masterman, "Mulberry Trees."

The reference in the OT (A) First Book of Maccabees is to "the juice of . . . mulberries" offered to elephants in preparation for a battle (1 Macc 6:34). There was a presupposition that mulberry juice would provoke the elephants to fight. Seeing and drinking the deep purple drink would remind them of the blood of their enemies they could shed if they gave all they had to the imminent battle.

The last reference to a mulberry tree in biblical literature is found in the CB (NT). Unique to Luke's Gospel, Jesus tells his apostles, "If you had faith the size of a mustard seed, you could say to this mulberry tree, 'Be uprooted and planted in the sea,' and it would obey you" (Luke 17:6). In this reference, the mulberry tree is used to indicate the strength of rootedness as contrasted to more-powerful faith. According to Karris, the mulberry is "a relatively large tree with an extensive root system. It would be difficult not only to uproot this tree but also to grow it in deep water."[5] What the Lukan Jesus is attempting to teach his apostles is that "[g]enuine faith can bring about quite unexpected things."[6] In other words, a strong faith can command a mulberry tree to jump out of the ground and into the sea!

Most people associate the mulberry tree with the production of silk mentioned in the CB (NT) Book of Revelation (18:12). Silk worms feed on the leaves of mulberry trees, which, by the time of the writing of Revelation (around 95 CE), had been imported into Palestine from China. "Lady Silkworm" is the myth of how Can Nu, the goddess of silkworms, appeared to ruler Huang Di "and offered him two delicately colored reels of the finest silk, one golden and the other silver."[7] While there are a number of tales as to how Can Nu became the silkworm goddess, the most prominent one begins with a beautiful daughter of a mortal man. Her father goes away for a year. After pining for his return, Can Nu sends a type of magic stallion to get him, promising to marry anyone who could find her father. The horse brings him home and keeps reminding Can Nu of her promise. She tells her father about her promise, and he kills the horse and lays its hide to dry. One day Can Nu is walking near where the hide is drying; suddenly it rises up and wraps itself around her and takes her to the country. When she is found, she is

> wrapped in the skin, hanging in an unfamiliar tree. . . . [S]he had been changed into a worm. As she wriggled she moved her head like a horse, and a fine thread spewed from her mouth. Can Nu's friend named the tree "mulberry," a word derived from "mourning." People experimented with the thread and found

---

5. Karris, "Gospel According to Luke," 709.
6. Ibid.
7. Littleton, *Mythology*, 416.

> they could use it to make fine cloths; they took tree cuttings and planted them, and, in time, learned how to breed silkworms for the thread.[8]

This tale serves as the foundation myth for the origin of silk. It has been noted that a silkworm can eat several times its own weight of mulberry leaves each day!

Another Chinese tale featuring the mulberry tree features the emperor Yao who had to face the emergence of ten suns in the sky. After praying to Di Jun, the god of the eastern heavens, that is, the god who "presided over the distant valley where the great Fu Shan tree grew. This was a giant mulberry in whose branches the ten suns, which in those days normally took turns to light up the sky, nested during the hours of night."[9] Littleton continues to narrate the tale, stating, "The suns chose to take their rest among the boughs for inside them were mystic birds, the jun-ravens, whose pinions carried the suns on their daily journey across the sky."[10] For some reason, the suns, which previously had taken turns each day, decided to rise all at once; their combined heat was scorching the earth. Di Jun sent his greatest bowman, Yi, from heaven to earth to shoot all the suns in the mulberry tree but one. After accomplishing his task, he was hailed by the emperor and humankind as a hero.

Two English language nursery rhymes use the mulberry tree. "Here We Go Round the Mulberry Bush" begins: "Here we go round the mulberry bush, / The mulberry bush, / The mulberry bush. / Here we go round the mulberry bush, / So early in the morning." Since mulberries do not grow on bushes but on trees, there was probably an earlier version of this rhyme featuring a bramble bush instead of a mulberry bush. Another version of the rhyme's last two lines may refer to Great Britain's struggles to produce silk in the eighteenth and nineteenth centuries: "Here we go round the mulberry bush, / On a cold and frosty morning." Bryson notes:

> The Chinese ferociously guarded the secrets of silk production; the punishment for exporting a single mulberry seed was execution. The Chinese needn't have worried too much about northern Europe, because mulberry trees were too sensitive to frost to thrive there. Britain tried hard for a hundred years to produce silk, and sometimes, got good results, but ultimately couldn't overcome the drawback of periodic harsh winters.[11]

8. Ibid., 417.
9. Ibid., 419.
10. Ibid.
11. Bryson, *At Home*, 381.

The other rhyme that mentions a mulberry tree is the American version of "Pop! Goes the Weasel." One stanza states: "All around the mulberry bush, / The monkey chased the weasel. / The monkey stopped to pull up his sock. / Pop! goes the weasel." The third line has variants, such as "The monkey stopped to scratch his nose," "The monkey thought 'twas all good fun," or "'twas all in good sport," "that it was a joke," "it was a big joke," or "'twas all in fun." While there are multiple interpretations as to the meaning of the rhyme and its variants, it was most likely dance music to which words were added later. Since the words were not specifically attached to the music, they changed through oral tradition as necessity and creativity allowed. The opening line of this rhyme may have been influenced by the opening line of the previous rhyme since both mention a mulberry bush.

The word mulberry may be derived from the Latin word for death, *mors*, and a Latin word for sorrow, *luctus*. It may also come from an Indo-European base word, *mull*, meaning *to pulverize* or *to crush*, referring to the way the berries were prepared for consumption as food or juice. Despite its role in rhymes, the mulberry tree with its purple fruit serves as a landmark for forbidden love which results in lovers's deaths, death in battle, death in not being able to grow deeper in faith, and death in a horsehide. Accompanying death is usually sorrow. Thus, the sacred mulberry's name as well as its purple berry serves as a reminder of blood shed in death and the sorrow that usually accompanies it.

Journal/Meditation: With what tree do you associate sorrow? Explain the association.

Prayer: Heavenly Father, source of all gifts, especially that favor of trust in your Son, Jesus Christ, increase my faith. Make it strong enough to cast the mulberry tree into the sea. Hear me through the same Jesus Christ, who lives and reigns with you and the Holy Spirit, one God, forever and ever. Amen.

Myrtle

Text: "... [T]he word of the LORD came to the prophet Zechariah ... and Zechariah said, In the night I saw a man riding on a red horse! He was standing among the myrtle trees in the glen; and behind him were red, sorrel, and white horses. . . . [T]he man who was standing among the myrtle trees [said], 'They are those whom the LORD has sent to patrol the earth.' Then they spoke to the angel of the LORD who was standing among the myrtle trees, 'We have patrolled the earth, and lo, the whole earth remains at peace.'" (Zech 1:8, 10–11)

Reflection: In the first of eight visions in the HB (OT) Book of Zechariah, the prophet narrates seeing four horses which represent God's heavenly patrol. There are four horses to represent earthly totality. In the passage's historical context, the horsemen "assigned to patrol the earth report on the situation of the Persian Empire."[1] Kodell states: "After the eruption of events surrounding the death of Cambyses II and the accession of Darius, the earth is at rest. But in contrast to this, Judah and her inhabitants are still suffering the consequences of the destruction [of Jerusalem] and the Exile."[2] While Zechariah assigns no meaning to the color of the horses, red and sorrel, a reddish brown, usually signify blood shed in war, and white stands for victory or conquest. Thus, while much blood has been shed through the destruction of Jerusalem and the temple, the Persian ruler Cambyses II (529–522 BCE)—who himself shed a lot of blood of other people, not to mention the wound he inflicted on himself that caused his death—has been succeeded by Darius (521–486 BCE)—who kills a pretender to the throne

1. Kodell, *Lamentations*, 67.
2. Ibid.

who may have been his brother and, once he is crowned, spends many years stopping rebellions, until a long period of peace has begun.

The horses, the man, and the angel stand among the myrtle trees. Myrtle trees, which signify life and fertility, possess dark green, lance-shaped leaves and sport multi-stemmed trunks. As an aromatic evergreen, delicate starry white flowers appear in the spring and turn into purple-black colored berries in the fall. The fruit of the myrtle may be what enabled it to be associated with the Feast of Booths or Tabernacles, marking the end of the harvest. Nehemiah instructs those who have returned from Babylonian exile to Jerusalem, to collect, among other branches, "myrtle . . . to make booths" (Neh 8:15). What is interesting is that myrtle is not mentioned among the braches of trees to be gathered before the exile (Lev 23:40). It seems to have been the custom of the harvesters to build temporary shelters of branches in which to live in the fields when gathering the harvest. Thus, myrtle was used in the construction of such huts because it signified the life and fertility that would result from the harvest. When Isaiah describes the new exodus that will occur when the Jews leave Babylonian captivity, he depicts the LORD stating that he will put myrtle in the wilderness (Isa 41:19a); instead of the brier shall come up the myrtle (Isa 55:13a). In other words, those Jews returning to Jerusalem would find life and fertility on their way home, and so they should celebrate the same during the Feast of Booths by using myrtle to build their huts.

Myrtle is also associated with Aphrodite (Venus), as "the myrtle tree was sacred" to her.[3] Myrtle was considered a potent aphrodisiac; hence Aphrodite's worshipers often wove crowns of it and put them on their heads, as well as on statues of Aphrodite at her festivals. As the goddess of love and sex, Aphrodite played a major role in prenuptial rituals and wedding nights; thus, myrtle was often used in bridal bouquets. The *Bible Dictionary* notes that the formal act of Israelite betrothal often consisted of the future bride being escorted to the home of her future husband by friends who carried myrtle branches.[4] Tresidder summarizes this entry on myrtle, stating that it represents "sexual love, marital happiness, longevity, and harmony."[5] He continues: "Perhaps because of its purple berries, this fragrant evergreen . . . was widely associated with love goddesses, especially the Greek Aphrodite (in Roman myth, Venus), and with rituals surrounding marriage and childbirth. . . . Aphrodite once covered herself in its leaves to hide from Satyrs."[6]

---

3. Witcombe, "Trees and the Sacred."
4. *Bible Dictionary*, "Marriage."
5. Tresidder, *Dictionary of Symbols*, 332.
6. Ibid.

The association of myrtle with life, fertility, prenuptials, weddings, sexual love, marital happiness, longevity, and harmony sheds some light on the HB (OT) Book of Esther. The Jewish name "Hadassah, that is, Esther" (Esth 2:7), means *myrtle*. This historical fiction book recounts how a young Jewish woman becomes queen in the royal Persian court. Furthermore, it shows her influence in winning the right to fight genocide of her Jewish people. Thus, while the Persian king desires her beauty (sexual love and marital happiness) as his queen, she brings life and harmony to the Jews. That is why she is named Myrtle.

Most biblical stories mentioning the myrtle tree are set during the Persian period of Jewish exile. In the midst of death and no future, biblical stories proclaim life and fertility. This helps to understand the connection of myrtle to the harvest festival once the Jews return to Jerusalem from Babylon. In Jerusalem they will prosper in harmony for a while. All this is indicated by the sacred myrtle tree.

Journal/Meditation: What tree represents life and fertility for you? In what specific ways are you and that tree connected?

Prayer: In the vision of your prophet and in the story of your Jewess, LORD God, you offer life and fertility to your people. Keep me alive with your grace, and make me fruitful with your Holy Spirit. You live and reign as one God—Father, Son, and Holy Spirit—forever and ever. Amen.

Nest for Birds

Text: "Two birds with fair wings, knit with bonds of friendship, in the same sheltering tree have found a refuge. Where those fine birds hymn ceaselessly their portion of life eternal . . . there is the universe's mighty keeper, who, wise, has entered into me the simple. The tree [is] where the fine birds . . . rest and procreate their offspring . . . ." (*RV* 1:164:20a, 21–22a).

Reflection: While there is no tree named nest for birds, the point of this entry is that sacred trees are the places where birds—along with some other creatures—make their nests into which they lay their eggs and hatch their young. The two birds in the passage from *The Rig Veda* represent the vital and the supreme spirit dwelling in each person's body, referred to as a sheltering tree. While the supreme spirit is passive and the vital spirit enjoys the rewards of good actions, both praise the gods who keep the universe for the eternal life they enjoy. This life comes from drinking the sacred soma juice, made from a plant unknown today, which enters into both the wise and the simple. Within the body of the tree, the vital and supreme spirit rests and produces even more life, just like birds build their nests in trees, lay their eggs, hatch their young, and raise them.

The Rig Veda states that "at sunset . . . seeks each bird his nest" (*RV* 2:38:8); sometimes "on the fair-leafed tree rest birds" (*RV* 10:43:4); other times "sits the young bird on the tree rejoicing" (*RV* 10:29:1). In a hymn dedicated to Agni, the god of fire—in terms of sunrise—is "like a swift-winged bird" who finds "a home in every tree" (*RV* 10:91:2). And in a later hymn, Agni is to be praised "who, bird-like, rests upon a tree" (*RV* 10:115:3).

A number of hymns in *The Rig Veda* contain references to "birds [visiting] their nest upon the tree" (*RV* 1:127:4), "the nestling of a bird" (*RV*

1:130:3), or set down "as in her sheltering nest a bird" (*RV* 9:62:15). The HB (OT) Book of Psalms mentions the trees in which "the birds build their nests" (Ps 104:17). In the CB (NT), Jesus tells a parable about a mustard seed that grows and "puts forth large branches, so that the birds of the air can make nests in its shade" (Mark 4:32). In Matthew's Gospel, the mustard seed "becomes a tree, so that the birds of the air come and make nests in its branches" (Matt 13:32), whereas in Luke's Gospel it "became a tree, and the birds of the air made nests in its branches" (Luke 13:19). Only in Matthew's Gospel and in Luke's Gospel does Jesus use the fact that "birds of the air have nests" (Matt 8:20; Luke 9:58) as a contrast to the fact that he calls no place home.

While the psalmist declares that "the sparrow finds a home, and the swallow a nest for herself, where she may lay her young, at [God's] altars" (Ps 84:3), that is, the temple in Jerusalem, most birds nest in trees. For example, "starlings fly unto the forest trees" (*RV* 8:35:7), and "a hawk [sits] on trees" (*RV* 9:86:35). In the HB (OT), it is the eagle "who stirs up its nest and hovers over its young" (Deut 32:11a), who "mounts up and makes its nest on high" (Job 39:27; cf. Jer. 49:16), or who, in a poetic sense, makes its nest among the stars (Obad 1:4), that is, in the tallest of trees.

Thus, any tree in which birds build nests, lay their eggs, and hatch their young is a sacred tree. It provides shelter for winged creatures, who sing the praises of their creator. Even the sun can be compared to a bird in a tree as its rays flit on the large branches, even though it has "no nest to dwell in" (*RV* 10:55:6). The HB (OT) Book of Deuteronomy presents a conservation measure when it comes to finding a bird's nest in a tree. To the Israelites Moses says, "If you come on a bird's nest, in any tree . . . with fledglings or eggs, with the mother sitting on the fledglings or on the eggs, you shall not take the mother with the young. Let the mother go . . ." (Deut 22:6–7).

Journal/Meditation: In what sacred tree in your yard or near you do you find birds nesting? In what specific ways do the birds make the tree sacred?

Prayer: O LORD, my king and my God, your winged creatures build homes in the branches of the largest trees you have made. Give me a greater respect for those who make their nests in all woody plants. I ask this in the name of Jesus Christ, who had nowhere to lay his head; he is Lord forever and ever. Amen.

Oak

Text: "An oak that grew on the bank of a river was uprooted by a severe gale of wind, and thrown across the stream. It fell among some reeds growing by the water, and said to them, 'How is it that you, who are so frail and slender, have managed to weather the storm, whereas I, with all my strength, have been torn up by the roots and hurled into the river?' 'You are stubborn,' came the reply, 'and fought against the storm, which proved stronger that you, but we bow and yield to every breeze, and thus the gale passed harmlessly over our heads.'"[1]

Reflection: If there is one tree that is most sacred among all the trees, it is the oak. As "The Oak and the Reeds" above makes clear, the oak signifies strength; while such strength is usually considered a positive characteristic, sometimes the need to bend, as Aesop presents it, is more desirable. Nevertheless, in all types of literature, the oak tree represents "might, endurance, longevity, [and] nobility,"[2] not to mention strength of character, courage, and pride.[3] Caldecott states: "The oak is solid, dependable, [and] durable. It grows to a great age and spreads its branches wide. The great oak forests of ancient times would naturally lend themselves to thoughts of magic and mystery."[4] There is a fascination that occurs when a person realizes that "the growth of the mighty oak [comes] from the tiny acorn."[5] Furthermore, by quoting Hall, Caldecott states, "While the tree is apparently much greater than its own source, nevertheless

1. Aesop, 36.
2. Tresidder, *Dictionary of Symbols*, 348.
3. Witcombe, "Trees and the Sacred."
4. Caldecott, *Myths*, 113.
5. Ibid., 161.

that source contains potentially every branch, twig, and leaf which will later be objectively unfolded by the processes of growth."[6] This is why that for many ancient people the oak "probably symbolized the protection and fertility the worshiper hoped to receive from the deity."[7]

For the ancient Celts the greatest tree of all was the oak; it represented "seasonal death and re-growth."[8] The druids "believed that the interior of the oak was the abode of the dead."[9] Because of the oak's height, it "formed a bridge between the earth and the heavens,"[10] not to mention the fact that its roots went deep into the underworld. From the oak, the druids collected their "sacred mistletoe," which was cut with "a golden sickle" and caught "in a white cloak."[11] Mistletoe "growing high on the oak in the branches . . . appears to have fallen from heaven, . . . and it grows apparently without reference to earth," states Caldecott.[12]

Littleton narrates the tale of Lleu, in which the oak tree is associated with magic. In this Welsh myth, "oak blossom is one of the flowers used to conjure up Blodeu-wedd."[13] *Blodeu* means *flowers* or *blossoms*, and *wedd* means *face, aspect,* or *appearance*; therefore, the name means *flower face*. She is the wife of Lleu Llaw Gyffes in Welsh mythology. Magicians take the flowers of the oak, among others, to create a wife for Lleu because his mother has put him under a curse never to have a human wife. Later, after Blodeu-wedd has an affair with Gronw Pebr, she arranges Lleu's death at Gronw's hand. Lleu transforms into an eagle and perches high in an oak tree. One of the magicians lures him down from the oak and switches him back to human form.

Peck narrates a tale about a black oak tree that speaks. A farmer named Pete is interested in a pretty girl named Josie, but she will not go out with him. After getting a charm, she hung it on an old black oak tree. "Pretty soon she heard a voice away up in the air a-mumbling. Josie was kind of scared, but she stood still a minute and listened. There was some more mumbling, and then the voice says, 'You got to marry Pete.' Josie ran for home when she heard that . . . ."[14] This occurs two more times, and then Josie marries Pete.

6. Ibid., 161–2.
7. Bar, "Trees," 390.
8. Littleton, *Mythology*, 264.
9. Witcombe, "Trees and the Sacred."
10. Littleton, *Mythology*, 264.
11. Ibid.; cf. Freeman, "Tree Lore."
12. Caldecott, *Myths*, 107.
13. Littleton, *Mythology*, 264.
14. Peck, *North American Folktales*, 315.

Besides individual oak trees, oak groves were considered sacred places. The word *druid* may derive from the Celtic word for *oak* because the druids erected their stone circles "under the shadow of a grove or wide-spreading oak."[15] Witcombe thinks that the medieval Gothic cathedral of Chartres, France, was built on a site which was once sacred to the druids. He notes the acorns, oak twigs, and trees in the sculptural decorations on the South Portal which may allude to the original oak grove.[16] He also notes the origin of Gothic pointed arches and vaults may have come from "the interlacing of tree branches."[17] He likens the view down the nave of Chartres Cathedral "to a path through a wood of tall overarching trees" which "may deliberately resemble the path to the sacred grove that stood on the original site . . . ."[18]

A grove of oak trees in Dodana was sacred to Zeus (Jupiter). The legend is that a dove flew from Egypt to Greece and alighted in the oak trees, from where it began to speak profound philosophical and religious truths. Caldecott notes that the dove, representing the spirit infused with the ancient wisdom of Egypt, rustles the leaves of the great oak tree, which represents the growing, developing new wisdom of Greece.[19] Keeping in mind that Zeus is often depicted hurling a thunderbolt, that connection to the god may derive from the ancient belief that lightning was supposed to strike oak trees more than any other trees.[20] Similarly, in the HB (OT) Book of Psalms, the LORD's voice, that is, thunder, which accompanies lightning, "causes the oaks to whirl" (Ps 29:9).

An oak tree is a magical place to fall asleep and dream because it is a point of contact with the other worlds.[21] It is also the tree in which Vivien imprisons Merlin in Tennyson's poem.[22] For Native Americans the oak tree was considered sacred because it provided food (acorns are edible and delicious when prepared correctly) and medicine (made from the bark).[23] Furthermore, the Lenape (Delaware) Native Americans preserve a legend about one of their chiefs whose wife became gravely ill. The legend states:

> The tribe's wisest healers and medicine men administered herbal medicines, but to no avail. The woman's condition worsened.

15. Bulfinch, *Mythology*, 358.
16. Witcombe, "Trees and the Sacred."
17. Ibid.
18. Ibid.
19. Caldicott, *Myths*, 112.
20. Freeman, "Tree Lore."
21. Caldecott, *Myths*, 169, 173.
22. Ibid., 178.
23. Polizzi, "Sacred Medicine Trees."

In desperation the distressed chief traveled to the sacred oak. There, he prayed to the Great Spirit that his wife be saved, and upon his return to camp found that she was in good health. Years later, this same chief feared attack by a hostile tribe. Once again he traveled to the oak and offered up prayer. Heeding the guidance of the Great Spirit, the chief gathered blankets and beads of the finest quality and journeyed to the camp of the enemy. His offerings were accepted, and war was averted.[24]

Many important events take place under an oak tree in biblical literature. Usually, the oak tree is identified with the place where an event takes place. Bar states, "In the ancient world the phenomenon of trees associated with sacred places was well known."[25] For example, on his way to Canaan "Abram passed through the land to the place at Shechem, to the oak of Moreh" (Gen 12:6a). It may be the same oak that was near Shechem (Gen 35:4) under which Jacob hides all the foreign household gods that Rachel brought with her from Haran; the foreign gods are buried under a tree to send them to the underworld. In the Book of Deuteronomy, the oak of Moreh (Deut 11:30) becomes the landmark for finding two mountains. Abram "settled by the oaks of Mamre" (Gen 13:18; cf. 14:13), and "[t]he LORD appeared to [him] by the oaks of Mamre, as he sat at the entrance of his tent in the heat of the day" (Gen 18:1).

When Rebekah's nurse, Deborah, dies, she is buried under an oak below Bethel (Gen 35:8); this reflects "an ancient custom in which dead people were buried under trees."[26] Furthermore, "because trees served as landmarks in ancient times" burial under a tree "helped people to identify the burial site"[27] and to send the dead person to the underworld. One of the boundary markers for the tribe of Naphtali is the oak in Zaanannim (Josh 19:33). Once all the tribes of Israel have been allotted land, Joshua makes a covenant with the people and sets up a stone "under the oak in the sanctuary of the LORD" (Josh 24:26) at Schechem as a witness to the covenant. At this same place, that is, "by the oak of the pillar at Schechem" (Judg 9:6) Abimelech is made king. However, before that happens, Gideon experiences the angel of the LORD "under the oak at Ophrah" (Judg 6:11), where he presents an offering that is consumed in fire (Judg 6:19–21). Samuel tells the newly-anointed King Saul that he will meet three men under the oak of Tabor (1 Sam 10:3). Later, Saul will be buried under the oak in Jabesh (1 Chr 10:12).

24. "American Forests."
25. Bar, "Trees," 383.
26. Ibid., 384.
27. Ibid., 385.

One of the most memorable biblical stories involving an oak tree is the one narrating the death of King David's son Absalom, who attempted to take over his father's kingdom. While Absalom is fleeing from his father's forces, his mule

> went under the thick branches of a great oak. His head caught fast in the oak, and he was left hanging between heaven and earth, while the mule that was under him went on. A man saw it, and told Joab [, David's army commander], "I saw Absalom hanging in an oak." Joab . . . took three spears . . . and thrust them into the heart of Absalom, while he was still alive in the oak. (2 Sam 18:9–10, 14)

The prophet Isaiah uses the strength of the oak to demonstrate how much stronger the LORD is. He tells Jerusalem that she "shall be ashamed of the oaks in which [she] delighted" (Isa 1:29), and that she "shall be like an oak whose leaf withers" (Isa 1:30). "[T]he LORD of hosts has a day . . . against all the oaks of Bashan" states Isaiah (Isa 2:12–13); echoing Isaiah, 2 Nephi in *The Book of Mormon* states, ". . . [T]he day of the Lord shall come . . . upon all the oaks of Bashan" (2 Ne 12:13); according to Ezekiel, it is from the oaks of Bashan that oars are made for ships (Ezek 27:6a). Israel will be like "an oak whose stump remains standing when it is felled" (Isa 6:13b) because she burned "with lust among the oaks, under every green tree" (Isa 57:5). Ezekiel is even more negative when he records that God's fury will leave "their slain . . . among their idols around their altars, on every high hill, on all the mountain tops, under every green tree, and under every leafy oak, wherever they offered pleasing odor to all their idols" (Ezek 6:13). Likewise, the prophet Hosea criticizes those who sacrifice on mountains and make offerings on hills, under oak because its shade is good (Hos 4:13). Even the prophet Zechariah declares that the great and the powerful, signified by the oaks of Bashan, should wail, because the thick forest has been felled! (Zech 11:2b)

There is some hope, however. Isaiah records the LORD promising to rebuild Jerusalem. Those who mourn the city's destruction "will be called oaks of righteousness, the planting of the LORD, to display his glory" (Isa 61:3c). Likewise, while rehearsing the LORD's deeds of the past, the prophet Amos recalls the Amorites, who were as strong as oaks, but the LORD destroyed their fruit above, and their roots beneath (Amos 2:9). The Second Book of Nephi in *The Book of Mormon* also offers hope for a tenth of the people, who are compared to "an oak whose substance is in them when they cast their leaves; so the holy seed shall be the substance thereof" (2 Ne 16:13).

The "evergreen oak" (see Holm) is mentioned only in the OT (A) Book of Daniel. Furthermore, chapter 13 of Daniel appears only in the Septuagint (the Greek translation of the Hebrew Bible) and in the Vulgate (the Latin translation of the Hebrew Bible). Serving as a type of novella, the sixty-four verses are meant to portray the vindication of a righteous woman, who is accused of adultery by two corrupted Jewish elders. The elders want to have sex with Susanna, who is married to Hilkiah, but she refuses them. They plot a trap for her that consists of them lying that they saw her in the garden with a young man. Just as she is about to be executed for adultery—in a patriarchal culture the elders's truth will trump a woman's truth—Daniel enters the picture. He interrogates each of the two elders separately by asking under which tree in the garden they saw Susanna and the young man. One answers the mastic tree, and the other answers, "Under an evergreen oak" (Sus 1:58 [Dan. 13:58]). This discrepancy in testimony leads to the understanding that both are lying, and Susanna is saved.

Thus, the oak tree is a sign of strength, might, endurance, longevity, nobility, courage, and pride. It represents death and re-growth to many people. Some ancient people considered mistletoe as a gift from the gods that fell from heaven and was caught in the branches of the oak tree. Stories with oak trees abound; under a tree one can find a place to dream. Oaks provide food and medicine; they are places for sacred rites and prayer. Both Abram and Gideon experience God under an oak tree. In the Bible, the oak serves as a landmark, a place of death, and a burial place. Because the tree has roots that go deep into the earth and boughs that reach high into the heavens, it connects all levels of a three-storied universe, and that makes the oak a sacred tree.

Journal/Meditation: What aspect of the sacred oak caught most of your attention? In what specific ways are you like that aspect of the sacred oak?

Prayer: Heavenly Father, you revealed yourself to Abraham and Gideon under a sacred oak, and many more of your marvelous deeds occurred under the same tree. Give me the strength, courage, and endurance of the oak that I may serve you in the name of your Son, Jesus Christ, who lives and reigns with you and the Holy Spirit, one God, forever and ever. Amen.

Olive

Text: "[Noah] waited . . . seven days, and again he sent out the dove from the ark; and the dove came back to him in the evening, and there in its beak was a freshly plucked olive leaf; so Noah knew that the waters had subsided from the earth." (Gen 8:10–11)

Reflection: According to the biblical great flood story, the only tree to survive was the olive. The olive leaf not only signifies that God's punishment is over, but that Noah, his family, and all the animals in the ark with him have won the victory of life—and are at peace with the LORD. As *The Quran* makes clear, it is God who sends down water from the sky which makes olives grow for people (*Quran* 16:10–11). The olive, which is an evergreen tree, possesses a thick knotted trunk which becomes many branches as it grows to heights of fifteen to thirty-five feet. It can reach a great age, counting as many as five hundred years. Its leaves are grayish green, and its pale yellow blossoms appear in May with its fruit harvested in October.

In sacred literatures olive trees are often described as being in an olive orchard (Exod 23:11; 1 Sam 8:14, 2 Kgs 5:26; Neh 5:11, 9:25; *Quran* 80:29), an olive grove (Deut 6:11, Judg 15:5), an "olive garden" (*Quran* 6:99, 141), and, of course, among other olive trees (Deut 8:8, 28:40; 1 Chr 27:28; *Quran* 24:35, 95:1; *D&C* 98:6). Only the Mormon *Book of Doctrine and Covenants* contains the parable of the olive trees, even though it is very similar to the parable of the vineyard in the synoptic gospels (Mark 12:1–12; Matt 21:33–46; Luke 20:9–19). "A certain nobleman had a spot of land, very choice," begins the parable,

> and he said unto his servants, Go . . . and plant twelve olive trees;
> and set watchmen round about them and build a tower, that one

may overlook the land round about, to be a watchman upon the tower; that my olive trees may not be broken down, when the enemy shall come to spoil and take unto themselves the fruit .... Now the servants of the nobleman went and did as their lord commanded them; and planted the olive trees, and built a hedge round about, and set watchmen, and began to build a tower. And while they were yet laying the foundation thereof, they began to say among themselves, And what need has my lord of this tower? and consulted for a long time, saying among themselves, What need has my lord of this tower, seeing this is a time of peace? Might not this money be given to the exchangers? for there is no need of these things! And while they were at variance one with another they became very slothful, and they hearkened not unto the commandment of their lord, and the enemy came by night and broke down the hedge, and the servant of the nobleman arose, and were affrighted, and fled; and the enemy destroyed their works and broke down the olive trees. (D&C 98:6)

The image of the green olive tree is applied often to people. The psalmist declares that he is "like a green olive tree in the house of God" (Ps 52:8). In the OT (A) Book of Sirach, wisdom praises herself, declaring that she grew tall like a fair olive tree in the field (Sir 24:14b). In one of his sermons, the prophet Jeremiah addresses the people of Jerusalem and Judah and reminds them, "The LORD once called you, 'A green olive tree, fair with goodly fruit . . .'" (Jer 11:16). And the prophet Hosea describes those who return to the LORD as having shoots that spread out, whose beauty shall be like the olive tree (Hos 14:6). The psalmist echoes Hosea when he sings about those who fear the LORD having children like olive shoots around their table (Ps 128:3).

In the CB (NT), the best application of the olive tree image is found in Paul's Letter to the Romans. Paul is discussing the joining of Gentiles to Jews who believe that Jesus is the anointed one in whom God has reconciled the world and justified both Gentiles and Jews. Beginning with the statement that "if the root is holy, then the branches also are holy" (Rom 11:16), Paul draws out lessons from the olive tree. He begins with the Jews who do not accept Jesus as the Messiah (anointed), referring to them as branches broken off (Rom 11:17; 1 Ne 15:12). The Gentiles, "a wild olive shoot, were grafted in their place to share the rich root of the olive tree" (Rom 11:17). Paul admonishes the Gentiles to engage in no boasting about their faith because they do not support the root, but the root supports them (Rom 11:18). The Gentiles say, "Branches were broken off so that I might be grafted in" (Rom 11:19). Paul states: "That is true. They were broken off because of their unbelief; but you stand only through faith. So do not become proud, but stand in awe" (Rom 11:20; cf. 1 Ne 15:7).

Now, Paul makes a further application using the olive tree image. He tells the Gentiles: "... [I]f God did not spare the natural branches, perhaps he will not spare you. Note then the kindness and the severity of God: severity toward those who have fallen, but God's kindness toward you, provided you continue in his kindness; otherwise you also will be cut off" (Rom 11:21–22). Then, Paul reveals what he considers to be God's plan for the future. He states: "And even those of Israel, if they do not persist in unbelief, will be grafted in, for God has the power to graft them in again" (Rom 11:23; cf. 1 Ne 15:16). The apostle summarizes his reflection on the olive tree and presents one of his famous how-much-more arguments to the Gentiles, stating: "... [I]f you have been cut from what is by nature a wild olive tree and grafted, contrary to nature, into a cultivated olive tree, how much more will these natural branches be grafted back into their own olive tree" (Rom 11:25).

McKenzie notes the following about Paul's image of the olive tree:

> The cultivation of the olive included grafting the branch of the cultivated tree into the trunk of a wild olive tree .... The analogy of Paul in Romans 11:17–25 reverses the normal practice by speaking of the grafting of the wild olive into the cultivated olive; the inversion is no doubt deliberate and is intended to show the paradoxical character of the will of God to save the Gentiles while permitting the Jews to reject his salvation.[1]

Parallel use of the olive tree image is also found in *The Book of Mormon*. The Book of Jacob combines the Gospel of Luke's unique story about a fig tree (Luke 13:6–9), the Gospel of John's account of the vine and the branches (John 15:1–6), the parable of the vineyard owner (Mark 12:1–12; Matt 21:33–46; Luke 20:9–19), and several other stories and sayings with Paul's use of the olive tree to produce a very long allegory of the tame and wild olive tree (Jac 5:1–6:13). The allegory begins by comparing the "house of Israel" to a tame olive tree, which a man took and nourished in his vineyard; and it grew, and waxed old, and began to decay" (Jac 5:3). So, the man pruned the tree, hoed around it, and fertilized it. "... [A]fter many days it began to put forth somewhat a little, young and tender branches; but ... the main top thereof began to perish" (Jac 5:6). Next, the man plucked "branches from a wild olive tree" (Jac 5:7) and grafted them onto the tame olive tree (Jac 5:10). He "hid the natural branches of the tame olive tree [which he cut off] in the nethermost parts of the vineyard" (Jac 5:14). Meanwhile, "the tree in which the wild olive branches had been grafted ... had sprung forth and

---

1. McKenzie, *Dictionary*, 625-6.

begun to bear fruit" (Jac 5:17)—"tame fruit" (Jac 5:18). Likewise, going to where the tame olive branches had been planted, the man found that they had taken root and were bearing fruit (Jac 5:20) even though it was a poor spot to plant them in the vineyard (Jac 5:21–22).

The man continues to plant two more tame olive branches in poor spots in his vineyard (Jac 5:23–24). Then, he plants one in good ground, but part of the tree bears good fruit and part bears wild fruit (Jac 5:25). The man decides to cut off the branches that bear wild fruit, but his servant asks for time to hoe and fertilize the tree (Jac. 5:26–29). After a long time, the man and his servant visit the vineyard and discover that the olive tree "whose natural branches had been broken off and the wild branches had been grafted in" was producing lots of fruit (Jac 5:30), but all of it was bad (Jac 5:32). The man determines that "the wild branches have grown and have overrun the roots" (Jac 5:37).

Meanwhile, the man and his servant go to the nethermost parts of the vineyard to see what the natural branches that were planted have produced. They discover that those branches have produced bad fruit, too (Jac 5:39). The man realizes that all the olive trees in his vineyard are producing bad fruit. So, he decides that they should be cut down (Jac 5:42, 46–49). However, the servant proposes that they take the tame olive branches and graft them back onto the tame olive tree's trunk (Jac 50–58). The man explains that "perhaps the roots [of the tame olive tree] may take strength because of their goodness; and because of the change of the branches, that the good may overcome the evil" (Jac 5:59; cf. 5:60). The vineyard owner notes that this is his last attempt to get good fruit from his olive tree (Jac 5:62).

The story continues by explaining the hoeing, fertilizing, and grafting process in which the man and his servant engage (Jac 5:63–69). Various groups of servants go and work in the vineyard (Jac 5:70–72), and "there began to be the natural fruit again in the vineyard; and the natural branches began to grow and thrive exceedingly; and the wild branches began to be plucked off and to be cast away; and they did keep the root and the top thereof equal according to the strength thereof" (Jac 5:73). Suddenly, God is introduced in the story: ". . . [T]he Lord had preserved unto himself . . . the trees [that] had become again the natural fruit; and they became like unto one body; and the fruits were equal; and the Lord of the vineyard has preserved unto himself the natural fruit, which was most precious unto him from the beginning" (Jac 5:74). The Lord invites the servants to join him in rejoicing over the good olive fruit (Jac 5:75–76). Should evil fruit appear again, the Lord declares that he will gather the good and the bad; the good he will preserve, but the bad he will cast away. Then, the end will come (Jac 5:77).

The application of the lengthy allegory is given in chapter 6. The house of Israel is the tame olive tree. God has tried many times to recover his people, remembering both roots and branches; some have hardened their hearts, whereas others are to be saved. The reader is urged to repent so as to enter into God's kingdom (Jac 6:1–13).

The HB (OT) Book of Zechariah preserves a vision in which the prophet sees "two olive trees, one on the right of the bowl [on top of a lamp stand] and the other on its left" (Zech 4:3). An angel explains that the two olive trees "are the two anointed ones who stand by the Lord of the whole earth" (Zech 4:14). In other words, one olive tree represents the high priest, and one represents the political leader; both are commissioned to work together to rebuild the temple. The author of the CB (NT) Book of Revelation uses Zechariah's image of two olives trees: "These are the two olive trees . . . that stand before the Lord of the earth" (Rev. 11:4). Keeping in mind that two witnesses are required to verify the truth (Deut 19:15), in Revelation the two represent the kingly and priestly people of God along with the two great HB (OT) prophets: Moses and Elijah.

Ancient people did not eat olives;[2] they pressed them for their oil. However, before the oil could be extracted, the olives had to be harvested, usually from October through November. The olive tree laden with fruit (Sir 50:10) was shaken or beaten (Deut 24:20; Isa 17:6; 24:13a) with hands, clubs, or long sticks.[3] The olives were then put into a press or tread (Mic 6:15). Only the "pure oil of beaten olives" (Exod 27:20; Lev 24:2) could be used for sacrificial offerings and the lamp in the tent of meeting.[4] In the HB (OT) Book of Judges, olive oil is referred to as rich oil (Judg 9:9). In the First Book of Chronicles, the author explains that David put a man named Joash over the stores of oil (1 Chr 27:28). The OT (A) Book of Tobit narrates how Tobit offered a tenth of the olive oil at the temple in Jerusalem (Tob 1:7). These notations lead to the understanding that olive trees represent wealth or its loss.[5] The prophets Amos, Habakkuk, and Haggai (Amos 4:9; Hab 3:17; Hag 2:19) along with the Book of Revelation in the CB (NT) (Rev. 18:13) see olive trees and oil as the loss of wealth. However, the parable of the dishonest manager in Luke's Gospel presents olive oil as a means of measuring wealth. After the manager decides to reduce the bill of his master's creditors, he asks one, "'How much do you owe my master? He answered, 'A hundred jugs of olive oil.' He said to him, 'Take your bill, sit down quickly,

---

2. Ibid., 626.
3. Ibid.; cf. Murphey, *Dictionary of Biblical Literacy*, 348.
4. Murphey, *Dictionary of Biblical Literacy*, 349.
5. Taylor, *How to Read a Church*, 208.

and make it fifty'" (Luke 16:5–6). Likewise, in the Book of Revelation a voice states that the olive oil is not to be damaged (Rev. 6:6).

Olive oil was used as a cosmetic (Sus 1:17 [Dan 13:17]), and the branches of the olive tree were used to make wreaths (Jdt 15:13) and the huts constructed to celebrate the Feast of Booths (Neh 8:15). The Second Book of Maccabees contains a story about a certain Alcimus, "who had formerly been high priest," going to King Demetrius and presenting, among other things, "some of the customary olive branches from the temple" (2 Mac 14:3, 4). Doran notes that while olive branches were "used as tokens of friendship," the reference here may be to a payment.[6] Finally, in one of his speeches Eliphaz tells Job that the fate of the wicked is like the olive tree that casts off its blossoms (Job 15:33).

Not to be forgotten in this reflection on olive trees is the Mount of Olives. McKenzie notes the "[t]he name indicates the number of olive trees which grew on its slopes in ancient times."[7] Murphey adds, "The villages of Bethany and Bethpage flanked its slopes with Gethsemane at the foot of the hill."[8] The word *Gethsemane* means *oil press*, and refers to the place where olives were pressed for their oil. The Mount of Olives is first mentioned in the Second Book of Samuel when King David is fleeing from his son, Absalom. David went up the ascent of the Mount of Olives, weeping as he went, with his head covered and walking barefoot (2 Sam 15:30). The prophet Zechariah also mentions it when describing the day of the LORD. The prophet writes: "On that day his feet shall stand on the Mount of Olives, which lies before Jerusalem on the east; and the Mount of Olives shall be split in two from east to west by a very wide valley; so that one half of the Mount shall withdraw northward, and the other half southward" (Zech 14:4). While the prophet Ezekiel does not mention it by name, it is clear that he is referring to the Mount of Olives when he describes the cherubim as stopping on the mountain east of the city of Jerusalem (Ezek 11:23).

In the CB (NT), the Mount of Olives is the place where Jesus begins riding the donkey that will take him to Jerusalem (Mark 11:1; Matt 21:1; Luke 19:29, 37). It is also the place where he delivers his apocalyptic discourse in which he explains why Jerusalem fell to the Romans in 70 CE (Mark 13:3; Matt 24:3). After Jesus celebrates the Passover with his disciples, he goes out to the Mount of Olives (Mark 14:26; Matt 26:30; Luke 22:39), specifically Gethsemane (Mark 14:32; Matt 26:36), to pray. The author of Luke's Gospel and the Acts of the Apostles states that Jesus "would go out and spend the

---

6. Doran, *2 Maccabees*, 268.
7. McKenzie, *Dictionary*, 626.
8. Murphey, *Dictionary of Biblical Literacy*, 201.

night on the Mount of Olives" (Luke 21:37) and that his ascension occurred there, because his disciples "returned to Jerusalem from the mount called Olivet, which is near Jerusalem" (Acts 1:12). Before the woman caught in adultery is brought to Jesus in John's Gospel, the narrative states that he had gone to the Mount of Olives (John 8:1). The Mormon *Book of Doctrine and Covenants* states that when Jesus returns, "he shall stand upon the Mount of Olivet" (*D&C* 108:5).

In order to discover the mythology of the olive tree, one needs to go to Greece. The gods Poseidon (Neptune) and Athene (Minerva) were arguing over who had the right to name a new city being built. So, Zeus (Jupiter) proposed a competition to be judged by the other gods. "Each contestant was challenged to produce a novelty for humanity, something both useful and beautiful, and whoever came up with the finest invention would be given the new city as a prize."[9] Poseidon struck the ground with his trident and produced the first horse, "but Athene, smiling gently, instantly produced out of the rocky soil a tree with gray leaves and small oval green fruits—the olive."[10] Littleton continues the story this way:

> The olive, [Athene] pointed out, would provide both food for human beings and oil for sacrifices to the gods. The tree would be hardy and enduring, bearing fruit even in the roughest, driest ground. But what is more important, she said, is that the olive tree represents peace.... Surely peace was more useful to mortals and more beautiful than war.[11]

The gods declared Athene the winner, and she named the new city Athens. "Her olive tree was one of the most precious gifts the gods ever gave the people of Greece."[12] Bulfinch narrates this same mythology, except he uses the names of the Roman gods. Instead of Poseidon, he names Neptune, and instead of Athene, he names Minerva.[13] Likewise, Herzberg identifies Athene as Pallas Athena, who strikes "the earth with her spear, and hardly had the point of the spear left the ground when up from the soil sprang a noble tree, laden with glossy black fruit, the olive."[14]

In the first "Consecration of the Chrism" prayer in *The Roman Pontifical*, both the olive tree and olive oil are mentioned. The Roman Catholic bishop, who consecrates the chrism on Holy Thursday morning, prays to God,

9. Littleton, *Mythology*, 175.
10. Ibid.
11. Ibid.
12. Ibid.
13. Bulfinch, *Mythology*, 107.
14. Herzberg, *Myths*, 43–4.

saying: "In the beginning, at your command, the earth produced fruit-bearing trees. From the fruit of the olive tree you have provided us with oil for holy Chrism."[15] After a reference to King David, and continuing to address God, he says: "After the avenging flood, the dove returning to Noah with an olive branch announced your gift of peace."[16] Later in the prayer, he mentions "the anointing with olive oil" which makes people "radiant with . . . joy."[17]

Thus, the olive tree survives the great flood, and its branch becomes a sign of peace and prosperity. According to Sill, "In Sienese paintings of the Annunciation, Gabriel generally holds an olive branch rather than a lily, since the lily was a symbol of Florence, Siena's enemy during the early Renaissance."[18] Because of its abundance, it represents the generosity of the LORD and/or the gods. Olive trees are grouped together in orchards and groves. They are subjects of parables and analogies in attempts to foster unity between Jews and Gentiles. Onto the holy root of the tame Jewish olive tree were grafted the wild Gentile branches. People are like olive trees, when they grow and produce good fruit. From the fruit of the olive oil is pressed, and that makes the olive tree a sign of wealth. "Olive oil was one of the most important products in the economy and in the daily life of the people."[19] Olive trees were so abundant on a hill opposite Jerusalem that it was named the Mount of Olives, and it figures prominently in gospel stories about Jesus. According to Greek and Roman lore, the sacred olive tree was a gift from Athene (Minerva), who, like the biblical God, offered it to humanity as something both useful and beautiful.

Journal/Meditation: Since it is highly possible that there is no olive tree growing near you, of what use do you make of olives and olive oil? What do olives, olive oil, and olive branches represent to you?

Prayer: I am like a green olive tree in your house, O God. I trust in your steadfast love. Grant that I may be laden with the fruit of good works and always grateful for your generous grace. I ask this in the name of your Son, Jesus Christ, who is Lord forever and ever. Amen.

---

15. *Roman Pontifical*, "Rites of the Blessing of Oils," par. 24:1.
16. Ibid.
17. Ibid.
18. Sill, *Symbols in Christian Art*, 206; cf. 119–20.
19. Murphey, *Dictionary of Biblical Literacy*, 348.

Palm

Text: "When [Mary] conceived [her son] she went away to a distance place. The birth pangs led her to the trunk of a date palm tree. 'Would that I had died before this,' she said, 'and become a thing forgotten, unremembered.' Then (a voice) called to her from below: 'Grieve not; your Lord has made a rivulet gush forth right below you. Shake the trunk of the date palm tree, and it will drop the ripe dates for you. Eat and drink, and be at peace.'" (*Quran* 19:22–26a)

Reflection: The unique story in chapter 19 of *The Quran* dedicated to Mary narrates how the voice of the divine directed her to shake the trunk of a palm tree in order to find food. The Gospel of Pseudo-Matthew contains a similar story featuring the baby Jesus as he, his father Joseph, and his mother Mary make their way to Egypt. The story begins "on the third day after they had started out" and "Mary was weary from too much sun in the wilderness, and seeing a palm tree she wanted to rest awhile in its shade" (Pseudo-Matt 20:1).[1]

The narrative continues:

> Joseph hastened to lead her to the palm and he had her descend from the donkey. When Mary sat down, she looked to the foliage on the palm and saw that it was full of fruit, and she said, "If only I could get some of that fruit from the palm!" Joseph said to her, "I am surprised that you're saying this, when you can see how high the palm is." . . . Then the young child Jesus, sitting in the lap of his mother, the virgin, cried out to the palm tree and said, "Bend down, O tree, and refresh my mother from your

---

1. Ehrman, *Apocryphal Gospels*, 107, 109.

fruit." Immediately when he spoke, the palm tree bent its top down to Mary's feet. Everyone gathered the fruit in it and was refreshed. After all its fruit had been gathered, the tree remained bent, expecting that it would rise up at the command of the one who had ordered it to bend over. Then Jesus said to it, "Stand erect, O palm, and be strong, and become a companion of my trees that are in the paradise of my Father. And open up from your roots the hidden springs, that water may flow from them to quench our thirst." Immediately, the palm stood erect, and from its roots springs of water began to come forth, clear, cold, and very sweet. They set out on the next day. But as they started their journey, Jesus turned to the palm tree and said, "I give you this privilege, O palm: one of your branches will be taken by my angels and planted in the paradise of my Father. Moreover, I will bestow this blessing on you, that whoever emerges victorious from a contest will be told, 'You have attained to the palm.'" While he was saying this, behold an angel of the Lord appeared, standing above the palm tree. Removing one of its branches it went flying away. (Pseudo-Matt 20:1–21:1)[2]

In a slightly different version of the Pseudo-Matthew story, known as "The Cherry Tree Carol," Joseph and Mary, on their way to Bethlehem, walk through an orchard in which they see cherries, which Mary asks Joseph to pick for her. From the womb, Jesus tells the cherry tree to bend, and it bows low to the ground so that they can pick cherries. After they do so, Joseph speaks to Jesus in Mary's womb, asking him when his birthday would be, and Jesus replies on January 6, the traditional date of Christmas in the Orthodox Church.[3]

Along with the oak and the olive tree, the palm tree is an often-mentioned tree in the Bible and *The Quran*. While the HB (OT) Book of Numbers refers to "palm groves" (Num 24:6), *The Quran* refers to an "orchard of date palm trees" (*Quran* 17:91), "gardens . . . surrounded by date palm trees" (*Quran* 18:32), and, "fields of . . . date palm trees" (*Quran* 13:4). The "tall date palms with their spathes [that is, leafy sheaths] pile on pile" (*Quran* 50:10) can reach heights of one hundred feet. On their slender stems grow feathery, pale, evergreen fronds which can extend from six to twelve feet in length. Palm trees can be cut (*Quran* 59:5) and the wind can blow strong enough to pull them out of the ground by the roots (*Quran* 54:20), leaving them to decay (*Quran* 69:7).

2. Ibid., 109; cf. Cavendish, *Legends*, 210.
3. "Cherry Tree Carol"; Cavendish, *Legends*, 191.

In Islamic culture and tradition, the palm tree signifies rest and hospitality. The presence of palm trees in an oasis represents that water is a gift of Allah. Furthermore, palm trees in a garden, as noted above, serve as images of paradise. Another Islamic tradition associates the palm tree with the Dome of the Rock. Mohammed may have built his house out of palm trees and leaned against them when speaking. The first mosque is thought to have had a roof placed on it of palm trees, and the first muezzin climbed a palm tree to call people to prayer; from the palm tree developed the minaret.

In a story unique to *The Quran*, Pharaoh threatens his magicians, who, after witnessing Moses' miracle of his staff turning into a snake, profess belief in the God of Moses and Aaron, saying, "I will have your hands and feet cut off on alternative sides and crucify you on the trunks of date palm trees" (*Quran* 20:71c). Another interesting tale featuring a palm tree is that of Nigeria's Yorbu people. The great god of the sky, named Olodumare or Olorun, looks down and sees that the earth is nothing but water. He sends two of his sons, Obatala and Oduduwa, into the world. "As they descended, he lowered a great palm tree that settled on the waters; when the brothers landed, they did so in the tree's branches. Almost at once Obatala began hacking at the bark of the tree and made a strong palm wine from its sweet sap. He soon became drunk and fell asleep."[4] The other brother proceeds to create the world from items his father had given to him. This mythology identifies the palm tree as an *axis mundi* because it reaches from the depths of the earth (underworld) to the heavens.

Palm trees represent abundance. At Elim, a place where the Israelites camped, there were seventy palm trees (Exod 15:27; Num 33:9). Jericho is known as "the city of palm trees" (Deut 34:3; 2 Chr 28:15). Deborah, a prophetess and female judge of Israel, is recorded as sitting under the palm of Deborah in the hill country to which the Israelites came up to her for judgment, that is, to settle disputes (Judg 4:5). Just as the LORD gives abundance represented by the palm tree, he can cut off the palm branch (Isa 9:14) or cause it to dry up (Joel 1:12). Thus, according to Ryken, "the palm tree was associated with an oasis, a place of fertility in the midst of the wilderness."[5]

Palm trees were carved into the walls of the temple (1 Kgs 6:29). The two doors featured carvings of palm trees covered in gold (1 Kgs 6:32) as were the doors into the nave (1 Kgs 6:35) and the stands (1 Kgs. 7:36). The carved palms covered in gold represent fertility. McKenzie suggests that the palm carvings were "the work of the Phoenician artists of Hiram."[6]

---

4. Littleton, *Mythology*, 626.
5. Ryken, *Dictionary*, 622.
6. McKenzie, *Dictionary*, 633.

According to Smith, "the word Phoenicia, which occurs twice in the New Testament—Acts 11:19; 15:3—is in all probability derived from the Greek word for a palm."[7] McKenzie adds, "[T]he palm grows abundantly in Phoenicia and appears on Phoenician coins...."[8] In one of his many visions, the prophet Ezekiel describes the new temple, whose pilasters had palm trees (Ezek 40:16, 26, 31, 34, 37), and other palm trees were the same size as one of the gates (Ezek 40:22). The pattern on the wall of the inner room and the nave consisted "of cherubim and palm trees, a palm tree between cherub and cherub. Each cherub had two faces: a human face turned toward the palm tree on the one side, and the face of a young lion turned toward the palm tree on the other side" (Ezek 41:18–19a). This same pattern appeared on the doors of the nave (Ezek 41:25).

Thus, not only do the palm trees represent abundance, but they are also signs of fertility. Tresidder notes that the palm "had feminine fecundity symbolism...."[9] He also notes that "palm motifs are associated ... with the sun cult of Apollo [and] with the goddesses Astarte and Ishtar."[10] The palm tree is sacred to Apollo because he was born under one on the island of Delos while his mother, Leto, clung to it. Astarte, a goddess worshiped in the city represented by a palm tree—Phoenicia—is also known as Ishtar in Assyria, where the palm tree is considered an *axis mundi*, just like it is for the Yorbu. Ishtar's travels to the underworld to retrieve her consort, Tammuz—the god of the date harvest—further emphasizes the palm as a sacred tree that unites the underworld, earth, and the heavens. Either as Astarte or Ishtar, the goddess represents fertility because she was thought to make dates abundant.

Another fertility goddess is Panaiveriyamman, also known as Taalavaasini. Named after panai, the Tamil name for the Palmyra palm, this Tamil tree deity offered the people of Tamil culture her blessings by bestowing upon them abundant fruit. Her latter name associates her with all types of palm trees.

Palm branches were carried in funeral processions in Egypt to represent immortality or eternal life. The god Huh, whose name means *endlessness*, represents infinity and time, long life and eternity. While he could be depicted as a man with a frog's head, he is also found painted as a man holding a palm branch in each hand. By 400 BCE, a palm branch had become the sign of victory in athletic contests as well as in military triumphs. A palm tree was supposed to have sprung up immediately when Julius Caesar

---

7. Smith, *Bible Dictionary*.
8. McKenzie, *Dictionary*, 633.
9. Tresidder, *Dictionary of Symbols*, 365.
10. Ibid.

secured his rise to power. Even Constantine I displayed palms on the coins he had issued to illustrate his victory over the known world.

In the Bible, the prescription for the Jewish Feast of Booths (Tabernacles, Sukkot) specifies taking the branches of palm trees (Lev 23:40), among three others, and rejoicing before God. Nehemiah emphasizes this, too, when he instructs that the Jews are to bring branches of palm, among four other types of trees, to make booths (Neh 8:15). The First Book of Maccabees in the OT (A) records the sending of a palm branch as a sign of friendship and peace by the high priest Simon to King Demetrius (1 Macc 13:37; cf 2 Macc 14:4). Once Simon frees the Jews from Syrian domination, they enter the citadel in Jerusalem carrying palm branches (1 Macc 13:51). Later, after purifying the temple, they enter it with fronds of palm (2 Macc 10:7). The OT (A) Book of Sirach describes Simon functioning as high priest with others around him who are like the trunks of palm trees (Sir 50:12b). The image of the palm appears on some Jewish coins, especially those issued by Rome when the Jews were under Roman domination. However, it also appears on coinage issued by Herod Antipas, and it is often found on Jewish ossuaries, where it represents eternal life and immortality.

In the CB (NT), only John's Gospel mentions that a great crowd "took branches of palm trees" (John 12:13) and met Jesus, who was riding into Jerusalem on a donkey. The only other place that palm branches appear in the CB (NT) is in the Book of Revelation. There, John of Patmos sees a multitude of people "standing before the throne [of God] and the Lamb, robed in white, with palm branches in their hands" (Rev 7:9). McKenzie notes that it is on the basis of Revelation 7:9 that "the palm in Christian liturgy and art has become the symbol of the martyr."[11] The Mormon *Book of Doctrine and Covenants* echoes the Book of Revelation. In a prayer, Joseph Smith asks God that the garments of his followers "be pure, that [they] may be clothed upon with robes of righteousness, with palms in [their] hands, and crowns of glory upon [their] heads, and reap eternal joy for all [their] sufferings" (*D&C* 109:76).[12]

Because of the extensive use of the palm tree and palm branches, it will come as no surprise that people are often compared to them. For example, Psalm 92 declares, "The righteous flourish like the palm tree" (Ps 92:12). Likewise, in the Song of Songs, the man tells the woman that she is stately as a palm tree which he wants to climb and lay hold of its branches (Song 7:7–8). With a lot less erotic intent, the prophet Hosea writes about seeing "Ephraim as a young palm planted in a lovely meadow" (Hos 9:13). The OT (A) Book of Sirach portrays lady wisdom as growing tall like a palm tree (Sir 24:14).

---

11. McKenzie, *Dictionary*, 633.
12. *Doctrine and Covenants*.

Once people are compared to palm trees, it only follows that they will be named after them. Thus, Tamar, a name meaning *palm*, is given to a Canaanite woman whom the patriarch Judah married to his son, Er (Gen 38:7). After Er died, he gave his second son, Onan, to her as a wife, but after Onan's death his third son, Shelah, was too young to be her third husband. In time, Tamar, disguised as a prostitute, seduced her father-in-law, Judah, and conceived and gave birth to twins: Perez and Zerah (Gen 38:12–30; 1 Chr 2:4; Ruth 4:12). The author of Matthew's Gospel in the CB (NT) includes Tamar in his list of the Messiah's ancestors (Matt 1:3). McKenzie explains: "The action of Tamar was taken to secure her rights as a widow, and for this reason Judah admitted that she was more in the right than he was (Gen 38:26). In the ancient world Tamar was admired as a woman of determination and adroitness."[13]

A daughter of King David and Maacah is named Tamar (2 Sam 13:1). Her half-brother Amnon falls in love with her and sets in motion a plot to rape her (2 Sam 13:1–14). After hearing what happened to his sister, Absalom, David's son, set in motion his own plot to have Amnon killed (2 Sam 13:14–29). After this, he sired a daughter, whom he named Tamar (2 Sam 14:27). Finally, the prophet Ezekiel two times mentions a town named Tamar (Ezek 47:19; 48:28).

Thus, the sacred palm tree that can live for two hundred years is a sign of longevity and abundance; it grows in groves, orchards, gardens, and fields. Those who are tired can find not only food, but rest and hospitality under a palm tree. Because of its abundance, it is also a sign of fertility. When it grows in height, it becomes an *axis mundi* connecting all three levels of the universe. As such, its roots reach into the underworld, and its branches reach into the heavens representing immortality, eternal life, and resurrection. Its branches are awarded as signs of victory, supremacy, and fame in sports, in war, and in martyrdom. A palm branch can be sent as a token of friendship and peace. Those who live righteous lives flourish like the sacred palm tree.

Journal/Meditation: How are you like a palm tree? What characteristics that describe palm trees also describe you? If you were a palm tree, what would you do?

Prayer: Almighty God, from your generous hand you have given the palm tree to people. Grant that I may flourish in righteousness like this sacred tree that one day I may receive the palm branch of victory for eternal life. I ask this in the name of Jesus Christ, your Son, who lives and reigns with you in the unity of the Holy Spirit, one God, forever and ever. Amen.

---

13. McKenzie, *Dictionary*, 867.

Pine

Text: "Duke Ai asked Tsai Yu about the holy ground. Tsai Yu replied, 'The Hsia sovereigns marked theirs with a pine, the men of Yin used a cypress, the men of Chou used a chestnut tree, saying, "This will cause the common people to be in fear and trembling."' The Master hearing of it said, 'What is over and done with, one does not discuss. What has already taken its course, one does not criticize; what already belongs to the past, one does not censure.'"[1]

Reflection: Duke Ai of Lu ruled a state in China from 494 to 468 BC. After asking Tsai Yu, a disciple in whom Confucius was greatly disappointed, about holy ground—an earth mound at the borders of a town or village, often associated with a sacred tree or grove which served as a resting place for spirits—Tsai Yu replies that the Hsia (Xia) Dynasty (about 2070–1600 BCE) rulers planted pine trees; the Yin (Shang) Dynasty (about 1558–1046) rulers planted cypress trees, and the Chou (Zhou) Dynasty (about 1046–256 BC) planted chestnut trees, trees bearing an inauspicious name. The Master (Confucius), using a tri-part formula makes it clear that it makes no difference what tree what dynasty considered sacred in the past. It is best not to censure events of the past.

The focus of this reflection is the sacred pine tree, "the most important of all resinous evergreens, representing immortality or longevity."[2] According to Tresidder, "it was linked with incorruptibility and was planted around Chinese graves."[3] The pine also represents creativity, peace, harmony, courage, resolution, and good luck. There are multiple species of pine tree, but

1. *Analects* 3:21.
2. Tresidder, *Dictionary of Symbols*, 390.
3. Ibid.

all are evergreen, coniferous, and resinous. They can grow from three to almost three hundred feet tall and live from one hundred to five thousand years. As evergreens, pines do not lose their needles (leaves) in the winter. They reproduce by growing cones which, when mature, release seeds. Pines can secrete resin, a solid or semi-solid substance in their sap that has a transparent or translucent quality and a yellow or brown color. Most people experience the sap as so sticky that it will not easily come off of the skin or be taken out of clothes. Sometimes, resin keeps the pine cone closed until a forest fire melts it and releases its seeds.

Besides being grown as timber and wood pulp, some pine trees produce large seeds used in cooking and baking. The soft, white, inner bark is also edible, raw or dried and ground into a powder to be used as a thickening agent in all types of food. Polizzi states that the inner bark can serve "as a survival food" and "an expectorant to lubricate the respiratory tract and ease a bad cough."[4] The Native American Adirondacks got their name from the Native American Mohawks's word for tree-eaters because they ate the bark of the pine tree. According to Polizzi, "pine pitch has powerful antibacterial and antimicrobial properties" and pine needles "are a great source of vitamin C, A, E, and a host of B vitamins."[5]

The Native American Iroquois had two great leaders who united five nations into the Iroquois Confederacy. They used a pine tree as a sign of their confederacy because it signified peace and friendship that had been established by their union. The branches of the tree represented protection. Below the roots of the tree they buried a weapon to indicate that there would be no more fighting among the Iroquois tribes.

The pine tree is considered sacred by the Roman goddess Cybele and her consort Attis. After Cybele fell in love with the long-haired beauty, he was sent by his parents to wed a king's daughter. However, Cybele appeared, Attis went mad, cut off his genitals, and died under a pine tree. However, Cybele, the mother goddess that she was, brought him back to life as her eunuch consort. In some sculptures, Attis wears a pine-garland crown as a sign of his immortality. In others he is depicted beneath a pine tree, gathering cones. In one of many forms of worship commemorating Attis's death under a pine tree, his followers cut down a pine tree and suspended from it an image of Attis. Then, they carried it to Cybele's temple.

Besides being sacred to Cybele and Attis, the pine tree was sacred to the god Dionysus (Bacchus), whose emblem is the thyrsus tipped with a pine cone. A thyrsus, a sign of prosperity, fertility, and pleasure, is a staff of giant

---

4. Polizzi, "Sacred Medicine Trees."
5. Ibid.

fennel covered with grape vines and leaves and topped with a pine cone. The thyrsus is a fertility phallus; the fennel represents an erect penis, and the pine cone represents the sperm or seed issuing forth. Tresidder states, "The cone itself is a phallic and flame symbol of masculine generative force."[6] He also notes that the thyrsus "was an emblem of the Mesopotamian hero god Marduk."[7] Caldecott notes that "for the Egyptians [the pine] was the emblem of Serapis, the bull god, continuously reincarnated."[8]

In the biblical world, the pine tree represents the new paradise; in a manner of understanding, it represents the fertility, abundance, and peace in the new world that the LORD promises to his people. Isaiah includes the pine tree among others in describing the new paradise that the LORD will create in the desert (Isa 41:19). The pine is included among those trees that will beautify the place of God's sanctuary (Isa 60:13). The Mormon *Book of Doctrine and Covenants* echoes this, when it states that the pine tree, among others, is to be brought to build a temple (*D&C* 107:10). The lovers in the Song of Songs consider their meeting place outdoors to have rafters of pine (Song 1:17).

McGinley narrates the tale of "The Pine Tree," a legend which explains how the pine became an evergreen tree. The story begins, "The pine tree was mortal once, like other trees that lift their boughs in air."[9] The legend continues to narrate how Joseph and Mary were fleeing Israel with Jesus to escape King Herod's slaughter of the innocent boys. "Houseless to the edge of a green wood [they came] where valorously stood a needled pine that every summer gave small birds a nest."[10] Joseph decides that under the pine is a good place to rest. "The pine tree, full of pity, dropped its vast protective branches down to cover them until the troops rode past . . . ."[11] The pine hid the three all night long. In the morning, the child Jesus "blessed the pine," saying, "Let you (and your brave race) who made yourself my rampart and my screen keep summer always and be ever green. For you the punctual seasons shall not vary, but let there throng a thousand birds to you for sanctuary all winter long."[12] The tale concludes stating that if one cuts a "pine cone part way through," one can "find it bears within it like a brand the imprint of his hand."[13]

---

6. Tresidder, *Dictionary of Symbols*, 390.
7. Ibid.
8. Caldecott, *Myths*, 59.
9. McGinley, *Wreath*, 13.
10. Ibid., 14.
11. Ibid.
12. Ibid., 15.
13. Ibid.

Caldecott narrates "Adam's Tree of Redemption" in which Seth, Adam's son, is sent to Eden to fetch "three seeds from the fruit of the tree" given to him by Mik-hael.[14] As Mik-hale hands the three seeds to Seth, he says, "Three days after your return home, your father will die. When he does, place these three seeds upon his tongue."[15] Three days after Seth got home Adam died, "and from his body three trees grew: a cypress, a pine, and a cedar."[16] Commenting on the pine, Caldecott states, "The pine represents strength of character and uprightness—the years during which Adam tried to live according to God's law to make up for what he had done."[17]

Thus, the pine tree signifies many different and similar things. When commenting on "The Old Tree," a Chinese tale, Caldecott quotes Jung, stating: "All pine trees are very much alike, yet none is exactly the same as another. Because of these factors of sameness and difference, it is difficult to summarize the infinite variations of the process of individuation. The fact is that each person has to do something different, something that is uniquely his [or her] own."[18] "The seed of a pine," writes Caldecott while quoting Jung,

> contains the whole future tree in latent form; but each seed falls at a certain time onto a particular place, in which there are a number of special features . . . . The latent totality of the pine in the seed reacts to these circumstances by avoiding the stones and inclining toward the sun, with the result that the tree's growth is shaped. Thus an individual pine slowly comes into existence, constituting the fulfillment of its totality, its emergence into the realm of reality.[19]

The pine tree was chosen by the Hsia (Zia) Dynasty of China to mark the holy ground of cemeteries for almost five hundred years, because it represents immortality, longevity, and incorruptibility. The myth that a Greek goddess's consort died under a pine tree and was raised to life there further enhances the pine's representation of immortality and incorruptibility. The tree, used for timber, has an edible bark and seeds and can be used for medicine. Among Native Americans it is a sign of harmony, representing the unification of many diverse tribes. Because the cone of the pine tree contains seeds, it is also a sign of fertility and abundance. Thus, the sacred

---

14. Caldecott, *Myths*, 132.
15. Ibid.
16. Ibid.
17. Ibid., 133.
18. Jung, *Man*, 164; cf. Caldecott, *Myths*, 43.
19. Jung, *Man*, 162; cf. Caldecott, *Myths*, 43.

pine tree and its cones add to the beauty of God's multiple dwelling places and signify simultaneously how all people are alike and different.

Journal/Meditation: What objects in your home are made from pine? How do those objects foster peace and harmony, longevity and creativity? Do you have a basket of pine cones anywhere? Why? Why not?

Prayer: As a sign of the new paradise that you promised your people, O LORD, you included the pine among the precious trees that you would grow in your new garden. Grant me many creative years in your service on earth and immortality in your kingdom, where you live and reign with my Lord Jesus Christ and the Holy Spirit, one God, forever and ever. Amen.

Plane

Text: "Two travelers were walking along a bare and dusty road in the heat of a summer's day. Coming presently to a plane tree, they joyfully turned aside to shelter from the burning rays of the sun in the deep shade of its spreading branches. As they rested, looking up into the tree, one of them remarked to his companion, 'What a useless tree the plane is! It bears no fruit and is of no service to man at all.' The plane tree interrupted him with indignation. 'You ungrateful creature!' it cried. 'You come and take shelter under me from the scorching sun, and then, in the very act of enjoying the cool shade of my foliage, you abuse me and call me good for nothing!'"[1]

Reflection: "The Travelers and the Plane Tree," the only fable in Aesop's collection to mention a plane tree, contains the following moral: "Many a service is met with ingratitude."[2] The plane tree, a tall deciduous tree that has leaves with pointed lobes, ball-shaped clusters of flowers and fruit, and bark that peels off in patches, has a name in Hebrew which means *naked*— because it sheds its outer bark annually. Aesop's fable is about ingratitude for the rapidly-growing, one-hundred-foot tall tree, known for its longevity and spreading crown and prized for its shade and the coolness it provides in the summer. It blossoms in April-May, and its fruit, often described as looking like a porcupine ball, features burrs or protruding dull thorns. However, it is the mottled brown and white bark which fascinates most observers. The thick trunk with numerous knots, especially in older trees, peels in patches and reveals what looks like white, brown, and green spots.

1. Aesop, 132.
2. Ibid.

This latter characteristic helps to understand the story in the HB (OT) Book of Genesis about Jacob taking "fresh rods of . . . plane" and peeling "white streaks in them, exposing the white of the rods" (Gen 30:37), and setting them in front of the flocks at the watering places. The idea was that when the animals bred, they would see the spotted branches of the plane tree and produce offspring that were spotted, and these would belong to Jacob. This experiment in primitive genetic engineering made Jacob a wealthy man!

The plane tree grows wild along river banks that contain water most of the year. In the OT (A) Book of Sirach, personified wisdom describes herself as growing tall like a plane tree beside water (Sir 24:14). This fact helps to understand the LORD's statement made to the prophet Isaiah: "I will set in the desert . . . the plane . . ." (Isa 41:19). The plane tree grows on river banks, not in the desert. But God's power is so great that for his people he will reverse the usual way of nature and provide for the return of the people from Babylonian captivity. Later the prophet records that the plane tree because of its height will be used to beautify the new temple, the LORD's sanctuary (Isa 60:13). Ezekiel, too, alludes to the height of the plane tree used in building projects (Ezek 31:8).

The plane tree was also sacred to Hippocrates, the father of medicine, because, according to legend, he taught the art of medicine to his students under one. The tree had many medicinal uses; its bark and leaves were used for burns, stings, bites, and infections. Just as the tree was sacred to Hippocrates, the plane was also sacred to Plato and the Athenian Academy. The philosopher founded the academy in a public garden or grove of plane trees in the suburbs of Athens. There, his students met to listen to their master. Witcombe notes that there was a sacred grove of plane trees at Lerna,[3] a region of springs on the east coast of the Peloponnesus, south of Argos. The plane tree was also planted near Hindu holy places dedicated to the goddess Bhavani, whose name means *the giver of life*, indicating the power of nature or the source of creative energy. Because of their love of water, plane trees were planted near such sources as streams, rivers, and fountains to mark central squares of villages, near tombs, and to serve as tall marvels emphasizing other human accomplishments, such as the building of elaborate palaces.

Thus, the tall plane tree is known for its shade produced by its spreading branches, under which both Hippocrates and Plato taught their students. In Hebrew it is named for its shedding bark which leaves the trunk with spots that make it look naked. It prefers to be planted near a water source which enables it to grow tall so that it can be used in construction

---

3. Witcombe, "Trees and the Sacred."

projects and to mark sacred places. The plane tree is not plain; it is a sacred tree to many people.

Journal/Meditation: Under what tree to you usually sit to avoid the summer sun? What memories do you associate with that tree? What is it about the tree that fascinates you? How do you express gratitude to the tree?

Prayer: Like the plane tree planted beside the flowing water, I grow tall in your presence, O LORD. Use me to build your kingdom that one day I may sit in your garden under the spreading branches of your love. I ask this in the name of Jesus Christ, my Lord. Amen.

Pomegranate

Text: "[King] Saul was staying in the outskirts of Gibeah under the pomegranate tree that is at Migron; the troops that were with him were about six hundred men." (1 Sam 14:2)

Reflection: In the verse above mentioning the pomegranate, the tree functions as a landmark. King Saul, the first king of Israel, is preparing for war with the Philistines, and he is camped under the pomegranate tree at Migron. The name of the tree and its fruit comes from two Latin words: *pomum*, meaning *apple*, and *granatum*, meaning *seeded*. Thus, the word *pomegranate* means *seeded apple*, and, of course, adequately describes the fruit which can contain between two hundred and fourteen hundred seeds. Technically, the fruit is a round berry with a thick reddish skin that is larger than a lemon but smaller than a grapefruit. The seeds are embedded in a white, spongy, astringent membrane.

The pomegranate tree, which can grow from sixteen to twenty-six feet tall, has multiple trunks and multiple spiny branches with glossy, narrow, oblong leaves. Because it is drought-tolerant, it can live up to two hundred years. Its bright red blossoms in the spring turn into green orbs which, when ripe, turn into reddish colored fruit which can be picked in late summer.

The first mention of pomegranate in biblical texts is found in the HB (OT) Book of Numbers in which it represents abundance and bounty. Furthermore, "on account of its vast number of seeds the pomegranate was often employed to represent natural fecundity."[1] When the Israelite spies return from reconnoitering the land of Canaan, among the items they bring are pomegranates (Num 13:23). Moses mentions the pomegranates in his

---

1. Hall, *Secret Teachings*, xcv; cf. Caldecott, *Myths*, 87.

speech to the Israelites before they crossed into the promised land (Deut 8:8). However, the people had become familiar with the pomegranate during their days of slavery in Egypt. In the wilderness of Zin, they complain to Moses, asking why he has led them to a place where there are no pomegranates (Num 20:5). Thus, the fruit of the pomegranate tree was eaten by the Hebrews in Egypt, where it represented prosperity and ambition, and in the land of Canaan. McKenzie thinks that it "was regarded as a delicacy."[2]

Images of pomegranates were used in embroidery. The HB (OT) Book of Exodus states that all around the lower hem of the robe of the ephod, a priestly garment worn by Aaron, is to be embroidered pomegranates of blue, purple, and crimson yarns (Exod 28:33; 39:24–26). The author of the OT (A) Book of Sirach mentions Aaron's robe encircled with pomegranates (Sir 45:9).

Images of pomegranates also appear in bronze work done for Solomon's temple. On top of the two pillars—one named Jachin and the other named Boaz—were placed capitals sculpted with two hundred pomegranates each (1 Kgs 7:20; 7:18) for a total of four hundred pomegranates (1 Kgs 7:42). The HB (OT) Book of Second Chronicles states that there were only one hundred pomegranates on each capital (2 Chr 3:16), yet corrects this later stating that there were two rows of pomegranates for a total of four hundred (2 Chr 4:13). These two pillars were broken by the Babylonians when they captured Jerusalem (2 Kgs 25:17). The prophet Jeremiah also records the pomegranates which encircled the top of the capitals, declaring that there were "ninety-six pomegranates on the sides; all the pomegranates encircling the latticework numbered one hundred" (Jer 52:23; cf. 5:22).

In the HB (OT) Song of Songs, pomegranates represent sexual temptation, fertility, and fecundity. The man states that the woman's "cheeks are like halves of a pomegranate" (Song 4:3b; cf. 6:7), that her channel—an intimate part of her body— "is an orchard of pomegranates with all choicest fruits" (Song 4:13). The woman responds, stating, that she went to the orchard to see whether the pomegranates were in bloom (Song 6:11; 7:12c). Later, she tells the man that she would give him the juice of her pomegranates (Song 8:2b). It doesn't take long to realize that the pomegranate is considered an erotic fruit by the author of the Song of Songs!

There are three more mentions of pomegranates in the Bible. The OT (A) Book of Tobit recounts how after deportation to Assyria he continues to make a trip to Jerusalem to offer the tithe of a tenth of the pomegranates (Tob 1:7). The prophet Joel sees the withering of the pomegranate tree as a sign of disaster (Joel 1:12), as does the prophet Haggai (Hag 2:19).

2. McKenzie, *Dictionary*, 681.

In Jewish tradition, the pomegranate represents righteousness because it is supposed to contain six hundred thirteen seeds which represent the six hundred thirteen commandments of the Torah. However, in *The Quran* the pomegranate represents Allah's generosity. The "gardens of . . . pomegranates" (*Quran* 6:99) are a gift from God. "It is he who grew the gardens, trellised and bowered, and . . . pomegranates, alike and yet unlike" (*Quran* 6:141). Pomegranates even grow in the two gardens of paradise (*Quran* 55:68).

In the Greek world, the pomegranate represents eternity, love, and marriage. "It was sacred to love goddesses, such as Astarte and Aphrodite (Venus in Roman myth),"[3] according to Tresidder. After Venus discovers that Adonis is dead, she sprinkles nectar on his blood "and in an hour's time there sprang up a flower of bloody hue like that of the pomegranate."[4] The pomegranate, "predominantly a fertility symbol linked with love, marriage, and many children," is also linked to "the maternal and agricultural goddess Hera (Juno), who holds a pomegranate as a marriage symbol."[5] Hera is also the goddess of childbirth. Her serrated crown resembles the calyx of the pomegranate. Witcombe notes that the "headdress worn by one of the women buried in the tomb of Queen Puabi at the Sumerian site of Ur (around 2500 BCE) includes in the elaborate decoration clusters of gold pomegranates, three fruits hanging together shielded by their leaves . . . ."[6] Thus, the pomegranate is a sign of royalty because of its calyx, "its crown-like terminal,"[7] and its representation of eternity.

The pomegranate also plays a major role in the myth of Persephone (Proserpine), the goddess of the underworld. The daughter of Zeus (Jupiter), the king of the gods, and Demeter (Ceres), a great earth goddess, was so beautiful that Hades (Pluto), god of the underworld, kidnapped Persephone and took her with him to make her his queen. Zeus demanded that his brother Hades return her. Persephone was racked with hunger; however, it was a rule of the Fates that anyone who consumed food or drink in the underworld was doomed to spend eternity there. So, Hades set out to trick Persephone into staying with him. "See, here is a tree—a pomegranate tree," he said. "You are hungry. Eat."[8] Caldecott continues narrating the story: "In the midst of the black and blighted garden stood a green pomegranate tree laden with ripe and glowing fruit. . . . She picked. She ate. She sank to the ground and rested her-

---

3. Tresidder, *Dictionary of Symbols*, 394.
4. Bulfinch, *Mythology*, 67.
5. Tresidder, *Dictionary of Symbols*, 394.
6. Witcombe, "Trees and the Sacred."
7. Sill, *Handbook of Symbols*, 56.
8. Caldecott, *Myths*, 85.

self. She fell asleep."[9] In some versions of the myth, Persephone eats a certain number of pomegranate seeds, such as four or six to indicate the number of months she is condemned to spend in the underworld. When she awakens, she is in bed with Hades! However, Zeus negotiates with Hades to permit Persephone to spend half of the year on earth in order to guarantee its flower and fruit (spring and summer) and half a year in the underworld during its dormant and cold waiting (fall and winter).

Caldecott makes an important observation, stating: "Persephone voluntarily, though under persuasion, ate the pomegranate fruit that precluded her from going back to the pure life of the maiden. The pomegranate in Greek myth is the fruit of commitment to marriage and sexual maturity."[10] If the reader thinks that this story resembles the myth in the HB (OT) Book of Genesis about the first woman eating the forbidden fruit, he or she is correct. After both ate the forbidden fruit, their perceptions changed. Quoting Hall, Caldecott writes that the pomegranate in the story of Persephone "signifies the sensuous life which, once tasted, temporarily deprives man [and woman] of immortality."[11] Furthermore, according to Hall "the pomegranate was also considered to be a divine symbol of such peculiar significance that its true explanation could not be divulged. . . . Many Greek gods and goddesses are depicted holing the fruit or flower of the pomegranate in their hands, evidently to signify that they are givers of life and plenty."[12]

In Christianity the pomegranate became a sign of the fullness of Jesus' suffering and resurrection. The Christ child is often depicted holding a pomegranate. According to Taylor, "In the hands of Christian artists, the legend of the pomegranate was developed to become a symbol of new life and resurrection,"[13] and according to Sill, "The many seeds in blood-red juice . . . equate to life out of death."[14] "When the pomegranate appears opened, with the seeds evident, it becomes analogous to the resurrection, the opening of the tomb, allegory of hope," adds Sill.[15]

Likewise, a single pomegranate can represent the church "whose many parts are like the many seeds contained within a single whole."[16] According to Caldecott, "the pomegranate came to represent for the early Christians

---

9. Ibid.
10. Ibid., 86.
11. Hall, *Secret Teachings*, xcv; cf. Caldecott, *Myths*, 87.
12. Ibid.
13. Taylor, *How to Read a Church*, 209.
14. Sill, *Handbook of Symbols*, 56.
15. Ibid.
16. Ibid.

the unity of the church."[17] Many seeds are held together in one rounded fruit, just as the many different Christians are held together in one church.

As already narrated in the bramble entry, Aesop narrates only one fable including the pomegranate tree, which is having a dispute with the apple tree concerning which one has the better fruit. While the bramble doesn't settle the dispute, it does put a stop to the quarrelling.[18]

Thus, the red, extremely seeded fruit of the pomegranate tree is a delicacy. In sacred literatures, the tree can serve as a landmark and represent abundance, bounty, prosperity, ambition, sexual temptation, love, marriage, fertility, fecundity, many children, generosity, eternity, royalty, resurrection, and the church. Indeed, due to its many meanings, the pomegranate is a sacred tree bearing sacred fruit.

Journal/Meditation: What fruit of a tree represents abundance for you? What fruit of a tree represents love for you? What fruit of a tree represents generosity for you? What fruit of a tree represents resurrection for you?

Prayer: LORD God, you are bounteous beyond measure. I recognize one sign of your abundance in the fruit of the pomegranate tree. Send the Holy Spirit to me to make me fertile in good words and works. Grant this through my Lord Jesus Christ, whose resurrection is signified by the pomegranate. He lives and reigns with you, Father, and the Holy Spirit, one God, forever and ever. Amen.

---

17. Caldecott, *Myths*, 87.
18. Aesop, 83.

Poplar

Text: ". . . Jacob took fresh rods of poplar . . . and peeled white streaks in them, exposing the white of the rods. He set the rods that he had peeled in front of the flocks in the troughs, that is, the watering places, where the flocks came to drink. And since they bred when they came to drink, the flocks bred in front of the rods, and so the flocks produced young that were striped, speckled, and spotted." (Gen 30:37–39).

Reflection: In the trickster tale about Laban and Jacob in the HB (OT) Book of Genesis, Laban agrees that every speckled and spotted goat and lamb should belong to Jacob as his wages. But Laban removes all the speckled and spotted creatures before Jacob can claim them and separates a three day's journey from Jacob. However, Jacob is a trickster, too. He decides to place striped poplar branches in front of the goats as they mate. His assumption is that whatever they saw while they mated would determine the color of the offspring. His primitive experiment in genetic engineering made Jacob very rich!

    The poplar tree from which Jacob shaped the rods is deciduous; it grows up to one hundred sixty feet tall and can sport a trunk over eight feet in diameter. The bark of the poplar is smooth and white to greenish or dark gray in color. Jacob striped the bark from the poplar rods to reveal the white wood underneath. The top side of the leaf is green, and the underside of the leaf is white. This fact may be connected to the trickster story of Jacob's genetic manipulation of the flock so that all the lambs were speckled or spotted black on white. According to Tresidder, it certainly influences one of the stories concerning Herakles (Hercules) "who bound a poplar branch around his head for his descent into the underworld. Smoke darkened the top of the leaves while his sweat blanched their lower surfaces."[1] Caldecott adds to this mythology by stating that after Hades had taken Persephone to the underworld, she ran from chamber to chamber and "at last found her way to the garden. There black poplars stood around, no breeze stirring their shadowy leaves."[2] Caldecott's statement also echoes the funerary symbolism of the poplar, made popular by Herakles's bringing it back from the underworld.

In Chinese Daoism, the yin/yang dualism is signified by the poplar leaf "because the leaves of the white poplar are dark green on the upper (solar) side but appear white on the lower (moon) side, where they are covered with soft down."[3]

In the only other mention of poplar tree in the Bible, the prophet Hosea criticizes the worship of other gods by the Israelites. They make offerings under poplar because their shade is good (Hos 4:13), states the prophet. This practice brings God's condemnation for their unfaithfulness.

In what seems to be a retelling of the story of Hades and Persephone (see Pomegranate), the Greco-Roman myth of Leuce (Leuka), meaning *white poplar*, features Pluto falling in love with Leuce and taking her to the underworld. Leuce, the most beautiful of the nymphs and a daughter of Oceanus, dies there. Pluto creates a memorial of her love in the Elysian Fields, where he brings a white tree, a poplar, into existence. Some sources of the myth state that it was from this tree that Herakles created a crown to celebrate his return from the underworld. Likewise, celebrants of the Dionysan (Bacchic) rites wore a wreath of poplar leaves, and such a wreath or crown could be worn by victors in athletic contests held in honor of Herakles. In other mythology, poplar wood was used in sacrifices to Zeus because Herakles had imported it from the banks of a river and used it to burn the thigh bones of sacrificial victims.

In the story of Phaeton, the son of the Sun and Clymene, Phaeton asks his father to drive his chariot (the sun) for a day. After the Sun tries to convince him that he will not be able to wield it, the Sun has to grant his wish. However, when the horses drawing the chariot run wild, the Sun hurls thunderbolts at Phaeton, and he falls, flaming, to his death. Phaeton's mother and three sisters mourn him for many months.

> One day when Paethusa [one of his sisters] tried to fling herself upon the ground, she complained that she could not move her feet. Lampetie [another sister] would have gone to her

1. Tresidder, *Dictionary of Symbols*, 395.
2. Caldecott, *Myths*, 84.
3. Tresidder, *Dictionary of Symbols*, 395.

assistance, but she was held fast by roots which had suddenly formed. A third [sister] made to tear her hair, and plucked out leaves. One cried out that her legs were caught in the grip of a tree trunk, another was indignant to find her arms had become long branches. While they were marveling at this, bark surrounded their thighs, and gradually spread over womb and breast, shoulders and hands, till only lips remained, vainly calling for their mother.... The grove of trees had increased in size by the number of Phaeton's sisters.[4]

Bulfinch states, "His sisters, the Heliades, as they lamented his fate, were turned into poplar trees, on the banks of the river, and their tears, which continued to flow, became amber as they dropped into the stream."[5]

Thus, the dark bark of the poplar tree reveals white wood used in a primitive biblical engineering and trickster story. While the leaves of the poplar represent the eternal duality of Chinese yin and yang, they are more associated with funerary practices. Herakles makes a crown out of poplar branches either before he descends to the underworld or when he ascends from it. Pluto mourns the passing of Leuce by planting a poplar tree, and Phaeton's three sisters turn into poplar trees while mourning their brother's death at the hands of their father. This tree is sacred because of its association with the underworld.

Journal/Meditation: What tree do you associate with funerary rites? What does it represent for you?

Prayer: Father of the living and the dead, you promise those who remain faithful to your ways that you will bring them through dark death to light life. Hear my prayer this day, and grant that I may serve you faithfully in this life so as to share in the next. Hear me through Jesus Christ, your Son, who is Lord of both the living and the dead forever and ever. Amen.

---

4. Caldicott, *Myths*, 92.
5. Bulfinch, *Mythology*, 45; cf. Herzberg, *Myths*, 76.

Red Cedar

Text: "... Amaziah sent messengers to King Jehoash son of Jehoahaz, son of Jehu, of Israel, saying, 'Come, let us look one another in the face.' King Jehoash of Israel sent word to King Amaziah of Judah, 'A thornbush on Lebanon sent to a cedar on Lebanon, saying, "Give your daughter to my son for a wife"; but a wild animal of Lebanon passed by and trampled down the thornbush. You have indeed defeated Edom, and your heart has lifted you up. Be content with your glory, and stay at home; for why should you provoke trouble so that you fall, you and Judah with you?'" (2 Kgs 14:8–10; cf. 2 Chr 25:17–19)

Reflection: Amaziah is king of Judah from 800 to 785 BCE, and Jehoash (Joash) is king of Israel from 801 to 786 BCE. Judah is the southern kingdom and Israel is the northern kingdom of what had once been King David's and King Solomon's confederacy of tribes into one empire. After Solomon's death (around 930 BCE) the nation splits into two separate kingdoms. Amaziah in the south challenges Jehoash in the north to battle. Jehoash replies to Amaziah by telling a story about a thornbush telling a cedar to give its daughter as a wife to the thornbush's son. Before this could occur, however, the thornbush was crushed by a wild animal. A small, useless thornbush cannot tell a large, mighty cedar—especially one of Lebanon—what to do! The thornbush is so lowly that a wild animal can trample it.

When the confederacy split into two kingdoms, ten tribes formed the northern kingdom of Israel, and the two remaining tribes formed the southern kingdom of Judah. In the story, Jehoash in the north is the cedar, and Amaziah in the south is the thornbush. Jehoash's fable warns Amaziah that he may not be as important as he thinks he is. In fact, he is so small that a wild animal can trample him. Amaziah had just defeated ten thousand Edomites (2 Kgs 14:7), and this victory had puffed him up. Jehoash tells him to enjoy his glory and not make war with his kinsfolk. If he should do so, Jehoash knows that he will lose, and Judah will fall to Jehoash.

The fable features a cedar tree, of which there are many species. For example, the red cedar is a common sight throughout most of the plains in the United States along roads, in fence rows, and scattered across fields. Also known as a juniper, it is a coniferous evergreen with needle-like leaves and berry-like, dark purple-blue seed pods. Living up to nine hundred years, the red cedar tree features reddish-brown fibrous bark that peels off in narrow strips and aromatic reddish wood used to make cedar chests and to line cedar closets. The wood is rot resistant and repels moths.

There is also the Lebanon cedar or cedar of Lebanon that is mentioned often in the Bible. This species of cedar is native to the mountains of the Mediterranean region. It, too, is an evergreen coniferous tree growing up to one hundred thirty feet tall with an up to eight-foot trunk diameter and needle-like leaves. This species produces seed cones only every other year. Sometimes referred to as a Cedar of God, the timber of the Lebanon cedar was exported by Phoenicians, Egyptians, Assyrians, Babylonians, Persians, Romans, and Turks to be used as a building material to construct palaces, temples, and ships. And the resin was used in the mummification process.

This entry is concerned with the cedar tree—no matter if it be red cedar, a juniper, or a Lebanon cedar. Cedar is the common name both for any type of cedar tree and for the wood harvested from cedar trees that grow all around the world. The tall evergreen tree with spreading branches, needles, and cones is long-lived, rot resistant, and fragrant. It lends itself to a variety of meanings.

For example, the cedar represents pride. Tresidder refers to this as an "emblem of majesty and incorruptibility."[1] The singer of Psalm 148 calls upon all cedars to praise the LORD (Ps 148:9). The prophet Isaiah declares the punishment of all that is proud and lofty, of all that is lifted up and high; all the cedars of Lebanon, lofty and lifted up. God will punish (Isa 2:12–13). Likewise, the prophet Zechariah announced the destruction of wicked rulers stating that "the cedar has fallen, for the glorious trees are ruined!" (Zech 11:2a).

In the HB (OT) Book of Job, God compares the monster Behemoth's stiff tail to that of a cedar (Job 40:17) to indicate its strength. Psalm 29 declares that the strength of God's voice—thunder— "breaks the cedars; the LORD breaks the cedars of Lebanon" (Ps 29:5). According to Psalm 92, the

---

1. Tresidder, *Dictionary of Symbols*, 92.

strong and righteous "grow like a cedar in Lebanon. They are planted in the house of the LORD; they flourish in the courts of . . . God" (Ps 92:12–13). As already noted above, King Jehoash of Israel considers himself to be as strong as a cedar (1 Kings 14:9).

The cedar represents strength because of its height. The prophet Amos refers to this when he records the LORD's declaration about destroying Israel's enemy, the Amorites, whose height was like the height of cedars (Amos 2:9). The psalmist says that the oppression of wicked people is towering like a cedar of Lebanon (Ps 37:35), while lady wisdom describes herself as growing tall like a cedar in Lebanon (Sir 24:13). The prophet Ezekiel likens the defeat of Egyptian Pharaoh Hophra by Nebuchadnezzar of Babylon to a fallen cedar:

> Consider Assyria, a cedar of Lebanon, with fair branches and forest shade, and of great height, its top among the clouds. So it towered high above all the trees of the field; its boughs grew large and its branches long . . . . Therefore thus says the Lord GOD: Because it towered high and set its top among the clouds, and its heart was proud of its height, I gave it into the hand of the prince of the nations . . . . Foreigners from the most terrible of the nations have cut it down and left it. (Ezek 31:3, 5, 10–12a)

The height of the cedar tree fosters security. When Balaam sees Israel camping, he blesses the people referring to them like cedar trees beside the waters (Num 24:6b). This theme of God providing security is echoed in Psalm 104 which declares, "The trees of the LORD are watered abundantly, the cedars of Lebanon that he planted" (Ps 104:16). The prophet Jeremiah evokes the security of the tall cedar trees when he uses the phrase "nested among the cedars" (Jer 22:23). The *Mormon* Second Book of Nephi declares that "the cedars of Lebanon" rejoice because God has defeated the wicked "and no feller is come up against" them (2 Ne 24:8). The OT (A) Book of Sirach described Simon, Son of Onias (Simon II), a high priest as being like a young cedar on Lebanon (Sir 50:12) as he stood securely ministering at the altar in the temple.

The cedar tree is also a sign of wealth and prosperity. Sill states, "The cedars of Lebanon were prized and treasured tall trees that forested the plains and slopes of Mount Lebanon, and were a source of wealth."[2] The First Book of Kings declares that King Solomon "made cedars as numerous as the sycamores" (1 Kgs 10:27). The Second Book of Chronicles records that Solomon "made cedar as plentiful as the sycamore" (2 Chr 1:15; 9:27). The *Mormon* Second Book of Nephi declares that the LORD will change the sycamores into cedars (2 Ne 19:10). Similarly, the prophet Isaiah portrays

---

2. Sill, *Symbols in Christian Art*, 205.

God saying, "I will put in the wilderness the cedar" (Isa 41:19). Because cedar was a sign of luxury in King Jehoiakim's reign (609–598 BCE), Jeremiah reproved him for his desire to outdo others in paneling his house with cedar (Jer 22:14). The prophet asks Jehoiakim, "Are you a king because you compete in cedar?" (Jer 22:15) He should be engaged in justice and righteousness instead of prosperity and luxury.

Long before Jehoiakim's reign, King David used cedar to build his palace. "King Hiram of Tyre sent . . . cedar trees and carpenters and masons who built David a house" (2 Sam 5:11). The First Book of Chronicles refers to the building materials as cedar logs (1 Chr 14:1). David referred to his house of cedar (2 Sam 7:2; 1 Chr 17:1) when speaking to Nathan the prophet about building a temple. When Nathan consults God about this, he replies that he never asked the Israelites, "Why have you not built me a house of cedar?" (2 Sam 7:7; 1 Chr 17:6). While David was never permitted to build a temple for God, he nevertheless gathered together and stored cedar logs without number (1 Chr 22:4) for his son, Solomon, to use in the project.

After David's death Solomon wasted little time gathering the rest of the building materials he needed to construct the temple. "He would speak of trees," mentioning "the cedar that is in Lebanon" (1 Kgs 4:33). He sent a message to King Hiram of Tyre, just as his father David did, asking him to command that cedars from Lebanon be cut for him (1 Kgs 5:6). Hiram replied, "'I will fulfill all your needs in the matter of cedar . . . .' So Hiram supplied Solomon's every need for timber of cedar . . ." (1 Kgs 5:8, 10). King Solomon roofed the temple with beams and planks of cedar and using timbers of cedar connected the vestibule to it. He lined the walls of the house on the inside with boards of cedar and the rear of the house with boards of cedar from the floor to the rafters. The cedar within the house had carvings of gourds and open flowers; all were cedar. He also overlaid the altar with cedar, and he built the inner court with one course of cedar beams (1 Kgs 6:9, 10, 15a, 16, 18, 20, 36).

Solomon also built his own house—which took thirteen years to complete—and called it "the House of the Forest of the Lebanon" (1 Kgs 7:2); it was "built on four rows of cedar pillars, with cedar beams on the pillars. It was roofed with cedar" (1 Kgs 7:2–3). Within the palace there was the Hall of Justice, covered with cedar from floor to floor (1 Kgs 7:7). The great court had one layer of cedar beams all round; so had the inner court of the house of the LORD, and the vestibule of the house (1 Kgs 7:12). "At the end of twenty years, in which Solomon had built the two houses, the house of the LORD and the king's house, King Hiram of Tyre [had] supplied Solomon with cedar . . ." (1 Kgs 9:10–11). After the Babylonians destroy Solomon's temple and the rebuilding begins about sixty years later, the HB (OT) Book of Ezra notes that the Jews gave others money and other items to bring cedar trees from Lebanon (Ezra 3:7) to be used in the second temple. According to Ryken, "The cedars of Lebanon represent the finest of earthly materials."[3]

"The supreme beauty and earthly glory of the cedars"[4] is illustrated in the Song of Songs. "[T]he beams of our house are cedar" (Song 1:17), states the woman to the man when she describes their outdoor meeting place. She describes his appearance as being like Lebanon, choice as the cedars (Song 8:9), probably a reference to his height. At the end of the extended love poem are appended other poems. In one of these the poet states that if the woman is a door, she will be enclosed with boards of cedar (Song 8:9), a reference to her non-virginity. Thus, according to Ryken, the "ravishing beauty" of the cedar "heightens the eroticism of the Song of Songs."[5]

Cedar wood was used in purification rituals and healing. The HB (OT) Book of Numbers describes the purification ritual required for those who have touched a corpse. Once a red heifer is slaughtered, it is burned, and the priest takes cedar wood, among other items, and burns it with the heifer (Num 19:6). The HB (OT) Book of Leviticus presents the ritual for cleansing a leper; cedar wood, among other items, are brought to the priest, who dips it into the blood of a dead bird and sprinkles the once-leprous person with it, and he or she is declared clean (Lev 14:1–7). Cedar was used in a similar manner by Native Americans. In "Native Americans and Trees," the author notes that "cedar was and remains strongly associated with prayer, healing, and protection against disease."[6] After a new home was constructed, boughs of cedar "were brushed through the air and believed to cleanse the home's interior. Various parts of the tree were burned as incense for the purpose of purification, driving out negative energy and drawing in good influences. Pieces of the tree were also carried in medicine pouches to ward of sickness."[7]

In "The Legend of the Cedar Tree," Fox explains how the tree came to be regarded as sacred by the Native American Cherokee. After a lengthy tale explaining how day and night came into existence, he notes that many of the people had died.

> The Creator placed their spirits in a newly created tree. This tree was named . . . [the] cedar tree. When [one] smells the aroma of the cedar tree or gazes upon it standing in the forest, [he or she] remembers that if [he or she is] Cherokee, [he or she is]

---

3. Ryken, *Dictionary*, 499.
4. Ibid.
5. Ibid.
6. "Native Americans and Trees."
7. Ibid.

looking upon [an] ancestor. Tradition holds that the wood of the cedar tree holds powerful protective spirits for the Cherokee. Many carry a small piece of cedar wood in their medicine bags worn around the neck. It is also placed above the entrances to the house to protect against the entry of evil spirits.[8]

Likewise, in Runge's "The Juniper Tree," the cedar tree possesses a "therapeutic power," according to Tatar.[9] "The oil, ashes, berries, leaves, and bark are used in many cultures for healing purposes."[10] In Runge's tale, the juniper grows in front of the house in a garden. A rich man's wife, who was childless, peeled an apple under the tree and asked for a child. After she conceives, "the woman sat under the juniper tree" and "her heart leaped for joy because the tree was so fragrant. . . . When the sixth month had passed, the fruit grew large and firm, and she became very quiet. In the seventh month she picked the berries from the juniper tree and gorged herself on them until she became miserable and ill."[11] She told her husband that if she should die, she wanted to be buried under the juniper tree. Sure enough, after giving birth to a son, she died and "the woman's husband buried her under the juniper tree."[12]

The lengthy story moves on (see Apple) narrating how the man married a second wife, who bore him a daughter named Marlene, although Grimm names her Marjory.[13] Marlene's mother decides to kill the man's son, chop his body, cook him, and serve him to his father for dinner. As his father unknowingly eats his son, he tosses the bones under the table. The story continues:

> Little Marlene went to her dresser and got her best silk kerchief. She picked up all the bones from beneath the table, tied them up in her silk kerchief, and carried them outside. . . . She put the bones down in the green grass under the juniper tree. . . . The juniper tree began stirring. Its branches parted and came back together again as through it were clapping its hands for joy. A mist arose from the tree, and in the middle of the mist a flame was burning, and from the flame a beautiful bird emerged and began singing gloriously. It soared up in the air, and then

---

8. Fox, "Legend of the Cedar Tree."
9. Tatar, *Classic Fairy Tales*, 158.
10. Ibid.
11. Runge, "Juniper Tree," 160.
12. Ibid., 161.
13. *Grimm's Complete Fairy Tales*, 270.

vanished. The tree was as it had been before, but the kerchief with the bones was gone.[14]

There is no doubt that the juniper tree is the source for the boy's mother and the boy's transformation. His mother is changed from being barren to being fruitful. The boy is changed from death to life. The fairy tale also echoes "The Legend of the Cedar Tree" narrated above. While the spirit of the mother and her son do not live within the tree, they are buried beneath it, and the boy's spirit emerges from it to be reincarnated as a beautiful bird. In biblical tradition, God's Spirit is often presented as a dove (Mark 1:10; Matt 3:16; Luke 3:22), a type of beautiful bird!

The destruction of the cedar signifies defeat. The prophet Jeremiah uses this image when he addresses the King of Judah. He tells the king that God will send destroyers to Jerusalem who will cut down his choicest cedars and cast them into the fire (Jer 22:7). Isaiah warns the ten destroyed tribes of Israel against pride and complacency. The Assyrians conquered them, but in their arrogance they declare that they would rebuild with cedars (Isa 9:10). Later, Isaiah taunts the king of Babylon in death, writing that since the cedars of Lebanon were laid low, no one comes to cut them down. Sheol, the place where the dead lived, is stirred up to meet him when he comes (Isa 14:8–9a). The king's power in life, represented by the mighty cedar, is contrasted to his lack of power as he heads to Sheol, the underworld. The much-in-demand cedar has been reduced to the common lot of the dead. Isaiah also taunts King Sennacherib of Assyria by reporting the words of the LORD God: "By your servants you have mocked the Lord, and you have said, 'With my many chariots I have gone up the heights of the mountains, to the far recesses of Lebanon; I felled its tallest cedars, its choicest cypresses; I came to its remotest height, its densest forest" (Isa 37:24; 2 Kgs 19:23). In other words, even though the arrogant and boastful Sennacherib has been able to do all these mighty things, he has mocked and reviled the Holy One of Israel, the LORD, and the king of Judah has retained his throne, and Jerusalem has survived intact. The prophet Zephaniah explains God's judgment of Assyria stating that its cedar work will be laid bare (Zeph 2:14). In *Mormon's* Second Book of Nephi, the writer declares that "the day of the Lord shall come upon all the cedars of Lebanon, for they are high and lifted up" and "the haughtiness of men shall be made low; and the Lord alone shall be exalted in that day" (2 Ne 12:13, 17). Ezekiel laments the destruction of Tyre by portraying her as a well-built ship with a mast made from a cedar from Lebanon (Ezek 27:5). Isaiah reproves the idols made from cedar (Isa 44:14–15); a human carpenter cannot create a god from a felled tree.

---

14. Tatar, *Classic Fairy Tales*, 165.

Because the cedar signifies pride, God destroys it. The prophet Zechariah states: "Open your doors, O Lebanon, so that fire may devour your cedars!" (Zech 11:1) The same image is used by Jotham in his fable about trees in the HB (OT) Book of Judges. The bramble passes judgment on all other trees, declaring that fire should come out of the bramble and devour the cedars of Lebanon (Judg 9:15).

The prophet Ezekiel narrates an allegory featuring a cedar tree:

> A great eagle, with great wings and long pinions, rich in plumage of many colors, came to the Lebanon. He took the top of the cedar, broke off its topmost shoot; he carried it to a land of trade, set it in a city of merchants. Then he took a seed from the land, placed it in fertile soil; a plant by abundant water, he set it like a willow twig. It sprouted and became a vine spreading out, but low; its branches turned toward him, its roots remained where it stood. So it became a vine; it brought forth branches, put forth foliage. (Ezek 17:3–6)

The great eagle is the king of Babylon, Nebuchadnezzar, who takes the topmost part of the cedar—King Jehoiachin of Judah—to Babylon. Keeping in mind that the royal palace in Jerusalem is known as the House of the Forest of Lebanon, Nebuchadnezzar takes a seed and plants it in Jerusalem; the seed is King Zedekiah, whom Nebuchadnezzar installed as king in place of Jehoiachin. Zedekiah, Jehoiachin's uncle, identified as a twig in the allegory, ultimately revolts, and Nebuchadnezzar kills his sons and takes him to Babylon as a captive of war.

After explaining the allegory, Ezekiel records:

> Thus says the Lord GOD: I myself will take a sprig from the lofty top of a cedar; I will set it out. I will break off a tender one from the topmost of its young twigs; I myself will plant it on a high and lofty mountain. On the mountain height of Israel I will plant it, in order that it may produce boughs and bear fruit, and become a noble cedar. (Ezek 17:22–23a)

In other words, God promises to restore the royal house of Judah, the line of David.

The cedar plays a role in the legends of Gilgamesh, the fifth King of Uruk in Mesopotamia. One day Gilgamesh said to his friend, Enkidu, that he wanted his name to be remembered. Cavendish states, "Gilgamesh resolves that since immortality is denied to [hu]mankind, he will at least carve an immortal name for himself through heroic exploits."[15] Caldecott records

---

15. Cavendish, *Legends*, 92.

Gilgamesh saying, "I will go to the land of the living, to the cedar forests, and I will build a monument that will last forever."[16] Enkidu reminds him that there is a fearsome giant, named Humbaba (Huwawa), who guards the forest. There are various versions of how they finally get to the gate of the "forest of mighty cedar that stretched in every direction."[17] "Gilgamesh is determined to win immortal fame for himself and his . . . friend," states Cavendish.[18] "Together they go to the Cedar Forest to attack its terrible supernatural guardian Huwawa. They make their way to the center of the forest. Gilgamesh cuts down a cedar tree with an ax, at which the monster Huwawa himself appears."[19] Because he fears Humbaba, Gilgamesh appeals for help from the sun god, Shamash, who loosed great winds that made the huge cedar trees sway and pin back Humbaba. "Gilgamesh wielded his ax and felled another tree, and another, until seven cedars lay at the foot of the mountain and he stood directly before Humbaba."[20]

Humbaba acknowledges defeat and offers to serve Gilgamesh, but Enkidu persuades him to kill the giant.

> At last one Humbaba was dead: The guardian of the cedar forest lay dead! Now there was nothing and no one to stop the destruction of the forest. Gilgamesh wielded his ax again and again. Enkidu cleared the roots. All the way to the banks of the Euphrates there was no more forest. . . . [Then] he laid the great palaces and temples and cities that he had built of cedar at the feet of the god who had made him king.[21]

Caldecott notes that Gilgamesh misunderstood what immortality meant, and ended up ruining the environment. "When Humbaba, the green man, the guardian of nature, asks that his life be spared and suggests that he could be the king's servant, Gilgamesh, by listening to Enkidu's bad advice, turns down the opportunity to work with nature to the benefit of both man and tree."[22] She adds, ". . . [T]he Gilgamesh story is about civilized, city-dwelling man destroying the natural environment because he fears it—because it is fierce and untamed and cannot be controlled."[23]

16. Caldecott, *Myths*, 19.
17. Ibid., 21.
18. Cavendish, *Legends*, 93.
19. Ibid.
20. Caldecott, *Myths*, 22.
21. Ibid.
22. Ibid., 24–5.
23. Ibid., 25.

As already seen in the entries on cypress and pine, one of the three seeds given to Adam's son, Seth, by Mik-hael or a cherub to be placed in Adam's mouth after he died, came from a mighty tree in paradise. Three days after Seth's return from seeing the tree, his father died, and Seth buried him with the three seeds in his mouth. Besides the cypress and pine, the cedar tree grew from his buried body. From the wood of the three intertwined trees, the Romans made the cross upon which Jesus was crucified.[24] Caldecott says, "The cedar represents nobility, incorruptibility, majesty, stateliness, and beauty."[25] Tradition also maintains that Moses' staff was made from that tree, that Aaron's flowering rod was made from that tree, that King David bewailed his sins under that tree, that Solomon used it as the main pillar supporting his palace and as a bridge over Kedron, and that the Queen of Sheba found it and Solomon buried it under a miraculous healing pool.[26]

Thus, the long-lived conifer evergreen known as the red cedar, the juniper, or the Lebanon cedar with rot-resistant fragrant wood represents pride, majesty, incorruptibility, immortality, strength, security, and prosperity. That is why it was used by King David to build his palace. That is why it was used by King Solomon to build his palace and temple complex. It is the finest of earthly building materials. It was also used for purification, healing, and protection, and it signifies transformation. Destroyed cedars represent defeat and restoration of the royal line of Judah. Mythology further enhances the dignity of the cedar by declaring it to be one of the three intertwined trees from which the cross was made. There can be no doubt that the cedar is a sacred tree.

Journal/Meditation: What has been your experience of the cedar tree? What does it represent for you? How do your experience and its meaning identify the cedar as sacred?

Prayer: Heavenly Father, you have taken a sprig from the lofty top of a cedar and planted it on a high and lofty mountain. Your son Jesus' death on the cross has produced boughs and borne fruit that have made it a noble cedar. Grant that I may live in its shade and find rest all the days of my life. I ask this through the same Jesus Christ, who lives and reigns with you and the Holy Spirit, one God, forever and ever. Amen.

---

24. Baring-Gould, *Curious Myths*, 107–10.
25. Caldecott, *Myths*, 133.
26. Ibid., 132; Baring-Gould, *Curious Myths*, 109–10.

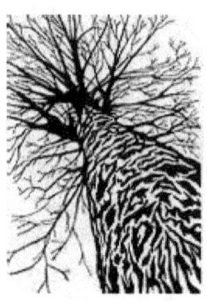

Sycamore

Text: "[Jesus] entered Jericho and was passing through it. A man was there named Zacchaeus; he was a chief tax collector and was rich. He was trying to see who Jesus was, but on account of the crowd he could not, because he was short in stature. So he ran ahead and climbed a sycamore tree to see him, because he was going to pass that way. When Jesus came to the place, he looked up and said to him, 'Zacchaeus, hurry down; for I must stay at your house today.' So he hurried down and was happy to welcome him." (Luke 19:1–5)

Reflection: There is a paucity of references to the sycamore in sacred literature probably because the tree was so common and plentiful. The only mention made of the sycamore in the CB (NT) is the story about Zacchaeus—whose name means *clean, the pure one,* or *the innocent one*—unique to Luke's Gospel. It is important to note that the tree the tax collector climbs in Jericho, the city of palm trees, is a sycamore! Johnson notes, "Zacchaeus seeks to see and does not know that he is being sought after and saved" by Jesus.[1] According to Bovon, "This particular kind of sycamore tree, a sycamore fig tree, which is unknown in the West, is a species that grows in plains, does not lose its foliage, possesses a short, wide trunk, and has thick low branches that spread wide. So it was not hard to climb it."[2] Because of the sycamore's association with Zacchaeus's desire to see Jesus, it signifies having a clear vision and ambition.

This type of sycamore, often spelled *sycomore,* can grow up to sixty feet tall and sports a dense crown of spreading branches which makes it ideal for shade. Its leaves are heart-shaped; the upper part of the leaf is dark green, and

---

1. Johnson, *Luke,* 285.
2. Bovon, *Luke 2,* 597.

the under part is lighter green with yellow veins; both surfaces are rough to the touch. The tree's bark is a green-yellow to orange and peels off in papery-like strips to reveal the yellow inner bark. Flowering and fruiting occurs all year producing large edible figs which appear in clusters like grapes.

In the HB (OT), the sycamore is mentioned only seven times. In the First Book of Kings, the large number of sycamore trees is used as a comparison for the numerous cedars—indicating prosperity—that King Solomon had (1 Kgs 10:27). The Second Book of Chronicles repeats this fact stating that Solomon made cedar as plentiful as the sycamore (2 Chr 1:15; 9:27). During Solomon's father's reign, King David had appointed Baal-hanan over the sycamore trees; this means that he functioned as a steward of the king's wealth (1 Chr 27:28) and may have been in charge of puncturing the fruit with a sharp instrument a few days before it was to be picked and eaten to enhance its sweetness. Isaiah describes the ruin caused by the invasion of the Assyrians into Israel stating that the sycamores have been cut down (Isa 9:10b). The Second Book of Nephi in *The Book of Mormon* echoes this statement: "... [T]he sycamores are cut down, but we will change them into cedars" (2 Ne 19:10). In recounting the LORD's works, the psalmist remembers the exodus, when God destroyed the Egyptian's sycamores with frost (Ps 78:47); however, no such deed is mentioned in the HB (OT) Book of Exodus!

The last biblical mention of sycamore trees in found in the prophet Amos, who identifies himself as "a dresser of sycamore trees" (Amos 7:14). Wolff states that Amos "has something to do with mulberry figs,"[3] another common name for the sycamore tree.

> The *ficus sycomorus* is dependent on a warm climate and prospers only in the lowlands—primarily in the Mediterranean coastal region and in the Jordan Valley—where it is very abundant [as noted above in 1 Kgs 10:27]. It bears fruit three or four times a year. *To slit* [the meaning of the Hebrew verb translated as *to dress*] designates the job of scratching the fruit, which is done with a nail or some iron instrument. Before it ripens, each fruit must be treated in this fashion for it to turn sweet. That was probably the work of poor people, entailing as it did much toil in comparison with a small reward.... We do not know whether the ... expression designates only someone who actually performed the work or might also refer to someone who supervised such labor. It is certain, however, that Amos is here pointing out a ... source of income.[4]

---

3. Wolff, *Joel and Amos*, 314.
4. Ibid.

In Egyptian mythology, the sycamore is associated with Ra or Re, Nut, Isis, and Hathor. The sun god Ra, a sign of daily renewal, rises each morning on the eastern horizon, the gate of heaven, between two sycamores of turquoise. The sky goddess Nut protects the world from the darkness outside it and all the demonic creatures that inhabit that darkness; the sycamore tree is considered her manifestation. Likewise, Isis, the major goddess of the Egyptian pantheon, is manifested by a sycamore tree. King Tuthmosis III is depicted being nursed by Isis in the form of a sycamore tree in a painting in his tomb. The sycamore tree is a sign of her protecting presence.

However, Hathor bears the title "Lady of the Sycamore." She is considered the royal family's mother goddess, a sign of love and fertility, possessing healing powers and associated with a certain sycamore at Heliopolis. In Memphis she was worshiped as the "Mistress of the Southern Sycamore," and in other places she was called "Mistress of the Sycamore in All Her Places." Her ability to heal is associated with the use of fig leaves for medicinal purposes and fig consumption, that is, the eating of the flesh of Hathor herself. She is often depicted as leaning down from the sycamore tree to offer food to souls in the afterlife; the deceased are often depicted sitting under a sycamore tree with Hathor sprouting from the trunk and offering food to them. This makes her associated with life and death. Furthermore, she gives birth to Horus, god of the sky, who made the sunrise possible every morning. Hathor's sycamore stood right at the boundary between this world and the afterworld with its branches reaching to the afterworld and its roots firmly planted in this world; this makes it a tree of life and an *axis mundi*. Each day Ra rises from the top of Hathor's sycamore to begin his migration across Hathor's sky. The sycamore represents the daily interplay between light and darkness, life and death; thus it represents renewal. Burial in a wooden coffin, especially made from sycamore, was seen as a return to the womb of the mother goddess Hathor.[5] Thus, the sycamore was seen by Egyptians as bearing life in the midst of death.

In Kenya, Africa, the largest ethnic group is the *kikuyu* people who refer to themselves as children of the huge sycamore tree. According to their mythology, they came from two original parents—*Gikuyu*, which means *a huge sycamore tree*, and Mumbi—who were created by a monotheistic god, named *Ngai*, a life companion to the sycamore. They are concentrated in the vicinity of Mount Kenya. All sacrifices to *Ngai* are performed under a sycamore tree. The reader will notice the similarity of this mythology to that of Norse mythology in which the first man was created from an ash tree and the first woman from an elder tree.

5. Witcombe, "Trees and the Sacred."

Caldecott records that Orpheus, the Greek poet, played his lyre after his bride, Eurydice, died of a snake bite. "All nature loved his music. . . . [B]efore he had finished his song the trees from the valleys had gathered round him and he was enclosed in a leafy glade rich in . . . sycamore . . . ."[6] She also refers to the "Christian legend [that] tells of how 'Mary and Jesus took refuge in the holy tree of Mataria, the sycamore of Isis-Hathor . . . .'"[7] Mataria is a district of Cairo in what was the ancient city of Heliopolis. Officially called Al-Matariyyah, the name comes from the Latin word for mother: *mater*. It refers to the tree of the Virgin Mary. According to this legend, the Holy Family found shelter under this sycamore tree on its way to Egypt. This story seems to be a variant of the one found in The Gospel of Pseudo-Matthew which mentions a palm tree doing exactly what the sycamore did: provide shade, bend down to offer fruit, and give water (Pseudo-Matt 20:1–21:1; see Palm). The legend attempts to replace two Egyptian mother goddesses, Isis and Hathor, with the Christian Virgin Mary.

Thus, the sycamore represents clear spiritual vision and ambition. It is not mentioned often in sacred literature, but it was numerous enough to be used as a comparative. Zacchaeus, a tax collector who makes a cameo appearance in Luke's Gospel, climbs one, and Amos, a prophet from the HB (OT), identifies himself as a dresser of sycamores. The sycamore was dear to one Egyptian god and three goddesses, representing life in terms of the sun, food, and fertility. Stemming from these attributes, the sycamore is sacred because it offers protection.

Journal/Meditation: What tree represents spiritual vision for you? What tree represents the daily interplay between life and death for you?

Prayer: LORD God, you made the sycamore plentiful for your people so that they could find shade and food beneath it. You inspired the tax collector Zacchaeus to climb one in order to enhance his vision of your Son, Jesus Christ. Grant that the Holy Spirit will make better my spiritual vision now that I may one day see you face to face in your eternal Trinity: Father, Son, and Holy Spirit, one God, forever and ever. Amen.

---

6. Caldecott, *Myths*, 89.
7. Ibid., 126.

Tamarisk

Text: "There was a sign for the people of Saba in their habitations: Two gardens, on the right and left. (And they were told) 'Eat of what your Lord has given you and be thankful. Fair is your land, and forgiving your Lord.' But they turned away. So we let loose on them the inundation of (the dyke of) al-'Arim, replacing their gardens with two other gardens which bore only bitter gourd, and tamarisks, and few sparse lote trees." (*Quran* 34:15–16).

Reflection: In *The Quran*, the tamarisk tree is mentioned only one time, as seen in the text above. Saba, a city of Yemen, was located near a dyke or dam named Ma'arib. Saba was prosperous; on either side of the irrigation canals were gardens, which produced all kinds of food. The text attributes the good food as a gift from Allah. However, the dyke burst, and the water was like a flood that destroyed the city; this is an historical fact. The original luscious gardens turned into bitter waste lands. The feathery-leaved tamarisk trees, good only for twigs and wattle-work, replaced the fragrant plants and flowers. The wild lote tree, a stunted kind of thorny bush, replaced the fruit trees. According to an online commentary,

> [T]he Sabeans, who were a highly prosperous and cultured people, . . . defied and disobeyed divine commandments and . . . incurred the displeasure of God and were destroyed by a mighty flood. . . . [T]heir . . . destruction . . . gives a warning to Muslims that great wealth, power, and prosperity will also be bestowed on them, but if in the hey-day of their glory they, like . . . the Sabeans, give themselves up to a life of luxury and ease, they will be punished like them.[1]

1. "Al Islam."

The tamarisk, among other named plants, represents waste.

There are over fifty species of tamarisk trees; some are evergreen, and some are deciduous. They can grow up to sixty feet tall and form dense thickets. Their slender, smooth, reddish-brown young branches with gray-green foliage become ridged, furrowed, bluish-purple as they age. Pink to white flowers appear on the branch tips which turn into seeds contained in small capsules which are adorned with a tuft of hair that aids in wind dispersal. With their long tap roots, tamarisks reach deep water tables even taking up salt which accumulates in their foliage. While *The Quran* considers the tamarisk as a waste tree, the wood may be used for carpentry or firewood. Tresidder notes that the tamarisk is "a resin-giving tree with sacred significance in desert regions."[2] Murphey adds that "it provided ample shade for desert travelers."[3]

In biblical literature, the tamarisk tree is mentioned only four times, and all are in the HB (OT). Three of the four uses of tamarisk tree serve as landmarks. In the Book of Genesis, after Abraham and Abimelech made a covenant, "Abraham planted a tamarisk tree . . . , and called there on the name of the LORD, the Everlasting God" (Gen 21:33). The planting of the tree establishes the site as a holy place. According to Bar, the tamarisk "is a tall tree that requires very little water and is suitable to the sandy soil of the northern Negev desert area. It is noted for its cool shade and ability to withstand heat and dry spells."[4] Because this is the only place in biblical literature where Abraham plants a tree, "the tree served as a landmark for a place where he called on his God."[5]

Similarly, in the First Book of Samuel, a tamarisk tree serves as a landmark for King Saul. David, the future king of Israel, has been building an army. The prophet Gad sent David to Judah. "Saul heard that David and those who were with him had been located. Saul was sitting at Gibeath, under the tamarisk tree on the height, with his spear in his hand, and all his servants were standing around him" (1 Sam 22:6). In other words, Saul is sitting in council under a sacred tree, a common practice in the ancient world, seeking advice from his servants as to what he should do about his son-in-law who is threatening his throne. This landmark tamarisk tree is connected to another later in the story. After Saul and his three sons die on Mount Gilboa after a battle with the Philistines, who cut off their heads, remove their armor, and fasten their bodies to the wall of Beth-shan, a few brave men from Jabesh-gilead remove the bodies from the wall and,

2. Tresidder, *Dictionary of Symbols*, 463.
3. Murphey, *Dictionary of Biblical Literacy*, 39.
4. Bar, "Trees," 385.
5. Ibid.

uncharacteristically, cremate them and take their bones and bury them under the tamarisk tree in Jabesh (1 Sam 31:13). The ancient custom of burying people under trees is attested in a variety of places; the tree serves as a grave marker and, because its roots reach deep into the earth, it becomes a medium of transport to the underworld.

In the prophet Isaiah is found the last biblical mention of tamarisk tree. It is in the section of the prophet which gives hope for the restoration of Jerusalem. Isaiah compares God's rainstorms in the desert, which transform it into fertile land, to God's ability to transform the people of scattered and weakened Israel. The prophet portrays the LORD telling Jacob, his servant, not to fear. He "will pour water on the thirsty land, and streams on the dry ground: [he] will pour [his] spirit upon [Jacob's] descendants, and [his] blessing on [Jacob's] offspring. They shall spring up like a green tamarisk . . ." (Isa 44:3–4). According to Baltzer, "the outpouring of water becomes an image for the outpouring and efficacy of the Spirit."[6] While the Spirit gives life, "[t]he subject is the revivification of the people and the return to the land."[7] The comparison of the fertility of Jacob's offspring to tamarisk trees indicates their abundance, and, as seen for the sycamore, presumes their common occurrence without mentioning it in biblical literature—or anywhere else for that matter.

The tamarisk tree is mentioned in the Egyptian myth of Osiris, who is trapped in a box by his brother Set and thrown into the Nile River.

> Currents bore [the box] to shore near Byblos, where it was washed up on the beach, its sharp edges cutting into the trunk of a tamarisk sapling. The young tree took strength from the buried god, and the wound healed over the leaden chest, the trunk soon closing over so completely that the box was lost to sight. Never before had a tamarisk grown to such a width or such a height. Never before had its flowers hung to profusely and for so long.[8]

Ultimately, the tamarisk is cut and installed as the central column of a great hall. Isis, Osiris's sister-wife, discovers where the tamarisk is and demands that it be split open. It is, and the coffin of Osiris is revealed. "Isis left the wood of the tamarisk tree with the king and the queen [of Byblos], for the tree had held the body of a god and was worthy to be venerated. But she took the coffin back with her to Egypt."[9] She opens the coffin and brings

   6. Baltzer, *Deutero-Isaiah*, 186.
   7. Ibid.
   8. Caledecott, *Myths*, 46.
   9. Ibid., 47.

Osiris back to life long enough for him to impregnate her with their son Horus. Set finds the coffin with the uncorrupted body of Osiris in it and chops the body into fourteen pieces, scattering them all over Egypt. After giving birth to Horus, Isis gathers the pieces and buries them.

Bulfinch narrates a similar myth. Instead of Set, Isis's and Osiris's brother is named Typhon, who is "filled with envy and malice" and decides "to usurp [the] throne"[10] of Osiris and Isis. After assembling a seventy-two member conspiracy, Typhon presents a chest "which had been made to fit exactly the size of Osiris, and declare[s] that he would give that chest of precious wood to whosoever could get into it."[11] No one fits in the chest except, of course, Osiris, who, as soon as he is in it, is flung into the Nile. The chest floats to Byblos, where it gets caught in a bush. Bulfinch does not mention the tamarisk tree; he states that "the divine power that dwelt in the body of Osiris imparted such strength to the shrub that it grew into a mighty tree, enclosing in its trunk the coffin of the god."[12] The king of Phoenicia has the tree cut and used as a column in his palace. Isis finds the column and with thunder and lightning strikes the column, causing it to split open and give her the coffin, which she conceals "in the depth of a forest, but Typhon discover[s] it . . . ."[13] He cuts the body into pieces, as in the other version of the story, and scatters them. Ultimately Osiris becomes ruler of the underworld.

The tamarisk tree, which grows miraculously to further entomb Osiris's coffin, makes him a god of renewal, regeneration, and resurrection. Through his double death, growing things regenerate. Furthermore, the tamarisk tree-become-column is a phallus, a sign of male power which only his female sister-wife can receive. The result of his resurrection is even more life, namely, that of Horus, his son. Thus, the tamarisk tree represents death in terms of serving as a second coffin, but it also represents life in terms of his astonishing growth around the coffin, Osiris's resurrection from it, and the impregnation of Isis with their son, Horus.

Another Egyptian god associated with the tamarisk is Wepwawet, a jackal-like funerary deity whose name means *opener of the ways*. He seems to have originally been a war deity, but ended up as a protector of the deceased as he led them through the underworld. He becomes associated with the tamarisk tree in his role as guide through the underworld because of its association with Osiris, namely, as protector of his body. Furthermore, soot

10. Bulfinch, *Mythology*, 293.
11. Ibid., 294.
12. Ibid.
13. Ibid.

from the tamarisk was often used to write the amulet inscription placed around the neck of the deceased on the day of burial.

Another association of the tamarisk with death is found in the Shahnameh (Epic of Kings). The legendary Iranian hero, Esfandiyar (Sepandiar) was the son and crown prince of the Kayanian King Goshtasp. Esfandiyar is best known from the tragic story of a battle with Rostam in this Persian epic. Rostam is the faithful military general, king-maker, and champion of champions. Zartosht (Zarathustra) gave Esfandiyar a chain and armor from heaven. The chain gave him the power to bind anyone, and the armor made him invincible. Esfandiyar's father, Goshtasp, sends him to capture and bring to him the aging Rostam in chains for his arrogance and disrespect toward the king. Esfandiyar reminds his father of Rostam's fame, great age, and service to the dynasty, and then he sets out towards Rostam's house. Rostam refuses to go with Esfandiyar, and they meet in combat. In this first battle, Esfandiyar is unaffected by Rostam's blows, while Esfandiyar wounds Rostam with his diamond arrowheads. After asking for time to dress his wounds, Rostam withdraws.

While mending, he consults Simurgh, a giant, winged monster in the shape of a bird with the head of a dog and the claws of a lion. Simurgh is so old that it has seen the world destroyed three times; thus, it has learned so much that it is thought to posses the knowledge of all ages. Simurgh tells Rostam that the only weapon that can affect Esfandiyar is a shot to the eyes from a special double-headed arrow made from the branch of a tamarisk tree. Simurgh reminds Rostam of Zartosht's curse on anyone killing Esfandiyar—suffering a cursed life and condemned to hell—and asks him to reconsider surrendering to Esfandiyar. Of course, Rostam refuses to accept either the shame of surrendering or being chained. Simurgh carries Rostam to the tamarisk tree, where he fashions the double headed arrow with one of Simurgh's feathers and a twig of the tamarisk tree. The next day the battle continues, and Rostam blinds and kills Esfandiyar with a tamarisk tree arrow shot through his eye.

Thus, no matter the origin of a story containing a tamarisk tree, it seems to be usually associated with death and the underworld. Turning two gardens into wasteland with tamarisks is a type of death of the land. Serving as an enclosure for Osiris's coffin makes the tamarisk a cause of Osiris's second death, but also protects him and, ultimately, gives him life. The same tree is a favorite of Wepwawet, who serves as the underworld explorer. And an arrow made from a branch of the tamarisk is the only weapon that can kill a Persian prince. While the tamarisk serves as a landmark in the Bible, the sacred tree functions more as a tombstone for death.

Journal/Meditation: What tree do you associate with death? How did you make that connection? With what else is that tree associated?

Prayer: LORD, everlasting God, when your patriarch Abraham first called upon your name, he planted a tamarisk tree to mark his experience of your presence. After the death of King Saul and his sons, their bones were buried under a tamarisk tree to guide their entrance to the underworld. Send your Holy Spirit to make me more aware of your presence, and, once my work on earth is finished, send your Son, Jesus Christ, to guide me to heaven, where he lives with you and the Holy Spirit, one God, forever and ever. Amen.

Terebinth

Text: "The LORD appeared to Abraham by the terebinth of Mamre, as he sat in the entrance of his tent, while the day was growing hot. Looking up, he saw three men standing nearby. When he saw them, he ran from the entrance of the tent to greet them; and bowing to the ground, he said: 'Sir, if I may ask you this favor, please do not go on past your servant. Let some water be brought, that you may bathe your feet, and then rest yourselves under the tree." (Gen 18:1–4, NAB)

Reflection: Abraham, as will be seen, is associated with two terebinths: the one at Mamre, as indicated in the text above, and the one at Moreh. A terebinth, according to Murphey, is "a large spreading tree . . . with reddish-green leaves and red berries in clusters."[1] Such simplicity might be enough if it weren't for the similarity of the tree's biblical name in Hebrew (*elah*) with the word oak (*elon*); thus in many English translations the word *oak* appears. "As the names suggest, both trees were deified by the ancients (*el*, "god"). And like the oak, terebinth stands were frequently honored as places of worship and as burial sites for esteemed dead."[2] Since the terebinth tree appears only in the HB (OT) books, some translators render the Hebrew word as terebinth and some use oak. For example, the *New American Bible* (NAB) uses terebinth eighteen times; the *New American Bible Revised Edition* (NABRE) uses terebinth fewer times and oak oftener; the *New Revised Standard Version* of the Bible (NRSV), employed throughout this book (except where noted), uses terebinth only three times, but when using oak, often contains a footnote stating that terebinth could be used. This leads to the conclusion, according

---

1. Murphey, *Dictionary of Biblical Literacy*, 39.
2. Meyer, *In the Shade*, 6.

to Masterman, that it is "not improbable that there was no clear distinction between oak and terebinth in the minds of the Old Testament writers; yet the two are very different trees to any but the most superficial observation."[3]

There is a tree named terebinth; it is deciduous and can grow a gray trunk up to thirty-two feet tall. It produces reddish-purple to green flowers in the spring which turn into small, globular fruit the size of a pea with a single seed; the fruit turns red to black when ripe. The oblong or egg-shaped leaves are bright green and leathery to the touch. All parts of the tree have a strong, bitter resinous smell which helps explain why it is a prime source for turpentine. However, its resin was also used as a wine preservative.

As can be deduced from the text above, Abraham was camped near the terebinth at Mamre. Earlier in the Book of Genesis the reader is informed that after Lot and Abram separate, Abram moves "his tents and [goes] on to settle near the terebinth of Mamre.... There he built an altar to the LORD" (Gen 13:18, NAB). After Lot was captured in a battle, a fugitive brought the news to Abram, "who was camping at the terebinth of Mamre" (Gen 14:13, NAB). The terebinth at Mamre is a sacred tree because Abram built an altar to the LORD there, and the LORD also appeared to Abraham under the tree. Bar states, "In the ancient world the phenomenon of trees associated with sacred places was well known."[4]

Abram is also associated with the terebinth at Moreh at first passing through the land "as far as the sacred place at Shechem by the terebinth of Moreh" (Gen 12:6; Deut 11:30, NAB). The Book of Judges notes the existence of this "terebinth at the memorial pillar in Shechem" (Judg 9:6, NAB). And it must be the same place where Joshua sets "a large stone ... under the terebinth that was in the sanctuary of the LORD" at Shechem (Josh 24:26, NABRE). Because the Hebrew word *Moreh* means *teacher*, "this name might be a reference [to] 'oracle giver.' Accordingly, the tree served as a place where oracles could be obtained."[5] However, "the terebinth of Moreh was [more of] a landmark and not a significant religious tree."[6]

In the Book of Judges, Gideon entertains "the angel of the LORD" who "came and sat under the terebinth in Ophrah" (Judg 6:11, NAB). After the angel instructs Gideon as to what he is called to do to defeat his enemies, Gideon prepares an offering of a "kid and an ephah of flour in the form of unleavened cakes. Putting the meat in a basket and the broth in a pot, he brought them out to [the angel] under the terebinth and presented them" (Judg 6:19, NAB). A fire, signifying the divine presence, comes up from the rock—a type

---

3. Masterman, "Terebinth."
4. Bar, "Trees," 383.
5. Ibid.
6. Ibid., 384.

of altar—and consumes the offering. Once Gideon recognizes that he has seen God, he builds a real altar under the terebinth, just like Abram did before him.

Other terebinths that serve as landmarks include one at Tabor (1 Sam 10:3, NAB) and one at Zaanannim (Judg 4:11, NAB). However, another very famous place is called "The Vale of the Terebinth" (1 Sam 17:2, 19; 21:10. NAB), otherwise called the "Valley of Elah" (1 Sam 17:2, 19; 21:9, NRSV). This is where large and shady terebinth trees grew and where the Israelites camped when David fought Goliath. There are other terebinths not associated with a specific place, such as the one under which a man of God sets (1 Kgs 13:14, NABRE) outside Bethel and "the branches of a large terebinth" into which Absalom, King David's son, gets his hair caught (2 Sam 18:9, NAB) and remains hanging until he is killed (2 Sam 18:10, NAB).

There is no doubt that the Israelites worshiped idols under terebinths. Isaiah records the LORD telling his people, "You shall be ashamed of the terebinths which you desired, and blush on account of the gardens which you chose" (Isa 1:29, NABRE). In these sacred groves the Israelites practiced idolatry, offering sacrifice and burning incense "beneath . . . [a] terebinth, because of [its] pleasant shade" (Hos 4:13, NABRE and NRSV). Isaiah also uses "a terebinth . . . whose trunk remains when its leaves have fallen" as an image of desolation (Isa 6:13, NABRE and NRSV). This prophetic use of terebinth is contrasted to Sirach's use in the OT (A) in which lady wisdom erotically states, "Like a terebinth I spread out my branches, and my branches are glorious and graceful" (Sir 24:16, NAB, NABRE, and NRSV).

Thus, the terebinth is mostly associated with Abraham; he often camps beneath one or declares the space beneath one a sacred place by erecting an altar there, as does Gideon. Terebinths serve as landmarks, just as road and street signs do today. The earliest patriarchs considered a large tree a sacred place, under which they could worship the LORD, their God. Some of their descendants also considered them sacred places to worship other gods. In either case, the terebinth is a sacred tree.

Journal/Meditation: Under what tree have you witnessed the appearance of God? Keep in mind that Abraham experienced God's appearance in the form of three men as the day was growing hot and offering them hospitality.

Prayer: LORD, God of Abraham, you revealed yourself to your servant Abraham while he sat under a terebinth. You revealed yourself to your servant Gideon while he was threshing wheat under a terebinth. Make yourself known to me this day in all I do and say. Hear my prayer in the name of your incarnate presence, Jesus Christ, who lives and reigns with you and the Holy Spirit, one God, forever and ever. Amen.

Vine (Vineyard)

Text: "The word of the LORD came to me [, Ezekiel]: O mortal, how does the wood of the vine surpass all other wood—the vine branch that is among the trees of the forest? Is wood taken from it to make anything? It is put in the fire for fuel. . . . [I]s it useful for anything? Therefore thus says the Lord GOD: Like the wood of the vine among the trees of the forest, which I have given to the fire for fuel, so I will give up the inhabitants of Jerusalem." (Ezek 15:1–2, 3a, 4, 6)

Reflection: In the above allegory of the useless vine, the HB (OT) prophet Ezekiel compares the inhabitants of Jerusalem to the wood of a vine, which is considered useless among the trees of the forest except for burning. Everyone knows that the answer to the rhetorical question about how does the wood of the vine surpass the wood of the trees of the forest is that it does not. The wood of the vine cannot be used to make anything, because the vine's branches are usually twisted and weak. Thus, like useless vine branches, according to Ezekiel, Jerusalem will be burned.

Although the woody vine is not a tree, its gnarled and twisted trunk grows as large as some small trees over the years. Furthermore, the vine is the most referenced plant in biblical literature. A vineyard, as the word suggests, is a yard planted with vines. More specifically, it is a plantation of grape-bearing vines grown mainly for winemaking. It is often characterized by its *terroir*, a French term loosely translated as *a sense of place* and referring to the geographical and geological characteristics of grapevine plantations which may be imparted in the wine. The French term is more accurate than one at first thinks, especially when it comes to the sense of place in the many stories featuring vineyards, which are usually located on gentle slopes of hillsides for access to direct sunshine. An old vine looks like a small, woody tree with branches that get their support from tendrils that climb, twine, or creep along a surface and attach themselves to the surface. The older the vineyard, the woodier the vines and the better the taste of the wine made from the grapes. Tresidder notes, "Vine and grapes are among the oldest symbols of fecundity and regeneration."[1]

Song of the Vineyard

The HB (OT) prophet Isaiah presents the epitome of vineyard stories. Bibles usually label Isaiah's tale as the song of the vineyard. In many ways it mirrors Ezekiel's allegory of the useless vine presented above, but it also reveals what went into creating, maintaining, and harvesting a vineyard. "Let me sing for my beloved my love-song concerning his vineyard," begins Isaiah's story.

> My beloved had a vineyard on a very fertile hill. He dug it and cleared it of stones, and planted it with choice vines; he built a watchtower in the midst of it, and hewed out a wine vat in it; he expected it to yield grapes, but it yielded wild grapes. And now, inhabitants of Jerusalem and people of Judah, judge between me and my vineyard. What more was there to do for my vineyard that I have not done in it? When I expected it to yield grapes, why did it yield wild grapes? And I will tell you what I will do to my vineyard. I will remove its hedge, and it shall be devoured; I will break down its wall, and it shall be trampled down. I will make it a waste; it shall not be pruned or hoed, and it shall be overgrown with briers and thorns; I will also command the clouds that they rain no rain upon it. For the vineyard of the LORD of hosts is the house of Israel, and the people of Judah are his pleasant planting; he expected justice, and he saw bloodshed; righteousness, but heard a cry! (Isaiah 5:1–7)

Literal Level

Roberts states that "the poem operates on several different levels and participates in several different genres. On the literal level, it is a song about a man's vineyard . . . ."[2] As the HB (OT) Book of Genesis states, "Noah, a man of the soil, was the first to plant a vineyard. He drank some of the wine

---

1. Tresidder, *Dictionary of Symbols*, 504.
2. Roberts, *First Isaiah*, 71.

and became drunk . . ." (Gen 9:20–21). *Mormon's* Book of Mosiah makes mention of a king Noah who "planted vineyards round about in the land; and he built winepresses, and made wine in abundance; and therefore he became a wine-bibber, and also his people" (Mos 11:15). Mormon's *D&C* makes perfectly clear that "it is not good, neither meet in the sight of [the] Father" for anyone to "drink wine or strong drink" (*D&C* 86:1). The *Book of Doctrine and Covenants* does not negate the establishment of vineyards; in fact, "the fruit of the vine" is "good for the food of man" (*D&C* 86:3). Only the making of wine from the grapes is frowned upon. In the Gospel of Thomas, Jesus states that he has stood in the midst of the people of the world and "found them all drunk" (Thos 28).[3] Here Jesus is referring to the inability of people to see. "Yet now they are drunk; when they shake off their wine, then they will repent," he states (Thos 28).[4] Bloom notes that in such gnostic and other texts, "the person who is ignorant and without knowledge is frequently said to be drunk."[5]

Love Song

Roberts also states that vineyard "is a standard metaphor for one's 'beloved' in Israelite love poetry" and "the song was probably heard metaphorically as a love song . . . of unrequited love."[6] Nowhere is this more evident than in the HB (OT) erotic love poem known as the Song of Songs or Song of Solomon. Ryken states, "Fertile vines produced luscious grapes, pleasing to the taste and, when fermented, intoxicating. It is not surprising, considering the general use of agricultural images for sexuality, that the vine is frequently employed in [this] most sensual of all biblical poems . . . ."[7] Vineyard serves as a metaphor for a woman's body. The unnamed woman states that her brothers made her keeper of the vineyards, but her own vineyard she has not kept (Song 1:6), that is, she has not remained a virgin or chaste. She compares her beloved to precious aromatic scents which she puts between her breasts, that is, a cluster of henna blossoms in the vineyards (Song 1:14). She declares her beloved to be fruit sweet to her taste (Song 2:3). He acknowledges that the vines are in blossom and give forth fragrance (Song 2:13), and he concludes her words declaring: "Catch us the foxes, the little foxes, that ruin the vineyards—for our vineyards are in blos-

3. Ehrman, *Apocryphal Gospels*, 319.
4. Ibid.
5. Bloom, *Gospel of Thomas*, 82.
6. Roberts, *First Isaiah*, 71.
7. Ryken, *Dictionary*, 916.

som" (Song 2:15). The little foxes in the song—a reference to the dangers of their lovemaking—also echo the story of Samson in the HB (OT) Book of Judges. Samson catches three hundred foxes, ties their tails together in pairs, places a lit torch between each pair of tails, and sets them loose to burn the vineyards of the Philistines (Judg 15:4-5), known as the vineyards of Timnah (Judg 14:5).

The vineyard serves as a setting for passionate lovemaking. The woman goes to the orchard to see whether the vines have budded (Song 6:11) and to meet the man. He, too, invites her to "go out early to the vineyards, and see whether the vines have budded, whether the grape blossoms have opened" for there he will give her his love (Song 7:12). He hopes that her breasts be like clusters of the vine (Song 7:7, 8b) and that her kisses be like the best wine that goes down smoothly, gliding over lips and teeth (Song 7:9). At the end of the poem the man declares that his vineyard, the woman, is better than Solomon's vineyard, whose fruit was worth much silver. His vineyard, his lover, belongs to him (Song 8:12). Similarly, Psalm 128, states that the wife of a man who fears the LORD will be like a fruitful vine within his house (Ps 128:3a).

"Israel was a land of vineyards," states Ryken.[8] ". . . [I]t is not surprising that the vine and the vineyard, so characteristic of this country's agricultural fertility, serve as a potent image for the land itself."[9] In his farewell speech, Jacob declares that his son Judah will bind "his foal to the vine and his donkey's colt to the choice vine," even washing "his garments in wine and his robe in the blood of grapes" (Gen 49:11). The inheritance of vineyards (Num 16:14), vineyards that the Israelites did not plant (Deut 6:11), a land of vines (Deut 8:8) is a land from which the Israelites eat the fruit of vineyards that they did not plant (Josh 24:13). In the Book of Numbers, "the angel of the LORD stood in a narrow path between the vineyards, with a wall on either side" (Num 22:24) in order to stop Balaam. The Book of Judges narrates how the people "gathered the grapes from their vineyards, trod them, and celebrated" (Judg 9:27). When the people wanted a king, the priest-prophet-judge Samuel reminded them that he would take the best of their vineyards and give them to his courtiers, and he would take one-tenth of their vineyards and give it to his officers and courtiers (1 Sam 8:14-15; 22:7).

When bargaining with Judah, the Rabshakeh, a representative of the king of Assyria, reminds the people that it is better to make peace, then every one of them will eat from his own vine (2 Kgs 18:31; Isa 36:16); otherwise the Assyrians will take them away to another land like their own, a land of vineyards (2 Kgs 18:32). Referring to the land of Judah, the prophet

---

8. Ibid., 914.
9. Ibid.

Ezekiel tells the princes of Judah in Babylonian captivity that their "mother was like a vine in a vineyard transplanted by the water, fruitful and full of branches from abundant water" (Ezek 19:10).

"The parable [song, allegory] of the vineyard . . . describes Israel as God's vineyard," states Ryken.[10] The prophet Hosea states this unequivocally: "Israel is a luxuriant vine that yields its fruit" (Hos 10:1). "It is God's not only because God loves it, but because he painstakingly prepared the land and planted it. He also carefully protected it. In this way the parable describes God's election of Israel as a nation (Deut 7:7–11) and his providential care of it."[11] The psalmist states this when he addresses God singing, "You brought a vine out of Egypt; you drove out the nations and planted it. You cleared the ground for it; it took deep root and filed the land. The mountains were covered with its shade, the mighty cedars with its branches; it sent out its branches to the sea and its shoots to the River" (Ps 80:8–11). Isaiah, too, echoes this theme when he describes the day of the Lord: "On that day: A pleasant vineyard, sing about it! I, the LORD, am its keeper; every moment I water it. I guard it night and day so that no one can harm it. . . . [L]et it cling to me for protection, let it make peace with me" (Isa 27:2–3, 5). Using the vine to represent the future fertility of Joseph, Jacob declares that Joseph is a fruitful bough by a spring, and his branches run over the wall (Gen 49:22). Likewise, one of Ezekiel's allegories begins with a seed, representing Zedekiah, who was set up as king of Judah by Nebuchadnezzar of Babylon. The seed

> sprouted and became a vine spreading out, but low; its branches turned toward him, its roots remained where it stood. So it became a vine; it brought forth branches, put forth foliage. And see! This vine stretched out its roots toward him; it shot out its branches toward him, so that he might water it. From the bed where it was planted it was transplanted to good soil by abundant waters, so that it might produce branches and bear fruit and become a noble vine. (Ezek 17:6, 7b–8)

Roberts notes that "Isaiah sings his love song about his friend's vineyard on behalf of his friend."[12] He adds, "Isaiah sings his love song for his friend, trying to convince the audience by the extended vineyard metaphor that it was through no fault of his friend that his friend's beloved did not reciprocate his love."[13] He continues:

10. Ibid., 915.
11. Ibid.
12. Roberts, *First Isaiah*, 71.
13. Ibid.

Isaiah's friend chose a fertile spur of hill country as the location for his vineyard. He did the necessary work of preparing the ground by digging it up to rid it of weeds and by removing the large stones that would impede growth. He planted the prepared vineyard with choice vine stock, built a tower within it to protect it from animal and human depredations, and hued out a wine vat in anticipation of the harvest. Then he waited for the well-tended vineyard to produce an abundance of grapes, but all it produced were sour, unripe, diseased berries.[14]

The HB (OT) Book of Proverbs uses a vineyard to illustrate the difference between laziness and industriousness. "I passed by . . . the vineyard of a stupid person; and see, it was overgrown with thorns; the ground was covered with nettles, and its stone wall was broken down," begins the proverb. "Then I saw and considered it; I looked and received instruction. A little sleep, a little slumber, a little folding of the hands to rest, and poverty will come upon you like a robber, and want, like an armed warrior" (Prov 24:30–34). As a further illustration of the lesson he learned, the author praises an industrious wife: "She considers a field and buys it; with the fruit of her hands she plants a vineyard" (Prov 31:16).

Suddenly in the prophet's love song "the friend himself speaks through Isaiah in the first person," states Roberts.[15] "Now, speaking as his friend, he invites [the audience] to judge between him and his 'vineyard.' Such judgment is still within the realm of a love song about unrequited love," states Roberts.[16] Isaiah's friend asks two rhetorical questions about what else could he do and was not his expectation reasonable. The same idea is expressed by God through the prophet Jeremiah: ". . . I planted you [, Israel,] as a choice vine, from the purest stock. How then did you turn degenerate and become a wild vine?" (Jer 2:21) "When I wanted to gather them, says the LORD, there are no grapes on the vine; . . . even the leaves are withered, and what I gave them has passed away from them" (Jer 8:13). As early as the Book of Deuteronomy in Moses' song the patriarch declared that the vine of Israel's enemies comes from the vinestock of Sodom, from the vineyards of Gomorrah. Their grapes are grapes of poison, and their clusters are bitter (Deut 32:32).

From this vineyard Isaiah's friend expected a good harvest. When he does not get it, according to Roberts, "He threatens to remove the hedge and wall around the vineyard so that the animals may graze and trample

---

14. Ibid.
15. Ibid.
16. Ibid., 72.

the unfruitful vineyard. He will no longer cultivate and prune the vineyard but will let it grow up in thorns and thistles like uncultivated wasteland. He will even command the clouds not to rain on it."[17] In the words of Isaiah, "[D]aughter Zion is left like a booth in a vineyard" (Isa 1:8a). Isaiah records other judgments using the vineyard metaphor. The LORD tells the elders and princes of his people that they have devoured the vineyard (Isa 3:14b); that ten acres of vineyard shall yield but one bath (Isa 5:10); that every place where there used to be a thousand vines will become briers and thorns (Isa 7:23); that foreigners shall dress their vines (Isa 61:5); that all the nations will wither like a leaf on a vine (Isa 34:4b) as at the gleaning when the grape harvest is ended (Isa 24:13b).

> ... [T]he vines of Sibmah, whose clusters once made drunk the lords of the nations; their shoots once spread abroad and crossed over the sea. Therefore I weep ... for the vines of Sibmah; for the shout over your fruit harvest ... has ceased. Joy and gladness are taken away from ... the vineyards; no songs are sung, no shouts are raised; no treader treads out wine in the presses; the vintage shout is hushed. (Isa 16:8abd–9ac, 10)

According to Ryken, there is irony here: "The irony is that a place where one normally finds joy has become a place of weeping."[18] Later, in Isaiah the LORD declares, "If [the vineyard] gives me thorns and briers, I will march to battle against it. I will burn it up" (Isa 27:4). A similar sentiment is found in *Mormon's* Second Book of Nephi: "And it shall come to pass in that day, every place shall be where there were a thousand vines at a thousand silverlings, which shall be for briers and thorns" (2 Ne 17:23).

The prophet Jeremiah employs the vineyard destruction metaphor. The LORD tells him, "Go up through [Israel's] vine-rows and destroy ... ; strip away her branches, for they are not the LORD's" (Jer 5:10). God promises to bring a nation to destroy Israel, and it will eat up her vines (Jer 5:17b). Many of her leaders "have destroyed [God's] vineyard, they have trampled down [his] portion, they have made [his] pleasant portion a desolate wilderness" (Jer 12:10). Echoing Isaiah's words about the vines of Sibmah, Jeremiah weeps. "Your branches crossed over the sea ... ; your summer fruits and your vintage the destroyer has fallen. Gladness and joy have been taken away from the fruitful land of Moab; I have stopped the wine from the wine presses; no one treads them with shouts of joy; the shouting is not the shout of joy" (Jer 48:32–33).

---

17. Ibid.
18. Ryken, *Dictionary*, 916.

Ezekiel approaches the destruction-of-the-vineyard metaphor using a series of questions, which he portrays the LORD asking about his vine: "Will it prosper? Will he not pull up its roots, cause its fruit to rot and wither, its fresh sprouting leaves to fade? No strong arm of a mighty army will be needed to pull it from its roots. When it is transplanted, will it thrive? When the east wind strikes it, will it not utterly wither, wither on the bed where it grew?" (Ezek 17:9–10) The psalmist echoes Ezekiel, when he sings to God asking, "Why then have you broken down [the vineyard's] walls, so that all pass along the way pluck its fruit? The boar from the forest ravages it, and all that move in the field feed on it" (Ps 80:12–13).

The prophet Hosea portrays God bluntly declaring, "I will lay waste [Israel's] vines . . . . I will make them a forest, and the wild animals shall devour them" (Hos 2:12ac). Joel describes how the wine-drinkers should wail and weep over the sweet wine because the plague of locusts has lain waste the vines (Joel 1:7), the wine dries up (Joel 1:10b), and the vinedressers should wail because the vine withers (Joel 1:12). Amos pronounces judgment on Samaria portraying the LORD declaring that he laid waste her vineyards (Amos 4:9); in all the vineyards there will be wailing (Amos 5:17). The prophet Micah pronounces judgment on Samaria portraying the Lord GOD saying, ". . . I will make Samaria a heap in the open country, a place for planting vineyards; I will pour down her stones into the valley, and uncover her foundations" (Mic 1:6). And the prophet Zephaniah pronounces judgment on Jerusalem, portraying the LORD saying, ". . . [T[hough they plant vineyards, they shall not drink wine from them" (Zeph 1:13c).

Before the prophets employed the destruction of a vineyard as a metaphor to describe God's judgment on the land and his chosen people, it was used by the authors of other HB (OT) books. For example, Moses makes clear that if the people disobey the LORD's commandments, they can plant a vineyard, but not enjoy its fruit (Deut 28:30); they can "plant vineyards and dress them, but [they] shall neither drink the wine nor gather the grapes, for the worm shall eat them" (Deut 28:39). In the Book of Numbers, the people complain to Moses about not having given them an inheritance of vineyards (Num 16:14) and the desert being no place for vines (Num 20:5). Recounting the plagues visited upon Egypt, the psalmist employs the destruction-of-the-vineyard metaphor as a judgment on Egypt: The Holy one of Israel destroyed their vines with hail (Ps 78:47; 105:33) but there is no such specific reference to this in the Book of Exodus.

In the CB (NT) Book of Revelation, God's judgment of the world is depicted as a harvest of a vineyard. The pseudonymous author, John of Patmos, describes the judgment this way: An angel called with a loud voice to [another angel] who had [a] sharp sickle, "Use your sharp sickle and gather the clusters of the vine of the earth, for its grapes are ripe." So the angel swung his sickle over the earth and gathered the vintage of the earth, and he threw it into the great wine press of the wrath of God. And the wine press was trodden outside the city, and blood flowed from the wine press, as high as a horse's bridle, for a distance of about two hundred miles. (Rev 14:18–20)

House of Israel and Judah

Keeping in mind that Isaiah's song of the vineyard is about a man's vineyard and can be considered a love song, Roberts states that "the third and deepest level of meaning" is that "Yahweh is the friend, and the vineyard is the house of Israel and the men of Judah.... Thus, the love song is not just an ordinary love song, ... but a theological love song and judicial parable rolled into one.... Yahweh looked for justice only to see bloodshed, for righteousness only to hear the cry of the oppressed."[19] With those three levels firmly in place, some further background is needed to get an even better grasp on the vineyard metaphor.

First, the vineyard has to be planted. Isaiah tells King Hezekiah, who was faced with the power of King Sennacherib of Assyria, that the sign that he had nothing to fear was a three-year program that included eating what grows of itself the first year, eating what springs from that the second year, and then in the third year sowing, reaping, planting vineyards, and eating their fruit (1 Kgs 19:29). In other words, King Hezekiah of Judah has a future. In a song of thanksgiving for deliverance from distress, the psalmist states that the LORD permits the hungry to plant vineyards and get a fruitful yield (Ps 107:37). Even though there are people who do not plant vineyards or even own one (Jer 35:7, 9), those who have are dispensed from warfare (Deut 20:6; 1 Macc 3:56). As Paul asks the Corinthians, "Who plants a vineyard and does not eat any of its fruit?" (1 Cor 9:7b)

Second, a vineyard gets to enjoy a rest every seventh year according to the HB (OT) Book of Exodus. For six years, Moses tells the Israelites, they may plant and gather the vineyard's yield, but on the seventh year, it is to lie fallow so that the poor of their people may eat (Exod 23:11). The Book of Leviticus explains: "... [S]ix years you shall prune your vineyard, and gather in [its] yield; but in the seventh year there shall be a Sabbath of complete rest for the land, a Sabbath for the LORD: you shall not ... prune your vineyard.

---

19. Roberts, *First Isaiah*, 72.

You shall not . . . gather the grapes of your unpruned vine" (Lev 25:3–5). However, Leviticus further specifies that every fiftieth year is a jubilee, and the people may not harvest the unpruned vines (Lev 25:11).

Third, a vineyard feeds the poor. God tells Moses to tell the Israelites that they "shall not strip [the] vineyard bare, or gather the fallen grapes of [the] vineyard; [they] shall leave them for the poor and the alien" (Lev 19:10). The Book of Deuteronomy reiterates that statement, declaring that when one gathers "the grapes of [the] vineyard," he or she does "not glean what is left; it shall be for the alien, the orphan, and the widow" (Deut 24:21). Furthermore, if a person goes into a neighbor's vineyard, he or she may eat his or her fill of grapes, as many as he or she wishes, but he or she shall not put any in a container (Deut 23:24). Before the destruction of Jerusalem, the prophet Jeremiah records the LORD of hosts reversing his previous commandments to Moses and declaring, "Glean thoroughly as a vine the remnant of Israel; like a grape-gatherer, pass your hand again over its branches" (Jer 6:9). Once Nebuchadnezzar destroys Jerusalem, Jeremiah records that he left "in the land of Judah some of the poor people who owned nothing, and gave them vineyards . . . at the same time" (Jer 39:10). The Second Book of Nephi in *The Book of Mormon* also associates the poor with the vineyard metaphor, stating, "The Lord will enter into judgment with the ancients of his people and the princes thereof; for [they] have eaten up the vineyard and the spoil of the poor in [their] houses" (2 Ne 13:14).

Fourth, unless the vineyard has been contaminated, that is, made unclean, by sowing a different kind of seed in it (Deut 22:9), violating the law of mixtures and causing impurity, it represents prosperity and wealth. It is so valuable that if someone causes a vineyard to be grazed over, restitution shall be made from the best in the owner's vineyard (Exod 22:5). Moses tells the king of Edom and the king of the Amorites that when the Israelites pass through their land, they will not pass through a vineyard, that is, they will not deviate from the road or destroy the vines (Num 20:17; 21:22). The First Book of Kings states that during King Solomon's reign, Judah enjoyed immense prosperity; the people lived in safety under their vines (1 Kgs 4:25). Some of Solomon's wealth was inherited from his father, King David, who had appointed officials over the vineyards and over the produce of the vineyards for the wine cellars (1 Chr 27:27). After the prophet Elisha tells Naaman the Syrian how to cure his leprosy, Naaman attempts to give gifts to Elisha, who refuses everything. However, Elisha's servant, Gehazi, tricks Naaman into giving him wealth, including a vineyard, for which Elisha punishes Gehazi with leprosy (2 Kgs 5:25–27). When faced with a famine after beginning the rebuilding of the temple in Jerusalem, the Jews complain to Nehemiah because they have to pledge their vineyards as collateral in order to get grain (Neh 5:1–3); this means that the vineyards are valuable, but that they may end up belonging to another (Neh 5:5). Nehemiah urges those who have taken vineyards to return them (Neh 5:11). In a speech in the Book of Nehemiah, Ezra the priest reminds the people that their vineyards are a gift from God (Neh 9:25). People sitting under their own vines represents prosperity (1 Macc 14:12).

Fifth, a vineyard represents pleasure beyond merely sitting under the vines. The author of the HB (OT) Book of Ecclesiastes explains how he decided to make a test of pleasure. So, he decides to cheer his body with wine and to plant vineyards for himself (Eccl 2:4). The Rabshakeh, the representative of the king of Assyria, equates making peace with eating from one's own vine and drinking one's own wine, but if the inhabitants of Jerusalem do not make peace, they will be taken to another land of wine and vineyards (Isa 36:16–17). The pleasure of the vine is denied to some of those whom God chooses. For example, the angel of God tells Manoah that his wife "may not eat of anything that comes from the vine" (Judg 13:14a). Lady wisdom's description of herself epitomizes the pleasure of the vineyard. She says, "Like the vine I bud forth delights, and my blossoms become glorious and abundant fruit" (Sir 24:17). And of course, the vineyard is a great place to lie in wait in order to capture a wife (Judg 21:20–21), who would have given her husband great pleasure!

In the HB (OT) Book of Job, Job describes evil people as those who "glean in the vineyard of the wicked" (Job 24:6). Later, in the same speech he states that "no treader turns toward their vineyards" (Job 24:18). Zophar, one of Job's friends, adds that the wicked "build their houses . . . like booths made by sentinels of the vineyard" (Job 27:18), and Eliphaz, another of Job's friends, declares that they "shake off their unripe grape, like the vine, and cast off their blossoms . . ." (Job 15:33). Using the vineyard metaphor, "these passages [among others] illustrate the use of the vineyard image in contexts of judgment."[20] In other words, such verses are the opposite of the pleasure the vineyard was supposed to give.

Other Vineyard Stories

The vine plays a role in one of the stories associated with Jacob's son, Joseph, who was sold into Egyptian slavery but rose through the ranks ultimately to be second in command to Pharaoh. While Joseph is serving as second in command to the chief jailer, he has the opportunity both to hear and interpret the chief cupbearer's dream.

20. Ryken, *Dictionary*, 916.

> So the chief cupbearer told his dream to Joseph, and said to him, "In my dream there was a vine before me, and on the vine there were three branches. As soon as it budded, its blossoms came out and the clusters ripened into grapes. Pharaoh's cup was in my hand; and I took the grapes and pressed them into Pharaoh's cup, and placed the cup in Pharaoh's hand." Then Joseph said to him, "This is its interpretation: the three branches are three days; within three days Pharaoh will lift up your head and restore you to your office; and you shall place Pharaoh's cup in his hand, just as you used to do when you were his cupbearer." (Gen 40:9–13)

Three days later on Pharaoh's birthday he restored the cup bearer to his previous position (Gen 40:20–23). In this story, the vine represents restoration or renewal. The number three indicates that God is present in the cupbearer's dream and directing the future of Joseph.

The vine also plays a role in Jotham's fable about the trees as already seen in the chapter on the bramble. When the trees decide to anoint a king to rule of them, "they said to the vine, 'You come and reign over us.' But the vine said to them, 'Shall I stop producing my wine that cheers gods and mortals, and go to sway over the trees?'" (Judg 9:12–13). In this fable, the vine represents the pleasure it gives through wine.

The First Book of Kings contains the story about "Naboth the Jezreelite" who "had a vineyard in Jezreel, beside the palace of King Ahab of Samaria" (1 Kgs 21:1). The story continues in this way:

> ... Ahab said to Naboth, "Give me your vineyard, so that I may have it for a vegetable garden, because it is near my house; I will give you a better vineyard for it; if it seems good to you, I will give you its value in money." But Naboth said to Ahab, "The LORD forbid that I should give you my ancestral inheritance." Ahab went home resentful and sullen because of what Naboth the Jezreelite had said to him; for he had said, "I will not give you my ancestral inheritance." He lay down on his bed, turned away his face, and would not eat. His wife Jezebel came to him and said, "Why are you so depressed that you will not eat?" (1 Kgs 21:2–4)

Ahab explained to her what had happened to him in his dealing with Naboth. "His wife Jezebel said to him, 'Do you now govern Israel? Get up, eat some food, and be cheerful; I will give you the vineyard of Naboth the Jezreelite'" (2 Kgs 21:7).

> So she wrote letters in Ahab's name and sealed them with his seal; she sent the letters to the elders and the nobles who lived with

Naboth in his city. She wrote in the letters, "Proclaim a fast and seat Naboth at the head of the assembly; seat two scoundrels opposite him, and have them bring a charge against him, saying, 'You have cursed God and the king.' Then take him out, and stone him to death." The men of his city, the elders and the nobles who lived n his city, did as Jezebel had sent word to them. Then they sent to Jezebel, saying, "Naboth has been stoned; he is dead."

As soon as Jezebel heard that Naboth had been stoned and was dead, Jezebel said to Ahab, "Go, take possession of the vineyard of Naboth the Jezreelite, which he refused to give you for money; for Naboth is not alive, but dead." As soon as Ahab heard that Naboth was dead, Ahab set out to go down to the vineyard of Naboth the Jezreelite, to take possession of it. (1 Kgs 21:8–11a, 14–16)

This story ends with the prophet Elijah meeting Ahab at the vineyard and accusing him of murder. Elijah tells him that his blood will be licked by dogs in the same place where Naboth was stoned. In this long account, the vineyard represents Naboth's ancestral inheritance, that is, a small portion of the land given by God to Abraham, Isaac, and Jacob and all their descendants.

There is also a very long story about a vineyard in the Book of Jacob (Jac 5:1–6:13) in *The Book of Mormon*. The analogy begins by likening the house of Israel to an olive tree, which a man planted in his vineyard. Since the vineyard is merely the setting for the story and the olive tree is the object of the analogy, it is fully treated in the chapter of this book on the olive tree. Similarly in the CB (NT), Jesus tells a parable about a man who had a fig tree planted in his vineyard (Luke 13:6). The focus of the parable is the fig tree and not the vineyard. So, the parable is covered in the chapter on the fig tree in this book. In both cases, however, it is important to note that either the authors did not know about the HB (OT) prohibition of mixtures (Lev 19:19; Deut 22:9), or the prohibition was ignored!

In the Bible, the vineyard metaphor is used by the major prophets as an image of restoration. Through Isaiah, God declares that on the day of the LORD "Jacob shall take root, Israel shall blossom and put forth shoots, and fill the whole world with fruit" (Isa 27:6). The destruction that ended the song of the vineyard in Isaiah 5:1–7 will be reversed. Likewise, when God creates new heavens and a new earth, people shall plant vineyards and eat their fruit (Isa 65:21). The prophet Jeremiah, too, portrays God declaring that his people "shall plant vineyards on the mountains of Samaria; the planters shall plant, and shall enjoy the fruit" (Jer 31:5); vineyards shall again be bought in the land (Jer 32:15). Likewise, the prophet Ezekiel declares that the Lord GOD's people shall plant vineyards (Ezek 28:26).

The minor prophets also use the vineyard to represent restoration. Once the LORD has lured his people back to the desert, he will give Israel her vineyards (Hos 2:15) and "they shall blossom like the vine, their fragrance shall be like the wine of Lebanon" (Hos 14:7b). The vine gives its full yield, states Joel (Joel 2:22). Amos is very clear: "I will restore the fortunes of my people Israel," declares the LORD, "and they shall plant vineyards and drink their wine" (Amos 9:14). In days to come states the prophet Micah, the people "shall all sit under their own vines" (Mic 4:4); they will blessed with the yield of the vine (Hag 2:19). Zechariah writes, "On that day, says the LORD of hosts, you shall invite each other to come under your vine" (Zech 3:10) for "the vine shall yield its fruit" (Zech 8:12). In the prophet Malachi, God states that the vine in the field shall not be barren (Mal 3:11). However, it is the prophet Habakkuk who summarizes the vineyard metaphor, writing, "Though . . . no fruit is on the vines, . . . yet I will rejoice in the LORD; I will exult in the God of my salvation" (Hab 3:17a, 18). This sentiment is echoed in the Third Book of Nephi in *The Book of Mormon*. The Lord of hosts states, "I will rebuke the devourer for your sakes, and he shall not destroy the fruits of your ground; neither shall your vine cast her fruit before the time in the fields, says the Lord of Hosts" (3 Ne 24:11).

In *The Quran*, a vineyard is part of the garden image of paradise. In the garden, among many other items, are vines (*Quran* 2:266). As the book repeatedly states, vineyards are among the signs of the Lord for those who reflect (*Quran* 13:4). Grapes serve as a sign to believe (*Quran* 17:91; 23:19). "There is a sign in the dead earth," states *The Quran*, from which God has "laid out gardens of . . . grapes upon it," (*Quran* 36:33a, 34). These ideas are echoed in the HB (OT) Song of Songs. Using the image of a garden, the man describes his beloved as "a garden locked" (Song 4:12).

Since this expose of vine and vineyard began with Isaiah's song of the vineyard, before moving on to the use of vine and vineyard in the CB (NT), it is good to look at the song of the vineyard in *The Book of Mormon*. It appears in the Second Book of Nephi:

> And then will I sing to my well-beloved a song of my beloved, touching his vineyard. My well-beloved has a vineyard in a very fruitful hill. And he fenced it, and gathered out the stones thereof, and planted it with the choicest vine, and built a tower in the midst of it, and also made a wine-press therein; and he looked that it should bring forth grapes, and it brought forth wild grapes. And now, O inhabitants of Jerusalem, and men of Judah, judge, I pray you, betwixt me and my vineyard. What could have been done more to my vineyard that I have not done in it? Wherefore, when I looked that it should bring forth grapes, it brought forth

wild grapes.... I will tell you what I will do to my vineyard—I will take away the hedge thereof, and it shall be eaten up; and I will break down the wall thereof, and it shall be trodden down; And I will lay it waste; it shall not be pruned nor [dug]; but there shall come up briers and thorns; I will also command the clouds that they rain no rain upon it. For the vineyard of the Lord of Hosts is the house of Israel, and the man of Judah his pleasant plant; and he looked for judgment, and behold, oppression; for righteousness, but behold, a cry. (2 Ne 15:1–7)

Vineyard Parable of the Tenants

In the CB (NT) there are only three major blocks of material that employ the vine and vineyard allegory. The first block builds on Isaiah's and Second Nephi's song of the vineyard. In the synoptic gospels of Mark, Matthew, and Luke, the material is known as the vineyard parable or the parable of the tenants. However, it is really an analogy. Originally written by the author of Mark's Gospel, it was copied and changed by both the author of Matthew's Gospel and the author of Luke's Gospel. The parable is also found in the Gospel of Thomas, which some scholars think represents another written source for the parable and other scholars think is dependent upon the synoptic gospels, especially Luke.

Beginning

In Mark's Gospel, the allegory begins: "Then [Jesus] began to speak to 'the chief priests, the scribes, and the elders' in parables. 'A man planted a vineyard, put a fence around it, dug a pit for the wine press, and built a watchtower; then he leased it to tenants and went to another country'" (Mark 11:27; 12:1). In Matthew's Gospel, this parable follows the analogy (parable) of a man having two sons, which will be treated below. Thus, Jesus continues to address the chief priests and the elders of the people (Matt 21:23), beginning, "Listen to another parable. There was a landowner who planted a vineyard, put a fence around it, dug a wine press in it, and built a watchtower. Then, he leased it to tenants and went to another country" (Matt 21:33). The opening line in Luke's Gospel indicates that Jesus is addressing only the people: "[Jesus] began to tell the people this parable: 'A man planted a vineyard, and leased it to tenants, and went to another country for a long time'" (Luke 20:9). The Gospel of Thomas, a collection of Jesus' sayings with no narrative structure or identification of an audience, begins, "[Jesus] said, 'A good man owned a vineyard and he leased it to tenant farmers so that they might work it and he might receive its produce from them" (Thos 65).[21] It is not difficult to see that Mark and Matthew (although slightly abbreviated) rely upon Isaiah 5:1b–2 for their beginnings of the allegory. Luke shortens the introductory line dramatically, as does Thomas.

First Slave(s)

"When the season came, [the vineyard owner] sent a slave to the tenants to collect from them his share of the produce of the vineyard," states Mark's Gospel (Mark 12:2). "But they seized him, and beat him, and sent him away empty-handed" (Mark 12:3). Matthew rewrites those two verses from Mark, recording: "When the harvest time had come, [the vineyard owner] sent his slaves to the tenants to collect his produce. But the tenants seized his slaves and beat one, killed another, and stoned another" (Matt 21:34–35). Luke's shorter version of the narrative states: "When the season came, he sent a slave to the tenants to collect from them his share of the produce of the vineyard. But they seized him, and beat him, and sent him away empty-handed" (Luke 12:2–3). And Thomas records: "[The vineyard owner] sent his servant so the farmers might give him the produce of the vineyard. They seized the servant and beat him: they almost killed him. The servant went and told his master. The master said, 'Perhaps he did not know them'" (Thos 65).[22] While Mark records the sending of a single slave, Matthew records the sending of at least three slaves (maybe even more), one of whom is beaten, one of whom is killed, and one of whom is stoned. As will be seen, the first slave that Luke records being sent will only be beaten and will be sent two more times. Thomas follows Luke in having only one slave sent and beaten, but the slave will return only one more time. The inner monologue that Thomas records the vineyard owner thinking is not clear. How could the slave not know the tenant farmers?

Second Slave(s)

Now according to Mark the vineyard owner "sent another slave to [the tenants]; this one they beat over the head and insulted" (Mark 12:4). According to Matthew, the owner "sent other slaves, more than the first; and [the tenants] treated them in the same way" (Matt 21:36). "Next he sent another

21. Ehrman, *Apocryphal Gospels*, 327.
22. Ibid.

slave; that one also they beat and insulted and sent away empty-handed," states Luke (Luke 20:11). Thomas records: "He sent another servant, and the farmers beat this one as well" (Thos 65).[23]

Third Slave(s)

"Then [the vineyard owner] sent another, and that one [the tenants] killed," states Mark. "And so it was with many others; some they beat, and others they killed" (Mark 12:4–5). Matthew does not record a third-sending of slaves, and neither does Thomas, but Luke does: "And he sent still a third; this one also they wounded and threw out" (Luke 20:12).

Owner's Son Sent

Finally, the vineyard owner decides to send his son. Mark narrates: "He had still one other, a beloved son. Finally he sent him to them, saying, 'They will respect my son.' But those tenants said to one another, 'This is the heir; come, let us kill him, and the inheritance will be ours.' So they seized him, killed him, and threw him out of the vineyard" (Mark 12:6–8). Matthew shortens his Markan source, narrating: "Finally he sent his son to them, saying, 'They will respect my son.' But when the tenants saw the son, they said to themselves, 'This is the heir; come, let us kill him and get his inheritance.' So they seized him, threw him out of the vineyard, and killed him" (Matt 21:37–39). Luke adds to the inner dialogue of the characters, narrating: "Then the owner of the vineyard said, 'What shall I do? I will send my beloved son; perhaps they will respect him.' But when the tenants saw him, they discussed it among themselves and said, 'This is the heir; let us kill him so that the inheritance may be ours.' So they threw him out of the vineyard and killed him" (Luke 20:13–15a). Thomas's version of the narrative is shorter than Luke's. Thomas records: "Then the master sent his son and said, 'Perhaps they will show respect to my son.' Since those farmers knew that he was the heir of the vineyard, they grabbed him and killed him" (Thos 65).[24] In Mark's Gospel, the son is the fourth messenger to go to the vineyard. In Matthew's Gospel, the son is the third messenger to be sent to the tenants. Luke follows Mark and makes the son the fourth messenger, whereas Thomas follows Matthew and makes the son the third messenger to go to the tenant farmers. Into the vineyard owner's soliloquy about the

23. Ibid.
24. Ibid.

tenants respecting his son, only Luke adds the hope that perhaps they will do so. In Mark, the tenants kill the son in the vineyard and then throw him out; in Matthew and Luke they throw him out and then kill him; Thomas does not include these details. The earliest versions of the allegory (parable) probably ended with the death of the son or the death of the tenants.

Application 1

The allegory differs in its conclusion just as it differs in is details. Mark's version asks rhetorically, "What then will the owner of the vineyard do?" and answers, "He will come and destroy the tenants and give the vineyard to others" (Mark 12:9). Matthew poses the question to the hearers, who reply with an answer: "'Now when the owner of the vineyard comes, what will he do to those tenants?' They said to him, 'He will put those wretches to a miserable death, and lease the vineyard to other tenants who will give him the produce at the harvest time'" (Matt 21:40–41). Luke follows Mark's rhetorical question-and-answer scenario: "What then will the owner of the vineyard do to them? He will come and destroy those tenants and give the vineyard to others" (Luke 20:15b–16a). All that Thomas states is, "The one who has ears had better listen!" (Thos 65)[25]

Before moving on to the second application of the allegory a few notes are necessary. According to Ryken, the vineyard theme in the HB (OT) has been changed by the authors of the CB (NT). "It is no longer ethnic Israel that is God's vineyard, but the kingdom of God."[26] He adds, "The landowner, who is surely meant to represent God, plants and protects a vineyard and then rents it to tenants who end up abusing his servants. The parable ends with a threat against those who misuse the vineyard."[27] Meier states that anyone even remotely familiar with Isaiah's song of the vineyard

> would easily recognize the vineyard as Israel, the owner of the vineyard as God, the servants sent by the owner as the prophets, and those who reject and kill the servants as the evil leaders of Israel (or more specifically, of Jerusalem). In addition, early Christian hearers of . . . the parable would immediately recognize the only son as Jesus, his violent death as his crucifixion, the punishment of the tenants as the destruction of Jerusalem, and the citation of . . . Psalm 118:22–23 as the announcement of Jesus' vindication by way of his resurrection [which will be

---

25. Ibid.
26. Ryken, *Dictionary*, 916–17.
27. Ibid., 917.

examined shortly]. One would have to be totally ignorant of both Jewish and early Jewish-Christian traditions not to grasp most if not all of the allegory inherent in and throughout the parable. Far from some adventitious contrivance, this allegory lies at the very core of the parable and is inextricably bound up with it.[28]

Application 2

As indicated in Meier's comments above, there is another application at the end of the allegory. In Mark's Gospel, Jesus asks:

> "Have you not read this scripture: The stone that the builders rejected has become the cornerstone; this was the Lord's doing, and it is amazing in our eyes"? When [the chief priests, the scribes, and the elders] realized that he had told this parable against them, they wanted to arrest him, but they feared the crowd. So they left him and went away. (Mark 12:10–12)

Matthew is much more direct in his application of the allegory. Matthew narrates:

> Jesus said to [the chief priests and the elders of the people], "Have you never read the scriptures: 'The stone that the builders rejected has become the cornerstone; that was the Lord's doing, and it is amazing in our eyes'? Therefore I tell you, the kingdom of God will be taken away from you and given to a people that produces the fruits of the kingdom. The one who falls on this stone will be broken to pieces; and it will crush anyone on whom it falls." When the chief priests and the Pharisees heard his parable, they realized that he was speaking about them. They wanted to arrest him, but they feared the crowds, because they regarded him as a prophet. (Matt 21:42–44)

Luke shortens the material he took from Mark, narrating:

> When [the chief priests and scribes with the elders] heard this, they said, "Heaven forbid!" But [Jesus] looked at them and said, "What then does this text mean: 'The stone that the builders rejected has become the cornerstone'? Everyone who falls on that stone will be broken to pieces; and it will crush anyone on whom it falls." When the scribes and chief priests realized that he had

---

28. Meier, *Marginal Jew*, 86–7.

told this parable against them, they wanted to lay hands on him at that very hour, but they feared the people. (Luke 20:16b–19)

In Thomas, the application is found in the next saying: "Jesus said, 'Show me the stone that the builders have rejected: that is the cornerstone'" (Thos 66).[29]

In both Mark and Matthew, Jesus quotes Psalm 118:22–23. In Luke, he only quotes Psalm 118:22. Because Matthew presents the Jewish leaders answering Jesus' question, they pronounce judgment on themselves. Matthew specifically states that the vineyard, that was a sign of the land and the Israelites, will be taken away from the Jewish leaders and given to a people, the church, composed of Jews and Gentiles, bearing fruit. Thus, the parable concludes with a threat against those who misuse the vineyard. According to Meier,

> Thomas has intentionally redacted the synoptic parable to turn it into an allegory of the ignorant slaves of the owner versus the rebellious free agents who have knowledge. None of the three synoptics has the theme of not-knowing/knowing at the two points where Thomas enunciates them. . . . The sudden ending with no further elaboration, commentary, or scriptural reference fits in perfectly with the hidden meaning of Jesus' words that [Thomas] has inculcated from the prologue and first two logia of the work. . . . [T]he synoptic elaborations and commentary are replaced with Thomas's frequent refrain, calling on the possessor of true knowledge to seek and find the hidden message: "Let him who has ears hear."[30]

Thus, there are a number of meanings reassigned to the vineyard metaphor. First, in Mark's Gospel the vineyard allegory (parable) of the tenants serves as a prediction of the fall of Jerusalem. Since the author of Mark's Gospel most likely composed the allegory, he "has Jesus prophesying the destruction of Jerusalem, implicitly fitting the whole parable into the larger story of Jesus' ministry to his own people, his rejection by their leaders, and their subsequent punishment via the destruction of their ancient capital and temple" in 70 CE.[31] In Mark, the beloved son dies in the vineyard, and then he is thrown out. Thus, according to Mark, the reason Jerusalem fell to the Romans was because Jewish leadership failed to accept the authority of Jesus.

---

29. Ehrman, *Apocryphal Gospels*, 327.
30. Meier, *Marginal Jew*, 122.
31. Ibid., 123.

Given Matthew's strong anti-Jewish position, the author of this gospel places the allegory (parable) immediately after another one set in a vineyard, which will be examined below, clearly hinting that slaves represent the major and minor prophets in a line of three, the last being the son, Jesus. The first group of tenants represents the Jewish leadership, especially the Pharisees and to some degree the Sadducees in Matthew, who have rejected Jesus' teaching. The son's death, which takes place outside the vineyard, clearly echoes Jesus' death. Thus, for Matthew, the vineyard—now the kingdom of God—is given to a new group of tenants, namely, the Jews who believe in Jesus and the Gentiles, the components of Matthew's church.

The allegory (parable) of the vineyard in Luke's Gospel has been adjusted by the author to fit his own understanding. The Lukan Jesus tells the parable to the crowd, not to the chief priests, scribes, and elders who had just asked him about his authority to teach. In other words, Jesus turns away from them and tells the people listening to him about them. From a Lukan point of view this parable (allegory) is a very harsh condemnation of Jews in favor of Gentiles. Even the Jewish leadership is afraid of the people who believe in Jesus' teaching! Luke makes it clear that the beloved son is Jesus, who is taken out of the vineyard and killed. The shorter quotation from Psalm 118 serves as a summary-commentary about the death and resurrection of Jesus, indicating that the allegory (parable) in all three synoptic gospels is a post-Easter creation of the church. The stone worthless to a builder has become the cornerstone of a new vineyard filled with fruit-bearing Gentiles.

Both Matthew and Luke employ a saying from Q (meaning *Source*, and indicating a document used by both Matthew and Luke but unknown to Mark) about anyone falling on the rejected stone that has become the cornerstone will be broken, and that it will crush anyone upon whom it falls (Matt 21:44; Luke 20:18). This saying is probably an allusion to Daniel 2:34–35, 44–45, one of Daniel's dream interpretations about a stone destroying a statue, and Isaiah 8:14–15, a passage about the LORD being a stone one strikes against, a trap, and a snare for Jerusalem.

Meier accurately summarizes the three versions of the allegory (parable) stating:

> A Jewish-Palestinian audience of Jesus' time, listening to a well-known prophet and teacher as he addressed the religious leaders in the Jerusalem temple, could hardly miss the scriptural allusions, inherent in symbols like the vineyard, the owner of the vineyard sending his servants to make claims on those working in his vineyard, and the rejection of those servants by the workers. One would have to be ignorant not only of individual

scriptural texts but also of the master narrative governing the Jewish Scriptures to miss the reference.[32]

Likewise, Thomas's lack of any application of the allegory (parable) is best explained by Meier. He writes: "The sweep of a collective, people-oriented salvation history, understood as a pattern of prophecy and fulfillment and climaxing in the ministry and death of the earthly Jesus, is not a congenial theme to Thomas, a work dedicated to secret, saving, and timeless truths revealed only to the solitary initiate."[33] However, Meier also states, "For all his abbreviations, even Thomas does not succeed in suppressing the Old Testament allusions entirely."[34] Thus, Thomas is best understood "as a gnostic work," and the allegory (parable) is best understood as "a subversive allegory of free men with knowledge (the tenants) rightfully revolting against the evil Creator God and his slave/servants." One could also understand "the parable as an allegory warning against the murderous results of greed and desire for material possessions."[35]

Two Matthean Allegories (Parables)

After having mentioned Matthew's anti-Jewish polemic in the allegory (parable) of the tenants (vineyard) above, it is good to look at two other allegories (parables) unique to Matthew's Gospel. Usually referred to as M or Special M to indicate that both allegories are found only in Matthew's Gospel and/or that the author of Matthew's Gospel wrote the allegories himself, these allegories feature a vineyard. Matthew 20:1–16 precedes the allegory of the tenants in the vineyard. The parable begins specifically connecting the vineyard to the kingdom of God, which Matthew prefers to call the kingdom of heaven. "The kingdom of heaven is like a landowner who went out early in the morning to hire laborers for his vineyard. After agreeing with the laborers for the usual daily wage, he sent them into the vineyard" (Matt 20:1–2). The analogy progresses with the vineyard owner hiring more laborers at nine o'clock, at noon, at three o'clock, and at five o'clock and sending them to work in his vineyard (Matt 20:3–7).

When evening comes, the vineyard owner tells his manager to pay the day laborers by beginning with the last who were hired and ending with the first who were hired. Thus, a reversal is occurring. So, when the manager

---

32. Ibid.
33. Ibid.
34. Ibid.
35. Ibid., 115.

first pays the day labors hired last, those hired first expect to get more, but all receive the same daily wage. The first hired complain to the vineyard owner: "These last worked only one hour, and you have made them equal to us who had borne the burden of the day and the scorching heat" (Matt 20:12). The vineyard owner reminds them that he contracted with all the day laborers for the same daily wage (Matt 20:13).

If the reader understands the first day laborers as the Israelites (Jews) and the last as the Gentiles, with those in between being converts to Judaism, the parable is about God's (the vineyard owner's) graciousness towards all people. In other words, he invites all people—Jews and Gentiles—to work in his kingdom, no matter what time of the day they accept his invitation. Those Jews, maybe even Jewish-Christians, who are grumbling echo the various grumblings of the Hebrews, Israelites, and Jews throughout the HB (OT), too numerous to list here. This is why the parable ends with the vineyard owner, God, telling the grumbling laborers to take what they have earned and go. He is free to do whatever he pleases with what belongs to him (Matt 20:14–15a). He finishes by asking them: ". . . [A]re you envious because I am generous?" (Matt 20:15b). No answer is provided. Using the vineyard metaphor, which originally referred to the promised land and the Israelites, the Matthean Jesus has just moved back the metaphor's boundaries to the point that they encompass the whole world and its peoples and God's kingdom!

Appended to this allegory (parable) is one of the author's typical ways to end a story: "So the last will be first, and the first will be last" (Matt 20:16; cf. 19:30). While the day laborers hired last are the first to be paid, that is about the only application of the last line of the allegory. However, with the added context of Matthew's anti-Jewish polemic, it can refer to the Gentiles (the last) getting ahead of the Jews (the first) when it comes to the kingdom of heaven.

The other unique Matthean allegory immediately precedes the allegory (parable) of the tenants in the vineyard. Thus, even before examining it, it is safe to say that the author of this gospel sees some connection between the two stories. The allegory of the two sons emphasizes the importance of deeds or works while denigrating empty promises. However, it is set in a vineyard, which indicates that it also has something to say about the expansion of the understanding of Isaiah's song of the vineyard.

The Matthean Jesus begins by posing a question to the chief priests and the elders of the people, who had just questioned his authority to teach. He says:

> "What do you think? A man had two sons; he went to the first and said, 'Son, go and work in the vineyard today.' He answered, 'I will not'; but later he changed his mind and went. The father

went to the second and said the same; and he answered, 'I go sir'; but he did not go. Which of the two did the will of the father?" They said, "The first." (Matt 21:28–31b)

The man with two sons is a familiar story to Jewish ears. However, in this unique narrative, the first son represents the Gentiles, who at first said no to God, according to the popular Jewish perspective of the time, while the second son represents the Jews, who in Matthew's Gospel refuse to believe that Jesus is the Messiah. Again, attention must be given to the place of work: a vineyard. In Matthew's Gospel, the vineyard is one of the metaphors for the kingdom of heaven (God). Gentiles (the first son), who had at first not believed that Jesus is the Messiah, are entering Matthew's church, while Jews (the second son), who had been the recipient of Jesus' ministry, did not believe. So, when the Jewish leaders are asked to name which son did the will of the father, they end up indicting themselves with their answer; they declare that Gentiles are doing God's will!

The Matthean Jesus adds an explanation to the correct answer given by the Jewish leaders. "Jesus said to them, 'Truly I tell you, the tax collectors and the prostitutes are going into the kingdom of God ahead of you. For John came to you in the way of righteousness and you did not believe him, but the tax collectors and the prostitutes believed him and even after you saw it, you did not change your minds and believe him'" (Matt 21:31c-32). In other words, Jewish leaders heard the teaching of John the Baptist, but they rejected it, like the second son. However, the outcasts, the dirt of society, the tax collectors and prostitutes, accepted it, like the first son. Those who had placed themselves outside the acceptable standards of righteousness are declared by Jesus to be the righteous, and those who thought of themselves as righteous are declared to be unrighteous. Tax collectors were Jews who worked for the Roman occupation forces of Palestine; they made their living by raising the amount of the set Roman tax and pocketing the difference. They were considered apostates. Prostitutes are those who have received money for sexual intercourse or other sex acts; they are considered unclean because of their contact with blood and semen. There are new residents in the vineyard, and the original ones are not pleased to have the new ones there!

Fruit of the Vine

The second major block of vineyard material in the CB (NT) is a saying of Jesus found in Mark, Matthew, and Luke. In Mark's Gospel at the end of the Passover meal Jesus declares, "Truly I tell you, I will never again drink of the fruit of the vine until the day when I drink it new in the kingdom of God" (Mark 14:25). Matthew's version of the saying is this: "I tell you, I will never again drink of this fruit of the vine until the day when I drink it new with you in my Father's kingdom" (Matt 26:29). Luke's version portrays Jesus stating, "... I tell you that from now on I will not drink of the fruit of the vine until the kingdom of God comes" (Luke 22:18). It is important to note that in Luke's Gospel, Jesus blesses the cup two times; this saying is attached to the first blessing of the cup. In Mark and Matthew there is only one cup blessing, and so the saying is attached to it. The Mormon *Book of Doctrine and Covenants* portrays Jesus stating, "... [T]he hour comes that I will drink of the fruit of the vine with you on the earth, and with Moroni, whom I have sent unto you to reveal the Book of Mormon, containing the fullness of my everlasting gospel..." (*D&C* 26:2). In all accounts of the saying, vineyard serves as the background by labeling the wine the fruit of the vine. The vineyard represents a heavenly or messianic place of joy, much like the restorative descriptions found in the HB (OT) material above, especially the prophet Isaiah. While it is true to state that the saying reflects future joy in God's kingdom in Mark and Luke, for Matthew it is a turning point in salvation history; according to Matthew's allegories (parables), the kingdom has been given to others. Minimally, the kingdom is open to others. The only residents of the vineyard are no longer Jews. In *D&C*, the kingdom has arrived on the earth with the revelation given to Joseph Smith by Maroni in September 1830.

This last point is further emphasized in *The Book of Mormon*. In the Book of Alma, Alma calls the reader to repentance "for the day of salvation draws nigh" (Al 13:21). "Yes, and the voice of the Lord, by the mouth of angels, does declare it unto all nations" (Al 13:22). Because the Mormons and those who have joined them are "wanderers in a strange land," they are "highly favored, for [they] have these glad tidings declared unto [them] in all parts of [their] vineyard" (Al 13:23). And, therefore, they "see the great call of diligence of men to labor in the vineyards of the Lord; and thus [they] see the great reason of sorrow, and also of rejoicing—sorrow because of death and destruction among men, and joy because of the light of Christ unto life" (Al 28:14).

Jesus the Vine

The third major block of biblical material concerning the vine and the vineyard is found in John's Gospel. The Johannine Jesus tells his disciples:

> I am the true vine, and my Father is the vinegrower. He removes every branch in me that bears no fruit. Every branch that bears

> fruit he prunes to make it bear more fruit. You have already been cleansed by the word that I have spoken to you. Abide in me as I abide in you. Just as the branch cannot bear fruit by itself unless it abides in the vine, neither can you unless you abide in me. I am the vine, you are the branches. Those who abide in me and I in them bear much fruit, because apart from me you can do nothing. Whoever does not abide in me is thrown away like a branch and withers; such branches are gathered, thrown into the fire, and burned. My Father is glorified by this, that you bear much fruit and become my disciples. (John 15:1–6, 8)

It is not difficult to see that Jesus, not Israel, is now the true vine in the vineyard. The author of this discourse understood and employed the language of viticulture. The image is that of a vineyard, owned by God the Father, with a single, woody, tree-like vine growing in it. That vine is Jesus. From the vine grow branches that bear fruit. In order that the branches keep bearing fruit, they have to be pruned, cut back, cleansed, and the Father does this through Jesus' spoken (and written) word to his disciples. In order for the branches to remain alive, they cannot be cut from the vine. The Johannine language refers to this as *abiding in*. The vine is the source of life for the branches; the vine enables the branches to produce fruit. If the branch does not stay on the vine, it is thrown into a pile and burned. The goal of staying on the vine is great fruit production, which glorifies the Father and indicates that the branch is a disciple of Jesus.

After reminding the reader that metaphorically the vine is Israel in the HB (OT) and that "Israel is the vine as the peculiar object of the care of Yahweh, as the vine is the object of the care of its grower, and the plant from which he expects most fruit,"[36] McKenzie adds that "the vine is also a figure of luxuriant growth and of fertility."[37] Then, he discusses the Johannine replacement image of Jesus as the vine. "[I]t signifies the close union between Jesus and the disciples," states McKenzie. "The disciples derive their power to bear fruit only by a vital union with Jesus, a sharing of the same life which is the source of power and activity."[38]

There are two echoes of this image in *The Book of Mormon*. In the First Book of Nephi, the author refers to receiving "the strength and nourishment from the true vine" (1 Ne 15:15). A fuller echo of the image is found in the Book of Alma.

---

36. McKenzie, *Dictionary*, 913.
37. Ibid.
38. Ibid.

> [T]he Lord did pour out his Spirit on all the face of the land to prepare the minds of the children of men, or to prepare their hearts to receive the word which should be taught among them at the time of his coming—That they might not be hardened against the word, that they might not be unbelieving, and go on to destruction, but that they might receive the word with joy, and as a branch be grafted into the true vine, that they might enter into the rest of the Lord their God. (Al 16:16–17)

There is also an echo of the Johannine image in the Gospel of Thomas. "Jesus said, 'A grapevine has been planted outside of the Father. And since it is not strong, it will be pulled up by its root and perish'" (Thos 40).[39] While this may be a variant of Matthew 15:13, it reemphasizes the Johannine perspective that Jesus is the true vine of the vinegrowing Father; there can be no competitive vine. Bloom notes a similar saying in what he refers to as the Book of Thomas: "If the sun shines on a grapevine and it prospers, it will dominate the weeds; otherwise the master must pull them out."[40] In the Father's vineyard, there is no room for weeds; only the one vine, Jesus, can be there.

Another passage about grape vines is found in Papias:

> The days are coming when vines will come forth, each with ten thousand boughs; and on a single bough will be ten thousand branches. And indeed, on a single branch will be ten thousand shoots and on every shoot ten thousand clusters; and in every cluster will be ten thousand grapes, and every grape, when pressed, will yield twenty-five measures of wine. And when any of the saints grabs hold of a cluster, another will cry out, "I am a better cluster, take me; bless the Lord through me."[41]

This passage is found inserted after John 8:11 in some manuscripts. The amazing abundance mentioned in the passage points to messianic times, as described particularly by the prophet Isaiah. However, even he could not predict the fertility of the vines mentioned above!

Miscellaneous

There are but two fables about a vine in Aesop, both of which merely provide a setting for a longer story with a moral. In the first, titled "The Stag and the Vine," a male deer, pursued by hunters, "concealed himself under

---

39. Ehrman, *Apocryphal Gospels*, 321.
40. Bloom, *Gospel of Thomas*, 87.
41. Ehrman, *Apocryphal Gospels*, 359.

cover of a thick vine." The hunters pass by the deer's hiding place without seeing him. "Supposing all danger to be over, [the stag] presently began to browse on the leaves of the vine. The movement drew the attention of the returning huntsmen, and one of them, supposing some animal to be hidden there, shot an arrow . . . into the foliage. The unlucky stag was pierced to the heart, and, as he expired, he said, 'I deserve my fate for my treachery in feeding upon the leaves of my protector.'"[42] Aesop appends a moral to this fable, namely, "Ingratitude sometimes brings its own punishment."[43]

In the second fable, titled "The Fox and the Grapes," a hungry fox sees some bunches of grapes "hanging from a vine that was trained along a high trellis, and did his best to reach them by jumping as high as he could into the air. But it was all in vain, for they were just out of reach. So he gave up trying, and walked away with an air of dignity and unconcern, remarking, 'I thought those grapes were ripe, but I see now they are quite sour.'"[44] While no moral is appended to this fable, it is not difficult to see that the fox has created a psychological excuse to cover his inability to grab the fruit. Aesop may not have realized it, but many people have a repertoire of excuses like the fox!

In Egypt, Osiris is associated with the vine and vineyard. As has already been narrated in the chapter on the tamarisk tree, Osiris was put into a box, which was ultimately encased in a tamarisk, until his sister-wife released him. Frazer states that Osiris was a tree spirit; as such his worshippers were forbidden to injure fruit-bearing trees or vines.

> According to one legend, he taught men to train the vine to poles, to prune its superfluous foliage, and to extract the juice of the grape. . . . Osiris is depicted sitting in a shrine, from the roof of which hang clusters of grapes . . . and in front of a pool, from the banks of which a luxuriant vine, with many bunches of grapes, grows towards the green face of the seated deity.[45]

Furthermore, because of Osiris's association with death and resurrection, it is not difficult to see how he became associated with the grapes, which must be crushed or die in order to become wine or rise.

In Greek and Roman mythology, the vine and vineyard is associated with Dionysus or Bacchus (Liber). Under either name, he is the god of the grape harvest, winemaking, and wine. He carries a staff with a pine cone on its tip, and so he is also treated in the chapter on the pine tree. There are various mythological accounts of his death and rebirth. As a dying and rising

42. Aesop, 138.
43. Ibid.
44. Ibid., 1.
45. Frazer, *Golden Bough*.

god, like Osiris, he was associated with trees, which make him a type of tree spirit. That, in turn, associates him with the dying or crushing of grapes and their fermenting or resurrection into wine. In other myths he is said to have discovered the culture of the vine and the mode of extracting its precious juice, even making a trip to Asia to teach people the cultivation of the vine. Some biblical scholars have drawn parallels between Dionysus or Bacchus and Jesus, especially the dying-and-returning motif that characterize both of them, and in John's Gospel the unique story of Jesus turning water into wine (John 2:1–11). According to Herzberg, Dionysus or Bacchus not only "became the god of wine" but "of the fertility and bounty of vegetation. He was a joyous god and with his worship was associated constant merrymaking. His chief festival was celebrated in March of each year, when the wine was ready for drinking."[46] He is often depicted in a chariot drawn by leopards; his head is crowned with vine leaves, and in his hand he holds the thyrsus, the staff mentioned above.

Conclusion

Thus, the most prominent image in the Bible is the vine or vineyard image. It signifies Jerusalem, Judah, and Israel. When it refers to the whole nation of Israel, it gives the Israelites a sense of place. The song of the vineyard illustrates the elements of a vineyard. Usually planted on a hill, it had to be dug and the stones cleared and used to build a wall to protect it from wild animals. Then a watchtower was built from which a guard protected the vineyard from thieves. After the vines were planted a wine press was carved out of the stone, and a vat created to catch the pressed grapes at harvest time. Vinedressers cared for the vines and pruned them yearly. Once the vineyard metaphor is associated with Israel, God is understood to be the owner of the vineyard. The metaphor is further expanded into a love song, a place of rest, food for the poor, prosperity, and pleasure. After it becomes a sign of destruction, it emerges as a sign of restoration. Isaiah's song of the vineyard is the basis for the vineyard allegory (parable) of the tenants which shifts the identification from the land of Israel to God's kingdom as preached by Jesus of Nazareth. Underlying the allegory (parable) is the reason each evangelist thinks Jerusalem was destroyed by the Romans. By the end of the Bible, the vine and vineyard metaphor refers to the world; all people are invited to the messianic vineyard. Jesus himself becomes the new vine to which all the branches are connected. And so for all these reason, the vine and vineyard are considered to be sacred.

46. Herzberg, *Myths*, 99.

Journal/Meditation: What tree best represents for you all that is associated with the vine and vineyard? Does the vine and vineyard metaphor communicate to modern people the same way it did to ancient Jews and Christians? If so, how? If not, why not? When you see or buy grapes in the supermarket, what do you associate with them? When you drink wine, what do you associate with it?

Prayer: God of the vineyard, once you planted your people as choice vines on a fertile hill, building a watchtower, a wine press, and a vat. In later times, you revealed your Son, Jesus Christ, to be the true vine, from whom the branches get their life. Fill me with the life-giving energy of the Holy Spirit that I may safely arrive in the kingdom, where you live and reign as one God—Father, Son, and Holy Spirit—forever and ever. Amen.

Willow

Text: "By the rivers of Babylon—there we sat down and there we wept when we remembered Zion. On the willows there we hung up our harps. For there our captors asked us for songs, and our tormentors asked for mirth, saying, 'Sing us one of the songs of Zion!'" (Ps 137:1–3)

Reflection: Psalm 137 from the Book of Psalms in the HB (OT) originates from either during the Jews's exile from Jerusalem in Babylon or shortly thereafter. While sitting near the canals of the Euphrates River, they remembered Jerusalem and wept. Even though their taskmasters asked them to sing songs from their homeland, they hung their harps on the willows that grew near the canals and refused to sing the joyful songs that accompanied pilgrims on their ascent of Zion to the holy city.

    Several other biblical passages indicate that willows grew along streams. For example, when God describes Behemoth to Job, he states that the willows of the wadi surround it (Job 40:22). A wadi is a stream bed that may have been dry much of the year. The prophet Isaiah mentions the Wadi of the Willows (Isa 15:7), specifically connecting the stream "at the southern end of the Dead Sea"[1] and the tree. Later, he does it again when he writes about God restoring Israel by pouring his spirit upon Jacob's descendants, who will spring up like willows by flowing streams (Isa 44:4). In her myth about Orpheus, Caldecott notes, "[W]illows left the riverbank to gather round and hear his songs."[2] According to Tresidder, the willow is a tree of lamentation.[3] And this remark is

---

1. Roberts, *First Isaiah*, 235.
2. Caldecott, *Myths*, 89.
3. Tresidder, *Dictionary of Symbols*, 518.

quite true when considering the many tales of sorrow, disappointment, grief, and regret associated with the willow tree.

There are over four hundred species of willows, all of which are deciduous, growing in moist soils to a height of thirty to forty feet. Because they grow near water sources, they possess watery reddish-brown bark sap full of salicylic acid which makes the wood of the tree pliant but tough. The slender branches sporting elongated, round, or oval leaves are matched by the large, fibrous roots, which aggressively seek out moisture and clog all types of drains, tile pipes, and septic and sewer systems. The use of the leaves and bark to make tea ultimately resulted in what is today known as aspirin, while thin or split willow rods can be woven into wicker or baskets. Because of its association with lamentation, the willow also signifies inner wisdom, an open mind with the stability and strength of age and experience which arise because of human sorrow.

Before exploring several stories featuring the willow and lamentation, the concept is best captured in the popular song titled "Willow Weep for Me" written by Ann Ronell in 1932. Over the years various artists have made redactions to the original lyrics, but the basic lamentation remains in the love song and describes the willow tree accurately. The song begins: "Willow, weep for me . . . . / Bend your branches green along the stream that runs to sea. / Listen to my plea. / Hear me, willow, and weep for me."[4] In the next stanza the hearer discovers why the singer is asking the willow to weep, namely, because the lover's lover has left, and he or she is sad. After further explanation, the singer asks the willow tree to weep in symphony and to bow down its branches and cover him or her.[5] In the Greek tale of "Persephone and the Pomegranate Tree" (see Pomegranate), Caldecott mentions that in the underworld Persephone sees "barren willows hung limply over black water."[6] Here in the underworld garden, as in the song, the willows lament Persephone's fate.

Before Ronell popularized the sorrow of a lost love with the willow tree, Hans Christian Andersen did it with "Under the Willow Tree" written in 1853. In this very long fairy tale, Andersen sets the story in a little town of Kjoge, where, in one garden grew "an old willow, under which the children were very fond of playing. They had permission to do so, although the tree stood close by the stream . . . ."[7] The reader is introduced to a little girl named Joanna and a little boy named Knud, who often played together

---

4. Ronell, "Willow Weep for Me."
5. Ibid.
6. Caldecott, *Myths*, 84.
7. Andersen, "Under the Willow Tree."

in the garden mentioned above or in a road. "Along this road a row of willow trees had been planted to separate it from a ditch on one side of it.... The old willow tree in the garden was much handsomer, and therefore the children were very fond of sitting under it."[8]

As the tale progresses the reader is told that the "two children still continued to play together . . . under the willow."[9] As in most stories, the children grow into adults; Joanna became a rich entertainer, and Knud became a journeyman. However, they had fallen in love. Knud travels to Copenhagen to see Joanna, and when he finds her, she recalls their childhood play under the willow tree. The travel narrative continues from one town to another. Finally, Knud arrives in Nuremberg, where he gets a job.

> ... [J]ust opposite the workshop stood a great willow tree, which seemed to hold fast to the house for fear of being carried away by the water. It stretched its branches over the stream just as those of the willow tree in the garden at Kjoge had spread over the river.... There was something about the tree here, especially in the moonlight nights, that went direct to his heart; yet it was not in reality the moonlight, but the old tree itself. However, he could not endure it ....[10]

So, leaving the town, he continued journeying until he reached Milan, where he again found Joanna, but she did not recognize him. So, he decided to return to his village. "'Ah, under that willow tree,' he said, 'a man may live a whole life in one single hour.'"[11] As he was making his way home, he noticed a tree.

> A willow tree grew by the roadside, [and] reminded him of home. He felt very tired; so he sat down under the tree, and very soon began to nod, then his eyes closed in sleep. Yet still he seemed conscious that the willow tree was stretching its branches over him; in his dreaming state the tree appeared like a strong, old man . . . , who had taken his tired son up in his arms to carry him back to the land of home, to the garden of his childhood, on the bleak open shores of Kjoge. And then he dreamed that it was really the willow tree itself from Kjoge, which had travelled out in the world to seek him, and now had found him and carried him back into the little garden on the banks of the streamlet; and there stood Joanna, in all her splendor, . . . to welcome him

8. Ibid.
9. Ibid.
10. Ibid.
11. Ibid.

back. [He awoke.] He was still sitting under the willow tree in a strange land, on a cold winter evening, with snow and hail falling from the clouds, and beating upon is face.[12]

After he awoke, he acknowledged how delightful the dream had been; it was the dream of his life. It was the quest he had been on as long as he lived. So, he closed his eyes to sleep and dream some more. The next morning when the villagers were on their way to church, "by the roadside they found a workman seated, but he was dead! [He was] frozen to death under a willow tree."[13] And so ends Andersen's tale of love lost.

In Japanese tradition, the willow is often associated with ghosts. People suppose that ghosts appear wherever a willow grows, and, of course, this causes lamentation. This is best exemplified in "Willow Wife," a tale narrated by Caldecott. "Heitaro loved the willow tree that grew close to his hut," begins the story. While Heitaro had no riches, "the tree was treasure and temple and company enough for him, and each new season of the year seemed more beautiful than the last. When the wind blew through its branches, no music was finer."[14] When bridge-builders came to cut the tree and use it in their construction project, Heitaro found other wood for them to use. "That night as the moonlight shimmered on its leaves, he stood beneath the willow branches and gave his thanks to the gods that the tree had been spared."[15] While standing there, he saw a beautiful young woman, who appeared to him two more times under the willow. Ultimately, they married and had a daughter. ". . . [E]ach night they prayed in the willow temple. However, the emperor decided to build a temple to the goddess of mercy and "demanded the wood of the willow tree." As the villagers began to cut the tree, Heitaro's "willow wife lay dying. When the last blow on the tree was struck, he was alone with his daughter."[16]

Caldecott notes, "The profound love of the man for the tree and of the tree for the man speaks for itself. . . . [N]o temple built by man would ever be as holy as the willow tree. . . . The spirit of the tree [that is, the ghost,] is the true goddess and lives while the tree lives. Kill the tree and you kill the goddess. The temple is a poor substitute for the living goddess."[17] Furthermore, the cut tree signifies Heitaro's lamentation for his willow wife.

12. Ibid.
13. Ibid.
14. Caldecott, *Myths*, 149.
15. Ibid.
16. Ibid., 150.
17. Ibid.

In another Japanese folktale titled "Green Willow," the Lord of Noto sends Tomodata, a samurai, on a mission of trust with specific directions. After undergoing many hardships, Tomodata is caught in a ferocious storm and falls into despair. However, the great winds cease, the clouds disperse, the moon shines, and Tomodata sees a little hill. "Upon the hill was a small thatched cottage, and before the cottage grew three green weeping willow trees. . . . The three willow trees swayed and flung out their green streamers in the wind. Tomodata threw his horse's rein over a branch of one of them, and called for admittance to the longed-for shelter."[18]

The cottage door opened, and there appeared an old woman, who welcomed Tomodata. She said to him, "As to your horse, I see you have delivered him to my daughter; he is in good hands." Tomodata turned around. "Just behind him, in the dim light, stood a very young girl with the horse's reins thrown over her arm. Her garments were blown about and her long loose hair streamed out upon the wind." Tomodata went into the cottage and sat by the fire to dry.

> Presently the daughter of the house came in, and retired behind a screen to comb her hair and to dress afresh. Then she came forth to wait upon him. She wore a blue robe of homespun cotton. Her feet were bare. Her hair was not tied nor confined in any way, but lay along her smooth cheeks, and hung, straight and long and black, to her very knees. She was slender and graceful. Tomodata judged her to be about fifteen years old, and knew well that she was the fairest maiden he had ever seen.[19]

Forgetting what the Lord of Noto had told him, he looked at her between the eyes. Then, he asked her name. "They call me the Green Willow," she said. Falling in love immediately with her, he sang a song to her, and she responded with a song of her own for him. He was sick for love of the Green Willow. Nevertheless, he remembered his mission of trust. So, even while reciting her name over and over again, he left the cottage and continued his journey. Coming to a shrine with flowing water, he decided to wash his face. "There lay the Green Willow, prone upon the ground. A slender thing she lay, face downwards, with her black hair flung about her."[20]

Tomodata picked her up and took her to a town where they found a house. "Here they dwelt three years of happy days, and for Tomodata and the Green Willow the years were like garlands of sweet flowers." While watching the autumn moon one evening, Green Willow began to shake

---

18. "Green Willow."
19. Ibid.
20. Ibid.

and shiver. She told him that she thought she was dying. "He carried her to the stream's side . . . and laved her forehead with water." Urging her to live, she moaned and said, "The tree, the tree; they have cut down my tree. Remember the Green Willow." And with that "she slipped, as it seemed, from his arms to his feet; and he, casting himself upon the ground, found only silken garments, bright colored, warm and sweet, and straw sandals, scarlet-thonged."[21]

In the following years, Tomodata became a traveling holy man. "Once, at nightfall, he found himself upon a lonely moor. On his right hand he beheld a little hill, and on it the sad ruins of a poor thatched cottage. The door swung to and fro with broken latch and creaking hinge. Before it stood three old stumps of willow trees that had long since been cut down."[22] Thus, this Japanese ghost story returns to the place where it began by featuring a young woman, who has a close spiritual connection with a willow tree, which leads Tomodata to love and lamentation. The influence of the divine is found in the three willow trees, the three years the lovers live together, and the three stumps of willow trees.

The same lamentation is found in part of the Flemish tale titled "The Orange Grove and the Enchanted Canary." While the whole story is not the topic under discussion here, a prince tells an old man that he has had a dream about a sunny land in which there was an orange grove and in one of the oranges he would find the woman who would be his wife. After receiving instructions about where to find the grove, the old man tells him not to open the three oranges he is to pick until he leaves the grove. He finds the orange grove, and he overcomes a number of difficulties to pick three oranges that will become three princesses. Of course, he opens the first two oranges before leaving, and each turns into a canary and flies away. Finally getting out of the place, he finds a river and opens the third orange. Out flies a canary, which drinks from the river and turns into a beautiful princess. In order to give her a proper reception in his father's castle, he tells the princess to wait in the forest by a pool. As the prince goes on, the princess spies "an ugly, lazy, and bad-tempered girl" coming to the pool. "Afraid of the stranger, the princess hid in a willow tree, but as she peeped out her reflection fell on the still surface of the pond." At first the ugly girl thought it was her reflection in the water, but then she spied the princess in the tree. "She enticed the shy princess down from the willow tree, and on hearing that she was to be the prince's bride, she offered to dress her hair so that she would look prettier at the wedding." While so doing, the ugly girl stuck a pin into

21. Ibid.
22. Ibid.

her head, and "the princess turned back into a bird and flew away." When the prince returned, he unknowingly took the ugly girl with him to the castle. When the guests were gathered for the wedding feast, a canary appeared. When the prince noticed the pin in its head, he removed it "and the canary became the beautiful princess again."[23] This tale of transformation from an orange to a canary, to a princess, to a canary, to a princess results in the sorrow of the ugly girl caused by a princess's reflection while sitting in a willow tree. The reader will also note that the prince picks three oranges!

"The Wisdom of the Willow Tree" is an Osage Nation story about a young man who seeks answers from a willow tree. "What is the meaning of life? Why is it that people grow old and die?" Those are the questions Little One asks the elders of his tribe. The elders tell him that "he would have to seek the answers in his dreams." So, he begins his vision quest by leaving the tribe and traveling to a stream.

> ... [A]s he walked along that stream, he stumbled and fell among the roots of an old willow tree.... "Grandfather," he said to the willow tree, "it is not possible for me to go on." Then the ancient willow spoke to him. "Little One," it said, "all the Little Ones always cling to me for support as they walk along the great path of life. See the base of my trunk, which sends forth those roots that hold me firm in the earth. They are the sign of my old age. They are darkened and wrinkled with age, but they are still strong. Their strength comes from relying on the earth. When the Little Ones use me as a symbol, they will not fail to see old age as they travel along the path of life." Those words gave strength to Little One's spirit. He stood again and began to walk. Soon his own village was in sight, and as he sat down to rest for a moment in the grass of the prairie, looking at his village, another vision came to him. He saw before him the figure of an old man. The old man was strangely familiar, even though Little One had never seen him before.... Then Little One looked, and as he looked, the lesson shown him by the willow tree filled his heart.... Little One said, "You are firm and rooted to the earth like the ancient willow." ... [H]e knew that the old man he had seen was himself. The ancient man was Little One as he would be when he became an elder, filled with that great peace and wisdom which would give strength to all of the people.[24]

Here, the willow tree represents wisdom, the fulfillment of the wishes of the heart learned from inner vision and dreams.

23. Ibid., 167.
24. "Wisdom of the Willow Tree."

This same point is made in a Chinese custom in which people carry willow branches to the tombs of their ancestors on the Tomb Sweeping Festival, which is similar to All Saints Day, November 1, and All Souls Day, November 2, in some Christian celebrations; the Celts marked a similar day on October 31, today known as Halloween. The Chinese believe that the ruler of the underworld permits the spirits of the dead to return to the earth. Willow branches keep them away! The goddess of mercy, Guanyin, is often pictured sitting on a rock with a willow branch in a vase of water at her side. Much like holy water in some Christian churches, the sprinkling of water with the willow branch puts demons to flight. In Taoism, a small carving made from a willow branch can be used to communicate with the dead.

According to Tresidder, in Buddhism, the willow is "an emblem of humility and compassion."[25] It also serves as "a symbol of the springtime of love, feminine grace, and the sorrow of parting.... It was a Daoist metaphor for patience, resilience, and immortality. In Tibetan tradition, it is the Tree of Life."[26]

As a sign of life—springtime or immortal—the willow can be cultivated from a twig. Even a branch lying on the ground can sprout into a new tree. A twig takes root rather quickly. In the Bible, the prophet Ezekiel states this when he compares the planting of a seed to the setting of a willow twig (Ezek 17:5b). There is a legend that Alexander Pope took a twig from a parcel tied with willows and sent from Spain to Lady Suffolk. He planted the twig, which rooted and thrived. The legend is that all England's willows are descended from that one twig.

The willow is one of the four named trees from which branches are taken to celebrate the Jewish festival of booths or tabernacles, a feast of thanksgiving in the fall for the harvest that will sustain life. The HB (OT) Book of Leviticus records the LORD telling Moses that the Israelites are to gather willows of the brook on the first of seven days and rejoice before the LORD (Lev 23:40).

In one version of the Osiris story, "it was the willow which sheltered his body after he was killed."[27] After he was lured into a box, which was sealed and thrown into the Nile, the coffin washed to the shore of Byblos, where a willow grew around it.[28] In other versions of the story, it is a tamarisk tree (see Tamarisk). "Many towns in Egypt with tombs in which a part of the dismembered Osiris was believed to be buried had groves of willows associated with them."[29]

---

25. Tresidder, *Dictionary of Symbols*, 518.
26. Ibid.
27. Witcombe, "Trees and the Sacred."
28. Dunn, "Tree Goddesses."
29. Witcombe, "Trees and the Sacred."

Thus, while the willow tree is primarily associated with lamentation, sorrow, disappointment, and grief, it is also a sign of life. It's most valuable trait is its flexibility. It reminds people that adaptability is the key ingredient in most life experiences. The ability to be flexible and adapt is what nourishes insight or inner wisdom. While the trunk of the tree is firmly planted in the ground with roots that reach far and wide, the branches remain flexible; they are able to sway in the wind and bend without breaking. Those on a spiritual path know that surrendering to life rather than fighting it is what gives a person a deeper understanding of himself or herself. The adaptability of the sacred willow is the teacher of this great truth.

Journal/Meditation: What tree represents adaptability for you? Does that tree also signify sorrow, disappointment, and regret? How? Does it signify inner wisdom? How?

Prayer: Father of my Lord Jesus Christ, you summoned your people to celebrate the life that you gave them by rejoicing before you with branches from the willow trees that grew near streams. You also made the willow a sign of lamentation so that your people might learn your wisdom from their suffering. With the assistance of the Holy Spirit make me flexible and wise. I ask this through the same Jesus Christ, my Lord. Amen.

Yew

Text: "Old yew, which graspest at the stones / That name the underlying dead, / Thy fibers net the dreamless head, / Thy roots are wrapped about the bones. / ... And gazing on thee, sullen tree, / Sick for thy stubborn hardihood, / I seem to fail from out my blood / And grow incorporate into thee."[1]

Reflection: The two strophes above from Alfred Lord Tennyson's "In Memoriam A.H.H." are a part of a poem consisting of over one hundred thirty sections, each section consisting of three to five, four-line strophes. Subtitled "Obiit MCDDDXXXIII" (literally, *he died 1833*), the poem is an elegy for Arthur Hallam, Tennyson's closest friend and his sister's fiancée, who died suddenly at the age of twenty-two. The two strophes quoted above present the yew tree, which appears in the 1849 final edition of the poem, and illustrates the association of the yew with death, transformation, eternal life, and immortality.

The slow-growing yew tree is a conifer that can grow from thirty-three to sixty-six feet tall and display a trunk six to seven feet in diameter. The brown bark is thin and scaly, often coming off the trunk in small flakes. The dark-green, needle-like leaves are flat. Each of the soft, bright red berry-like seed cones contains a single seed. The sacred yew's primary association with death, transformation, eternal life, and immortality stems from its exceptional longevity. Trees can live for four hundred to six hundred years of age, and some arbor experts think that they can make it to over one thousand years old. One characteristic contributing to its longevity is its ability to split under the weight of advanced growth without succumbing to disease in the fracture and dying, as do many other trees. A second characteristic

---

1. Tennyson, "In Memoriam A.H.H.," 1849, section 2, lines 1–4, 13–16.

contributing to its longevity is its ability to give rise to new shoots from cut surfaces, even in its advanced age. Third, when its branches get long and touch the ground, they send down roots and send up new shoots, becoming separate but linked trunks. Fourth, ". . . the old center of the tree rots and fresh seeds grow again from within the soft center."[2] Besides propagating itself, new trees can be started from cuttings, seeds, grafting, or layering as long as the soil is moist, fertile, sandy, and loamy. The tree's association with death stems from the fact that all parts of the yew are toxic to people.

Furthermore, the yew's association with death, transformation, eternal life, and immortality either stems from the fact that trees were planted in churchyards and cemeteries and associated with the dead, or people planted them in churchyards and cemeteries because of their association with death, transformation, eternal life, and immortality. In other words, it is difficult to determine if yew trees were planted to serve as landmarks for graves or if graves were dug near yew trees because of their association with death. What may have begun as the tradition of bringing a branch of the yew tree to the tombs of the dead on All Souls Day (November 2) may also have contributed to the planting of such trees in cemeteries. Because they retain their needles year-long, yew trees, like other evergreen trees, are associated with immorality. Their longevity and toxicity would have also added to their association with immortality and death.

As noted above, in literature the yew, while it grows in other places and because of its longevity often serves as a landmark, is usually located in churchyards and cemeteries. Tennyson writes about its branches grasping the headstones in the cemetery, while under the stones lay the dead. The extensive root system, according to Tennyson, wrap around the head of the deceased, which indeed they did before the invention of modern coffins and vaults. It did not take long for the roots to pierce a wooden coffin and weave themselves through the deceased's bones. Tennyson even envies the sullen, stubborn roots of the tree which will one day incorporate him through the tree to his best friend. Caldecott reemphasizes this last statement, writing, "The Bretons believe that each corpse in the graveyard has a root of the yew tree growing in its mouth."[3]

About a hundred years before Tennyson, Robert Blair wrote a seven hundred sixty-seven line poem titled "The Grave." Its blank verse illustrated the subject of death and the graveyard featuring the yew tree. He writes about the grave this way: "Well do I know thee by thy trusty yew, / Cheerless, unsocial plant! that loves to dwell / 'Midst skulls and coffins, epitaphs

2. Caldecott, *Myths*, 192.
3. Ibid.

and worms: / Where light-heel'd ghosts, and visionary shades, / Beneath the wan cold moon (as fame reports) / Embodied, thick, perform their mystic rounds: / No other merriment, dull tree! is thine!"[4]

In 1803 William Wordsworth had written a thirty-three line poem titled "Yew Trees." The poem begins by identifying the tree's longevity. Wordsworth states that its branches were used to make weapons.[5] As will be seen later in this entry, the yew tree branches were used to make bows and longbows, and the arrows were tipped with the poison produced by the tree. That is what the poet is alluding to when he mentions weapons.

Wordsworth continues to describe the old tree and how it sends out new shoots. He mentions four yew trees "Joined in one solemn and capacious grove; / Huge trunks! and each particular trunk a growth / Of intertwisted fibers serpentine / Up-coiling and inveterately convolved . . . ."[6] Wordsworth next describes the shade given by the yew and the cemetery in which it stands. He mentions the ghostly shadows formed by the branches that hover over the graves full of skeletons.[7]

About fifty years after Wordsworth's composition, Arnold wrote "Requiescat," a sixteen-line poem about the death of an unnamed woman. Arnold begins the poem, writing: "Strew on her roses, roses, / And never a spray of yew! / In quiet she reposes; / Ah, would that I did too!"[8] The poet indicates by the title, a Latin word meaning *may she rest*, that he prefers to think of this woman as resting instead of as being dead.

Before Tennyson and Wordswoth, in "Titus Andronicus," written 1588—90, Shakespeare portrays Tamora, Queen of the Goths, narrating how others had told her "they would bind [her] . . . unto the body of a dismal yew, and leave [her] to [a] miserable death."[9] And in "Macbeth," written in 1606, the bard portrays the third of three witches assembling items to be tossed into a cauldron. Among the many things are "slips of yew silver'd in the moon's eclipse"[10] or "slips of yew slivered in the moon's eclipse."[11] Here, Shakespeare is alluding to yew used in spells to raise the dead, which is what the witches are doing. Yew could also be burned to contact the spirits of the dead.

4. Blair, "The Grave," lines 21–7.
5. Wordsworth, "Yew Trees," lines 1–4.
6. Ibid., lines 15–18.
7. Ibid., lines 19–33.
8. Arnold, "Requiescat," lines 1–4.
9. Shakespeare, "Titus Andronicus," act 2, scene 3, lines 106–108.
10. Ibid., "Macbeth," act 4, scene 1, lines 27–28.
11. Harrison, *Shakespeare*, "Macbeth," act 4, scene 1, lines 27–28.

In 1907, naturalist Gilbert White noted that a yew tree is "an emblem of mortality by [its] funereal appearance."[12] White also may be alluding to the funerary custom of carrying sprigs of yew to the grave of the deceased and either throwing them into the grave under the body or throwing them in the grave on top of the coffin. And Thomas Gray's "Elegy Written in a Country Churchyard" in the eighteenth century witnesses to the presence of the yew in the cemetery. In the poem he mentions the "yew-tree's shade, / Where heaves the turf in many a mould'ring heap, / Each in his narrow cell for ever laid, / The rude forefathers of the hamlet sleep."[13] Likewise, in William Butler Yeats "Baile and Aillinn," the late nineteenth-early twentieth-century poet presents Baile, who dies out of grief for love of Aillnn. After he is buried, according to Yeats, "... poets found, old writers say, / A yew tree where his body lay."[14] After generations had passed, the poets "wrote on tablets of thin board, / made of ... the yew, / All the love stories that they knew."[15]

In "Macbeth," Shakespeare portrays Hecate, an ancient Greek goddess—her Roman parallel being Trivia—making an appearance at the witches's cauldron. Hecate is associated with ghosts, infernal spirits, the dead, and, of course, sorcery or witchcraft because she was the governess of the liminal regions or underworld among the many other things over which she is said to preside. Bulfinch refers to her as "the goddess of the underworld,"[16] and states that this occurred "after taking part in the search for Persephone."[17] Hades, the god of the underworld, had abducted Persephone and taken her to his realm, but Demeter, her mother, and Hecate went in search of her. Later, Hecate became Persephone's companion on her yearly journey to and from the underworld (see Pomegranate). So, it would come as no surprise that the yew tree, associated with death, was sacred to her. Suffness writes:

> Greeks held the yew to be sacred to Hecate.... Her attendants draped wreaths of yew around the necks of black bulls which they slaughtered in her honor, and yew boughs were burned on funeral pyres. The yew was associated with the alphabet, and the scientific name for yew today, *taxus*, was probably derived from the Greek word for yew, *toxos*, which is hauntingly similar to *toxon*, the word for bow, and *toxicon*, the word for poison. It is

12. "Churchyard Trees," *Saturday Review*, 331.
13. Gray, "Elegy," lines 13–16.
14. Yeats, "Baile and Allinn," lines 87–8.
15. Ibid., lines 95–7.
16. Bulfinch, *Mythology*, 134.
17. Ibid., 911.

presumed that the latter were named after the tree because of its superiority for both bows and poison.[18]

In one version of the Greek myth of Krokos (Crocus), he is the lover and rejected suitor of the nymph Smilax. In another version of the myth, he fails to notice the advances of Smilax, and she wastes away. And in a third version of the tale, Krokos witnesses the death of his beloved Smilax and the gods, pitying his grief, turn him into the saffron crocus and Smilax's corpse into a yew tree.[19]

Caldecott narrates the Celtic myth of "Deirdre and the Yew Tree." Deirdre, daughter of the bard Phelim, was so stunningly beautiful that Conor MacNessa, king of Ulster, decided to marry her. She, however, was in love with a young man named Naoise, with whom she fled to Scotland. After being lured back to Ireland, Naoise was killed, and she ended up as MacNessa's bride. Caldecott, quoting Delaney, writes: "In the end she committed suicide, and from her grave grew a yew tree. 'The branches twined and spread across the wide countryside until they found the branches of another yew which had grown from the grave of Naoise.'"[20] This love story illustrates not only the yew's connection to death, but also the tree's branches and roots incorporating all the dead as one.

Because of its strength, yew wood was particularly suited to making bows. The wood is classified as a closed-pore softwood, which makes it the hardest of the softwoods while also giving it an elasticity. Its deep golden orange with deep red core when polished made it the wood of choice once the longbow was invented. The arrows used in the bows could be tipped with poison made from the yew; the whole tree is poisonous except the fleshy part surrounding the seed. The druids with the belief in reincarnation preferred the wood of the yew tree for making their wands and saw the tree as a natural sign of everlasting life. There is even a tradition that the cross upon which Jesus of Nazareth was crucified was made from the yew tree; this most likely came from the yew's representation of immortality and from a yew tree in Wales that bled a red substance that looked like blood. Furthermore, the association of the wood of the cross with the yew tree could have come from the carrying of yew branches—probably because of their abundant availability—instead of palm branches on Palm Sunday. There is also a tradition of decorating churches with yew branches on Easter Sunday to represent Christ's immortality, that is, his resurrection from the dead. In a ballad titled "The Leaves of Light," the third verse specifically states that

18. Suffness, *Taxol*, 28.
19. "Crocus as Fertility Daemon."
20. Caledcott, *Myths*, 192; cf. Delaney, *Celts*, 157.

Jesus was crucified on a yew tree: "And they went down into yonder town / and sat in the Gallery. / And there they saw sweet Jesus Christ / Hanging from a big yew tree."[21]

The Native American Haida called the yew *haida*, denoting a bow-plant and indicating its primary use. However, it was also used by other various tribes to make harpoons, fish spears, fish clubs, war clubs, canoe paddles, halibut hooks, canoe bailers, dishes, bowls, spoons, needles, mauls, tool handles, spring poles for deer traps, awls, pegs, and drum frames. More recently, the leaves and the bark of the tree have been found to contain taxol, an anti-cancer agent that inhibits cancer cell growth.

Thus, there can be little doubt that the yew tree's primary association is with death, transformation, eternal life, and immortality. As early as 1636—long before the poets Tennyson, Blair, Wordsworth, Arnold, and Shakespeare associated the tree with death and gave it a sinister and morbid identity—Robert Turner, a seventeenth-century translator of many mystical and medico-chemical texts, had written: "If the yew be set in a place subject to poisonous vapors, the very branches will draw and imbibe them, hence it is conceived that the judicious [people] in former times planted it in churchyards . . . because those places [were] fuller of putrefaction and gross oleaginous vapors exhaled out of the graves by the setting sun . . . ."[22] Due to its longevity and its toxicity, the sacred yew tree has become a paradoxical emblem of mortality and immortality.

Journal/Meditation: With what tree do you associate mortality and immortality? With what tree do you associate death, transformation, and eternal life?

Prayer: Ever-living God, the evergreen yew signifies your eternity and the immortality for which I hope. Give me peace as I reflect on my own death and my desire to be transformed through it just like your Son, Jesus Christ, who lives and reigns with you and the Holy Spirit, one God, forever and ever. Amen.

---

21. Partridge, "Yew Trees."
22. Ibid.

Zaqqum

Text: "Is this better or the tree of Zaqqum which we have reserved as punishment for evil-doers? It is a tree that grows at the bottom of hell. Its spathes are like the prickly pear. They will eat and fill their bellies with it, washing it down with boiling water. Then to hell they will surely be returned." (*Quran* 37:62–68)

Reflection: The tree of Zaqqum appears only in *The Quran*, in which it is mentioned by name three times (*Quran* 37:62; 44:43; 56:52). This tree, identified earlier in the book as "the accursed tree of the *Quran*" (*Quran* 17:60) or as "the cursed tree (mentioned) in the *Quran*,"[1] is a tree Allah created; it is bitter and pungent and grows at the bottom of hell; it is "a tree that springs out of the bottom of hell fire."[2] It is reserved as punishment for evil-doers; it is "a trial for the wrong-doers;"[3] it is for "the erring and the deniers" (*Quran* 56:51) or those who "go wrong and treat (truth) as falsehood."[4]

According to *The Quran*, "The tree of Zaqqum will indeed be the food of sinners" (*Quran* 44:43–44) or "the food of the sinful."[5] That food is described as being like the leafy sheaths of prickly pears; "the shoots of its fruit stalks are like the heads of devils."[6] "It is like pitch. It will fume in the belly" (*Quran* 44:45); it is "[l]ike molten brass; it will boil in their insides."[7] Any

1. Quran, intratext.com, 17:60.
2. Ibid., 37:64.
3. Ibid., 37:63.
4. Ibid., 56:51.
5. Ibid., 44:44.
6. Ibid., 37:65.
7. Ibid., 44:45.

description communicates the idea that when the people in hell get hungry and come to get food from this tree, the food is difficult to eat and swallow. In other words, one of the punishments of hell is such intense hunger that it forces one to eat from the tree of Zaqqum and fill one's belly with this thorn-like food (*Quran* 56:53) which will burn lips, mouths, and insides.

Besides the intense punishment of hunger in hell, there is also the punishment of intense thirst. *The Quran* describes how the person in hell washes down the awful food with boiling water (*Quran* 44:46) or "a mixture made of boiling water;"[8] he or she drinks over the food "scalding water, lapping it up like female camels raging of thirst with disease" (*Quran* 56:54–55), or he or she "drinks boiling water on top of [the food] like diseased camels raging with thirst!"[9] In other words, the food boils and burns like molten brass in one's abdomen, and the resulting thirst forces the person in hell to drink boiling water.

After satisfying their hunger and thirst, evil-doers and sinners will be returned to hell, "to the (blazing) fire."[10] "'Seize him and drag him into the depths of hell,' (it will be said). 'Then pour over his head the torment of scalding water.' 'Taste it,' (they will be told). 'You were indeed the mighty and noble! This is certainly what you had denied'" (*Quran* 44:47–50). Another translation of the same verses states: "(A voice will cry): 'Seize . . . him and drag him into the midst of the blazing fire! Then pour over his head the chastisement of boiling water. Taste . . . (this)! Truly [were you] mighty, full of honor! Truly this is what [you] used to doubt!'"[11]

This description of the tree of Zaqqum and the tortures in hell that accompany those eating from it—identified as "those of the left hand" (*Quran* 56:9a)—are meant to be contrasted to the "gardens of tranquility" (*Quran* 56:12) with "such fruits as [the foremost] fancy" (*Quran* 56:20). Others, "those of the right hand" (*Quran* 56:27), "will be in (the shade) of thornless lote and acacia covered with heaps of bloom, lengthened shadows, gushing water, and fruits numberless, unending, [and] unforbidden" (*Quran* 56:28–32). Thus, while gardens of food await those who submit to God's will, the bitter, pungent, and sacred Zaqqum tree growing at the bottom of hell is the only source of food for the condemned.

8. Ibid., 37:67.
9. Ibid., 56:54–55.
10. Ibid., 37:68.
11. Ibid., 44:47–50.

Journal/Meditation: What tree represents hell for you? What characteristics of the tree enable you to associate it with hell?

Prayer: With your Holy Spirit, heavenly Father, guide me in your ways. Help me to learn from your Son, Jesus, how to do your will. After a life in your service on earth grant that I may be received into the kingdom where you live and reign with my Lord Jesus Christ and the Holy Spirit in perfect Trinity forever and ever. Amen.

Conclusion and Trees in Film

Text: "Trees are the earth's endless effort to speak to the listening heaven." (Rabindranath Tagore)

Reflection: Tagore's words animate trees, giving them a voice, much like Bradbury gave a voice to the hemlock tree in *The Hemlock Tree and Its Legends*. Just like the earth never gets tired of growing trees, so heaven never gets tired of listening to their words—and neither should we! Forty trees have been presented in the preceding pages; each of them is a part of the environment; each of them is permeated by Spirit and, thus, reveals the divine to us. That is why they are sacred. They embody spirit, and as part of the universe, they mediate spirit, that is, they mediate the divine. Writing in *Laudato Si'*, Pope Francis states: ". . . [T]he awareness that each creature reflects something of God and has a message to convey to us, and the security that Christ has taken unto himself this material world and now, risen, is intimately present to each being, surrounding it with his affection and penetrating it with his light" can enrich and "help nurture that sublime fraternity [we have] with all creation. . . ."[1]

Trees breathe in carbon dioxide and breathe out oxygen, while we do exactly the opposite. This fact alone reminds us of our dependence on trees to purify the air. In other words, trees are in us, and we are in trees. We are in relationship with trees—regardless if we desire it or not—because we share a common animating spirit. They can be counted among the "sparkly bits of the holy everywhere."[2] Francis writes: "The universe unfolds in God, who fills it completely. Hence, there is a mystical meaning to be found in a

---

1. Francis, *Laudato Si'*, par. 221.
2. Taylor, "Praying at the Edge," 264.

leaf.... The ideal is... to discover God in all things."³ Griffith quotes Siemen declaring, "Nature can no longer be treated as a thing or property that we humans have a right to dominate and exploit."⁴ Again, Francis writes:

> If we approach nature and the environment without ... openness to awe and wonder, if we no longer speak the language of fraternity and beauty in our relationship with the world, our attitude will be that of masters, consumers, ruthless exploiters, unable to set limits on their immediate needs. By contrast, if we feel intimately united with all that exists, then sobriety and care will well up spontaneously.... [N]ature [is] a magnificent book in which God speaks to us and grants us a glimpse of his infinite beauty and goodness.... The world is a joyful mystery to be contemplated with gladness and praise.⁵

Francis' approach to trees and the rest of creation is, thus, wonder. Employing Trinitarian thinking, he writes:

> The Father is the ultimate source of everything, the loving and self-communicating foundation of all that exists. The Son, his reflection, through whom all things were created, united himself to this earth when he was formed in the womb of Mary. The Spirit, infinite bond of love, is intimately present at the very heart of the universe, inspiring and bringing new pathways.⁶

He adds "that the Trinity has left its mark on all creation."⁷ In other places in *Laudato Si'* he encourages his readers "to think of the whole as open to God's transcendence,"⁸ to use the "environment as a way of expressing ... identity,"⁹ to see that "there is a nobility in the duty to care for creation through little daily actions" like "planting trees,"¹⁰ and to learn "to see and appreciate beauty."¹¹ He elaborates on this last point, writing, "If someone has not learned to stop and admire something beautiful, we should not be surprised if he or she treats everything as an object to be used and abused without scruple."¹²

---

3. Francis, *Laudato Si'*, par. 233.
4. Griffith, "Organic Habits," 16.
5. Francis, *Laudato Si'*, pars. 11–12.
6. Ibid., par 238.
7. Ibid., par. 239.
8. Ibid., par. 79.
9. Ibid., par. 147.
10. Ibid., par. 211.
11. Ibid., par. 215.
12. Ibid.

In other words, the pope is interested in a sound ecological spirituality in much the same way as this book has been focused on the spirituality of trees. Feldmeier states: "Spirituality... describes engagement in things transcendental. Ultimate aims. Ultimate goals. It has to do with one's connection with and commitment to ways of engaging transcendence."[13] Feldmeier adds, "In a theistic religion... this transcendence is God. Christian spirituality is engagement with God as God has revealed himself in Jesus Christ."[14] Francis says that "all sound spirituality entails both welcoming divine love and adoration, confident in the Lord because of his infinite power."[15]

Feldmeier states that "everyone has ideas about what [he or she thinks] makes life meaningful or how [he or she pursues] the ultimate, even if [he or she has not] articulated what exactly that means."[16] He explains that spirituality is humbly "seeking to encounter a living, personal God."[17] Francis adds, "A spirituality which forgets God as all-powerful and Creator is not acceptable. That is how we end up worshipping earthly powers, or ourselves usurping the place of God, even to the point of claiming an unlimited right to trample his creation underfoot."[18] A healthy ecological spirituality, according to Francis, is realizing "[n]ature is nothing other than a certain kind of art, namely God's art, impressed upon things, whereby those things are moved to a determinate end."[19] The art of God that we have examined in this book is the variety of trees that populate our earth.

Trees are not objects to be consumed; they are objects to be honored because they are spirit bearers. By exploring the connections between trees and religions, myths, legends, fables, tales, and other types of stories, we put into practice *Nostra Aetate*, the "Declaration on the Relation of the Church to Non-Christian Religions" issued by Vatican Council II on October 28, 1965. "Throughout history even to the present day," states the declaration, "there is found among different peoples a certain awareness of a hidden power, which lies behind the course of nature and the events of human life. At times there is present even a recognition of a supreme being. This awareness and recognition result in a way of life that is imbued with a deep religious sense."[20]

13. Feldmeier, "What Is Spirituality?" 20.
14. Ibid.
15. Francis, *Laudato Si'*, par. 73.
16. Feldmeier, "What Is Spirituality?" 20.
17. Ibid., 21.
18. Francis, *Laudato Si'*, par. 75.
19. Ibid., par. 80.
20. Flannery, *Declaration (Nostra Aetate)*, par. 2.

This reflection on spirituality is further developed. "The Catholic Church," states the document, "rejects nothing of what is true and holy in [other] religions. She has a high regard for the manner of life and conduct, the precepts and doctrines which, although differing in many ways from her own teaching, nevertheless often reflect a ray of that truth which enlightens all men [and women]."[21] Besides recognizing the truth that is found in Hinduism, Buddhism, Islam, and Judaism—with which Christians share "a common spiritual heritage"[22]—the church also "urges her sons [and daughters] to enter with prudence and charity into discussion and collaboration with members of other religions" and "acknowledge, preserve, and encourage the spiritual and moral truths found among non-Christians."[23] Through various texts, reflections, journal/meditation questions, and prayers all focused on sacred trees, we have done just that in this book.

Borrowing a phrase from Teilhard de Chardin, a twentieth-century mystic, we have discovered that we are living in the divine milieu. The universe is drenched, saturated with the divine, and trees are but one manifestation of the ongoing evolutionary process. Through the honor we show to trees, we are co-creators with God in the living system known as the universe. The spirit manifested through trees is like energy, spiritual energy, whose source is God. We see it in the bowing and the bending of trees in the wind, in the deep recesses of the earth where roots ground the trees, and in the leaves, blossoms, and fruit which the trees produce. It is not difficult to see how such awe led ancient ancestors to worship the tree instead of the One manifest in the spiritual energy in the tree.

Living in this divine milieu should lead us to ongoing transformation, the very purpose of spirituality. "Any spiritual path that doesn't lead to real transformation is, at best, useless," states Feldmeier.[24] He adds, "There's a lot of cheap spirituality with no transformation."[25] In other words, once we value the trees of the environment, then we change our minds and, consequently, our behavior concerning them. Francis repeatedly emphasizes the need for transformation in *Laudato Si'*. He states, "If we acknowledge the value and the fragility of nature and, at the same time, our God-given abilities, we can finally leave behind the modern myth of unlimited material progress."[26] Francis writes that each creature, and I would add each tree, "has

21. Ibid.
22. Ibid., par. 4.
23. Ibid., par. 2
24. Feldmeier, "What Is Spirituality?" 22.
25. Ibid., 23.
26. Francis, *Laudato Si'*, par. 78.

its own purpose. None is superfluous. The entire material universe speaks of God's love, his boundless affection for us. Soil, water, mountains [trees]: everything is, as it were, a caress of God."[27] Francis continues, writing that once we understand "that nature as a whole not only manifests God but is also a locus of his presence," then "discovering this presence leads us to cultivate the 'ecological virtues.'"[28] Among these virtues is that of universal communion. "... [A]ll of us are linked by unseen bonds and together form a kind of universal family, a sublime communion which fills us with a sacred, affectionate, and humble respect."[29] Another virtue entails "a distinctive way of looking at things, a way of thinking, policies, an educational program, a lifestyle, and a spirituality which together generate resistance to the assault of the technocratic paradigm,"[30] that is, "life ... becomes a surrender to situations conditioned by technology, itself viewed as the principal key to the meaning of existence."[31] Another ecological virtue is what the pope calls the "logic of receptivity"; that is, the environment "is on loan to each generation, which must then hand it on to the next."[32]

Francis writes, "The environment is one of those goods that cannot be adequately safeguarded or promoted by market forces."[33] He explains:

> The principle of the maximization of profits, frequently isolated from other considerations, reflects a misunderstanding of the very concept of the economy. As long as production is increased, little concern is given to whether it is at the cost of future resources or the health of the environment; as long as the clearing of a forest increases production, no one calculates the losses entailed in the desertification of the land, the harm done to biodiversity, or the increased pollution.[34]

Another ecological virtue that is needed is awareness of how the market manipulates people into being consumers. "Since the market tends to promote extreme consumerism in an effort to sell its products," writes Francis, "people can easily get caught up in a whirlwind of needless buying and spending."[35] The only way to stop this, according to Shapiro, is "the practice

27. Ibid., par. 84.
28. Ibid., par. 88.
29. Ibid. par. 89.
30. Ibid, par. 111.
31. Ibid., par. 110.
32. Ibid., par. 159.
33. Ibid., par. 190.
34. Ibid., par 195.
35. Ibid., par. 203.

of moving from alienation to integration, from the smaller self that insists it is apart from God to the greater Self that knows itself and everything else as a part of God."[36] Moore adds that we need more "prayers that articulate the privileged way the sacraments take up nature, enabling the natural world to be a means of mediating supernatural life. . . . [F]lora . . . [has] a direct bearing on the spirituality of believers."[37]

There is but one environment on the earth we share, and sacred trees are a part of it. Paul would probably not mind if we paraphrase a small part of his First Letter to the Corinthians: There are varieties of trees, but the same Spirit; and there are varieties of fruits, but the same Lord; and there are varieties of wood softness and hardness, but it is the same God who activates all of them in all the trees. To each tree is given the manifestation of the Spirit for the common good. To the fig is given through the Spirit the utterance of wisdom, and to the oak the utterance of knowledge according to the same Spirit, to the mulberry faith by the same Spirit, to the willow gifts of healing by the one Spirit, to the yew the working of miracles, to the bramble prophecy, to the olive the discernment of spirits, to the hemlock various kinds of tongues, to the palm the interpretation of tongues. All these are activated by one and the same Spirit, who allots to each one individually just as the Spirit chooses. For just as the earth is one and yet it has many trees, and all the trees of the earth, though many, form one environment, so it is with Christ (cf. 1 Cor 12:4–12).

36. Shapiro, "Roadside Assistance," 19.
37. Moore, "Let Justice Find a Voice," 209, 213.

Trees in a Few Modern Films

The Lord of the Rings: The Two Towers

In the last twenty-five years of film-making, trees have stared in movies, and they have illustrated care for the environment as well as an ecological spirituality. For example, who could forget Peter Jackson's *The Lord of the Rings* trilogy? In *The Two Towers* (2002), we meet Treebeard (John Rhys-Davies), a tree shepherd in Fangorn Forest. In the book, Gandalf, the White Wizard, describes him as "the eldest and chief of the Ents, and when [one] speaks with him, [he] ... hears the speech of the oldest of all living things."[38] In his dialogue with the hobbit named Pippin in the book, Treebeard explains: "Some of us are still true Ents, and lively enough in our fashion, but many are growing sleepy, going tree-ish, as you might say. Most of the trees are just trees, of course; but many are half awake. Some are quite wide awake, and a few are, well, ah, well getting Entish."[39]

Because of the constraints put on art—what can be done in a book cannot be done in film, and vice-versa—in Tolkien's book, Treebeard narrates some of the history of his kind.

> When the world was young, and the woods were wise and wild, the Ents and the Entwives—and there were Entmaidens then: ah! .... [T]he Ents gave their love to things that they met in the world, and the Entwives gave their thought to other things, for the Ents loved the great trees, and the wild woods, and the slopes of the high hills; and they drank of the mountain streams, and ate only such fruit as the trees let fall in their path; and they learned of the Elves and spoke with the trees. But the Entwives gave their minds to the lesser trees .... The Entwives ordered them to grow according to their wishes, and bear leaf and fruit to their liking .... So the Entwives made gardens to live in ....[40]

Later in the book, Pippin asks Treebeard about Entmoot, and he informs him that it is a gathering of Ents "which does not happen nowadays."[41] In the film, Treebeard names the trees which have come to the Entmoot: "Beech, oak, chestnut, ash .... Many have come."[42]

---

38. Tolkien, *Lord: Two Towers*, 164.
39. Ibid., 71.
40. Ibid., 79.
41. Ibid. 82.
42. Jackson, Screenplay: *Two Towers*, no page numbers.

After the Entmoot, the Ents decide to attack Isengard in order to destroy the evil that has taken root there. Treebeard explains this to Pippin after he comments about how quickly the Ents made up their minds to destroy Isengard. Treebeard says, "Indeed I have not seen them roused like this for many an age. We Ents do not like being roused; and we never are roused unless it is clear to us that our trees and our lives are in great danger."[43] To Merry Treebeard says, "[The Ents] are all roused now, and their mind is all on one thing: breaking Isengard."[44] Later, addressing both Pippin and Merry, Treebeard states, "Of course, it is likely enough, my friends..., likely enough that we are going to our doom; the last march of the Ents. But if we stayed at home and did nothing, doom would find us anyway, sooner or later. That thought has long been growing in our hearts; and that is why we are marching now."[45] In the film, seeing the tree stumps that Saruman has left at the edge of the forest, Treebeard says, "Many of these trees were my friends. Creatures I had known from nut and acorn."[46]

Ultimately, as Jackson displays in the film, the Ents destroy Isengard by releasing the water that Saruman (Christopher Lee) had dammed, thus creating a flood that destroyed all of his underground operations of creating Orcs and making weapons. In the book Pippin describes what he and Merry witnessed:

> [W]e sat high up above the floods and watched the drowning of Isengard. The Ents keep on pouring in more water, till all the fires were quenched and every cave filled. The fogs slowly gathered together and steamed up into a huge umbrella of cloud; it must have been a mile high. In the evening there was a great rainbow over the eastern hills.... It all went very quiet.... The Ents stopped the inflow in the night, and sent the Isen [River] back into its old course. And that was the end of it all.[47]

What Tolkien illustrated in the book and what Jackson interpreted into film is the ancient concept of sacred groves of trees. A small group of trees within a forest was considered sacred. As we have seen repeatedly in this book, people who practiced various religions revered and respected such sacred sites. In Tolkien's work, the Ents, a race of beings that closely resemble trees, take the side of good in order to destroy evil. The sacred grove awakens and wipes out Isengard.

43. Tolkien, *Lord: Two Towers*, 89.
44. Ibid.
45. Ibid., 90.
46. Jackson, Screenplay: *Two Towers*, no page numbers.
47. Tolkien, *Lord: Two Towers*, 177.

The Lord of the Rings: The Fellowship of the Ring

In *The Lord of the Rings: The Fellowship of the Ring*, the first book in Tolkien's trilogy, Lord Celeborn, Galadriel the Lady of Lorien, and the Silvan Elves live in trees. As the members of the fellowship had entered Lothlorien, Tolkien described one tree in the forest:

> The branches of the mallorn tree grew out nearly straight from the trunk, and then swept upward; but near the top the main stem divided into a crown of many boughs, and among these they found that there had been built a wooden platform .... It was reached by a round hole in the center through which the ladder passed.[48]

Once the fellowship got to the city of the Galadrim, Tolkien described

> the mightiest of all the trees; its great smooth bole gleamed like gray silk, and up it towered, until its first branches, far above, opened their huge limbs under shadowy clouds of leaves. Beside it a broad white ladder stood. ... At a great height above the ground [was a platform] like the deck of a great ship. On it was built a house, so large that almost it would have served for a hall of men upon the earth. ... [It was] a chamber of oval shape, in the midst of which grew the trunk of the great mallorn, now tapering towards its crown, and yet making still a pillar of wide girth.[49]

The script for the second film describes the fellowship standing on a hill.

> They look with wonderment at the vista spread before them. Several miles towards the south, a large hill rises out of the woods. Upon the hill rise many mighty mallorn trees, taller than any others. Nestled high in the crown of the mallorns is a beautiful city. It gleams in the low rays of the late afternoon sun—green, gold, and silver. ... The fellowship steps onto a wide fleet filled with a soft light. The walls are green and silver, the roof gold, and in its midst is the trunk of the mighty mallorn tree, now tapering toward its crown.[50]

---

48. Tolkien, *Lord: Fellowship*, 374.
49. Ibid., 387.
50. Walsh, Screenplay: *Fellowship of the Ring*, 99–100.

The Lord of the Rings: The Return of the King

Tolkien's third use of a tree in his *The Lord of the Rings* trilogy is found in *The Return of the King*. However, it is first mentioned in *The Fellowship of the Ring*. In Minas Tirith "in the courts of the king grew a white tree. . . . But in the wearing of the swift years of Middle Earth . . . the tree withered . . . ."[51] The white tree is mentioned in *The Two Towers* by Faramir, the younger son of Denethor, steward of Gondor, who states, "I would see the white tree in flower again in the courts of the kings . . . ."[52] In *King*, Gandalf and Pippin notice in the court a fountain, "but in the midst, drooping over the pool, stood a dead tree, and the falling drops dripped sadly from its barren and broken branches back into the clear water. . . . It looked mournful . . . and [Pippin] wondered why the dead tree was left in this place where everything else was well tended."[53] Finally, a great eagle brings tidings to the people of Gondor: ". . . [The] king shall come again, and he shall dwell among you all the days of your life. And the tree that was withered shall be renewed, and he shall plant it in the high places, and the city shall be blessed."[54] Later in the book, Gandalf instructs Aragorn where to find the new tree that is to be planted in the court of the king.[55] ". . . [T]he tree grew and blossomed."[56] However, in the translation of the book into film, Jackson portrays Gandalf and Pippin passing by the dead tree and Pippin's eye caught by the "dead tree that stands in the middle of the court of Minas Tirith."[57] The next time the tree is seen, a single blossom appears on the end of one branch, a camera shot that is not even recorded in the script! In the extended edition of the film, the scene is labeled "41. The Tomb of the Stewards." In the script, the scene is labeled "Ext. Minis Tirith, Court of the Kings,"[58] but there is no camera direction given as to a close up of the blossom on the dead tree. The third time the tree appears is a close up of Aragorn (Viggo Mortensen) "wearing a breast plate emblazoned with the white tree."[59]

---

51. Tolkien, *Lord: Fellowship*, 271.
52. Tolkien, *Lord: Two Towers*, 279.
53. Tolkien, *Lord: Return of the King*, 23.
54. Ibid., 245.
55. Ibid., 254.
56. Ibid., 256.
57. Walsh, Screenplay: *Return of the King*, 29.
58. Ibid., 94.
59. Ibid., 123.

The Chronicles of Narnia: Prince Caspian

Tolkien used many other trees in his other books and stories. However, these illustrate the point being made here: Sacred trees are used in books and film. Furthermore, C.S. Lewis, one of Tolkien's contemporaries, also used trees in his books which have been translated into films. Like Tolkien, Lewis incorporated trees in several of his books in *The Chronicles of Narnia* series. We limit our examination to *Prince Caspian* primarily because it is one of the three books in the *Narnia* series that has been turned into a film: *The Chronicles of Narnia: Prince Caspian* (2008).

In *Prince Caspian*, the Pevensie siblings—Peter, Susan, Edmund, and Lucy—return to Narnia, which they had visited before in *The Chronicles of Narnia: The Lion, the Witch, and the Wardrobe* (2005). Hundreds of years have passed in Narnia. They are enlisted to help ward off the evil King Miraz and restore the rightful heir to the throne, Prince Caspian. What interests us here is the use of trees. Thus, while rowing a boat on Glasswater Creek, Lucy (Georgie Henley), looking up at the trees, says to Trumpkin (Peter Dinklage), a dwarf, "They're so still." Trumpkin replies, "They're trees. What do you expect?" Lucy says, "They used to dance." Trumpkin says, "It wasn't long after you left that the Telmarines invaded. Those that survived retreated to the woods. And the trees have retreated so deeply inside themselves that no one has heard from them since."[60] The Telmarines are descendants of pirates who had invaded Narnia. There is no comparable material in the book.

---

60. Adamson, Screenplay, *Prince Caspian*, 15.

A few scenes later, "at dawn, Lucy hears a growl and wakes up.... She pushes branches out of the way as she makes her way through the forest. A dryad [, a spirit of a Narnian tree, sometimes also referred to as a hamadryad] floats past her laughing. The trees move aside, making way for her."[61] In the book, this scene is described by Lewis this way:

> Lucy's eyes began to grow accustomed to the light, and she saw the trees that were nearest her more distinctly. A great longing for the old days when the trees could talk in Narnia came over her. She knew exactly how each of these trees would talk if only she could wake them, and what sort of human form it would put on. She looked at a silver birch; it would have a soft, showery voice and would look like a slender girl, with hair blown all about her face, and fond of dancing. She looked at the oak; he would be wizened, but hearty old man with a frizzled beard and warts on his face and hands, and hair growing out of the warts. She looked at the beech under which she was standing. Ah!—she would be the best of all. She would be a gracious goddess, smooth and stately, the lady of the wood.[62]

After that lengthy scene-setting narrative, Lucy speaks, saying, "'Oh, Trees, Trees, Trees!' (though she had not been intending to speak at all). 'Oh, Trees, wake, wake, wake. Don't you remember it? Don't you remember me? Dryads and hamadryads, come out, come to me.'" The narrator continues, "Though there was not a breath of wind they all stirred about her. The rustling noise of the leaves was almost like words.... The rustling died away."[63]

During the next night, Lucy hears her name called and wakes from sleep. She sees the forest bathed in moonlight. She also sees a glade of trees at which she looks very hard.

> "Why, I do believe they're moving," she said to herself. "They're walking about." She got up ... and walked towards them. There was certainly a noise in the glade, a noise such as trees make in a high wind, through there was no wind tonight. Yet it was not exactly an ordinary tree noise either. Lucy felt there was a tune in it, but she could not catch the tune any more than she had been able to catch the words when the trees had so nearly talked to her the night before. But there was, at least, a lilt; she felt her own feet wanting to dance as she got nearer. And now there was no doubt that the trees were really moving—moving in and out through one another as if in a complicated country dance. ("And

61. Ibid., 24.
62. Lewis, *Prince Caspian*, 103.
63. Ibid., 103–4.

I suppose," thought Lucy, "when trees dance, it must be a very, very country dance indeed.") She was almost among them now.[64]

Lewis continues to narrate the scene:

> The first tree she looked at seemed at first glance to be not a tree at all but a huge man with a shaggy beard and great bushes of hair. . . . But when she looked again he was only a tree, though he was still moving. You couldn't see whether he had feet or roots, of course, because when trees move they don't walk on the surface of the earth; they wade in it as we do in water. The same thing happened with every tree she looked at. At one moment they seemed to be the friendly, lovely giant and giantess forms which the tree people put on when some good magic has called them into full life; next moment they all looked like trees again. But when they looked like trees, it was like strangely human trees, and when they looked like people, it was like strangely branchy and leafy people—and all the time that queer, lilting, rustling, cool, merry noise. 'They are almost awake, not quite,' said Lucy. She knew she herself was wide awake, wider than anyone usually is.[65]

Lucy dances among the trees, gradually making her way through them to a central open space "with dark trees dancing all round it."[66] And there she meets the huge lion, Aslan. After some dialogue between the two, they pass through the trees. Lewis narrates: "The trees parted to let them through and for one second assumed their human forms completely. Lucy had a glimpse of tall and lovely wood gods and wood goddesses all bowing to the Lion; next moment they were trees again, but still bowing, with such graceful sweeps of branch and trunk that their bowing was itself a kind of dance."[67]

Before the great battle, Lewis narrates: "The sound, deep and throbbing at first like an organ beginning on a low note, rose and became louder, and then far louder again, till the earth and air were shaking with it."[68] Lewis continues:

> What Lucy and Susan saw was a dark something coming to them from almost every direction across the hills. It looked like a black moss creeping on the ground, then like the stormy waves of a black sea rising higher and higher as it came on, and then, at last, like what it was—woods on the move. All the trees of the world

64. Ibid., 121.
65. Ibid., 121–2.
66. Ibid. 122.
67. Ibid. 126.
68. Ibid., 135.

> appeared to be rushing towards Aslan. But as they drew nearer they looked less like trees, and when the whole crowd, bowing and curtsying and waving thin long arms to Aslan, were all around Lucy, she saw that it was a crowd of human shapes. Pale birth girls were tossing their heads, willow women pushed back their hair from their brooding faces to gaze on Aslan, the queenly beeches stood still and adored him, shaggy oak men lean and melancholy elms, shock headed hollies (dark themselves, but their wives all bright with berries) and gay rowans, all bowed and rose again, shouting, "Aslan, Aslan!" in their various husky or creaking or wave-like voices. The crowd and the dance round Aslan (for it had become a dance once more) grew so thick and rapid that Lucy was confused. She never saw where certain other people came from who were soon capering about among the trees.[69]

In the film version, Aslan roars, and the battle continues. In the meantime, the awakened trees enter into the fray. According to the film script, "a tree root grabs [Caspian] and pulls him away. Peter (William Moseley) helps Caspian (Ben Barnes) out of the pit... and they see that the trees have come. Telmarines continue launching rocks, and one of them knocks over a tree. Another tree sticks a root into the ground. It comes up further down, taking out a trebuchet."[70]

Lewis is more descriptive. The Old Narnians shriek, "The Wood! The Wood!"[71] Lewis narrates: "But soon neither their cries nor the sound of weapons could be heard any more, for both were drowned in the ocean-like roar of the Awakened Trees as they plunged through the ranks of Peter's army, and then on, in pursuit of the Telmarines." Seemingly now to address the reader, Lewis writes:

> Have you ever stood at the edge of great wood on a high edge where a wild south-wester broke over it in full fury on an autumn evening? Imagine that sound. And then imagine that the wood, instead of being fixed to one place, was rushing at you; and was no longer trees but huge people; yet still like trees because their long arms waved like branches and their heads tossed and leaves fell round them in showers. It was like that for the Telmarines. It was a little alarming even for the Narnians.[72]

And thus the awakened Narnian trees help win the battle and restore Caspian to his throne.

69. Ibid., 136–7.
70. Adamson, Screenplay, *Prince Caspian*, 48.
71. Lewis, *Prince Caspian*, 167.
72. Ibid., 167–8.

Avatar

Four trees have starring roles in James Cameron's *Avatar* (2009). The script for this film was also written by Cameron. Jake Sully (Sam Worthington) goes to the distant world of Pandora, upon which lives the Na'vi in Hometree which sits "right over the richest unobtanium deposit" on the planet.[73] Sully infiltrates the Na'vi with the use of an avatar and falls in love with Neytiri (Zoe Saldana). Our interest in this film revolves around the trees in it.

The first, as already mentioned above, is Hometree. According to the script, Hometree is "Neytire's village, which is sheltered inside one of the great trees. Hometree is 250 meters [820 feet] tall, with a trunk four times the diameter of the largest Sequoia, and a base of massive mangrove-pillars."[74] It has a "helical core, . . . a kind of natural spiral staircase."[75] It is "like a gothic cathedral . . . . Sunlight streams down through gaps in the towering vault."[76] When the viewer gets to look down "the central shaft of Hometree, 80 meters [262 feet] to the ground, villagers are ant-like. [Sully] tries to keep up with Neytiri as she leaps up the core trunk like a lemur. He climbs the last section, arriving out of breath beside her. She leads him outside, onto a large branch. Through gaps in the foliage, [Sully] can see other great trees scattered across the landscape, like enormous umbrellas above the rainforest. Neytiri strides out across the branch . . . ."[77] Grace Augustine

---

73. Cameron, Screenplay: *Avatar*, 52.
74. Ibid., 44.
75. Ibid., 46.
76. Ibid., 54.
77. Ibid., 60.

(Sigourney Weaver) explains that Hometree is the Na'vi's "ancestral home. They've lived there since before human history began."[78]

Once Sully finds out the miners intend to destroy Hometree, he tells the Na'vi that they "have to get out of Hometree [and] run to the forest."[79] Miles Quaritch (Stephen Lang), who is in charge of security on Pandora, orders his helicopters to fire on Hometree.

> The inside of Hometree erupts with multiple explosions of teargas. . . . The villagers pour out of Hometree. Everyone is yelling. Piercing screams [are heard with]in the boiling gas. Inside, Hometree is a burning smoky hell. Flames roar up the insides like a chimney. Stragglers scramble outside, coughing and dragging wounded with them.[80]

Then,

> the base of Hometree vanishes in a chain of high-explosive blasts. The massive pillars fragment into matchsticks, and . . . Hometree groans and starts to move. In a cacophony of cracking, splintering roots, the mighty tree topples with agonizing slowness. . . . Hometree hits the ground like the end of the world, raising a great cloud of dust and pulverizing debris.[81]

And that is the end of Hometree.

The second tree in *Avatar* is simply referred to as the Great Tree; later it will be identified as the Mother Tree. In a scene early in the film,

> several woodsprites float down through the trees, . . . descend[ing] silently toward [Sully] and Neytiri. . . . The woodsprites, pulsing with purpose, gloat right towards [Sully]. They dance gently around his shoulders and head. . . . More woodsprites gather around him. Several alight on him. [Sully] holds still . . . . He spreads his arms. More sprites come, landing all over his arms, hands, body.[82]

He asks Neytire, "What are they?" She responds. "Atokirina. Seeds of the Great Tree—very pure spirits." The script continues, "Jake, now a pulsing, glowing, fluttering mass of light, moves one hand slowly, not wanting to break the spell. He studies one of the sprites dancing on his palm until . . . the woodsprites

78. Ibid., 81.
79. Ibid., 107.
80. Ibid., 107–8.
81. Ibid., 109.
82. Ibid., 42.

whirl up and away, scattering into the darkness."[83] In the context of the film, this is Sully's anointing scene. The Great Tree is choosing him for a mission, which, of course, is not clear early in the film. This scene is similar to those in biblical literature featuring someone pouring oil over the head of a leader or someone hearing the voice of God and responding in the affirmative. A little later in the story, Neytiri explains the epiphany she witnessed with Scully as being a sign that needs to be interpreted by the Tsahik.[84] The clan leader, Neytiri's father, wants to know why Neytiri did not kill Sully, and she explains: "I was going to kill him, but there was a sign from Eywa."[85] She adds, "Father, many atokirina came to [Sully]."[86] Suddenly the Tsahik, Neytiri's mother, appears; she is "the one who interprets the will of Eywa."[87]

Sully, as well as the viewer, wants to know who Eywa is. The name may come from the Proto-Germanic word for yew: *iwa*. Ewya is the Na'vi's deity, "the great mother, the goddess made up of all living things."[88] Sully reports that Neytiri speaks a lot "about the flow of energy—the spirits of the animals and what not . . . ."[89] After hunting and making a kill, Sully tells the dead animal, "Your spirit goes with Eywa; your body stays behind to become part of the people."[90] Once Sully understands that Eywa is the channel of energy through all living things, he is able to dance "from the inside," to channel "the primal energy."[91] He explains: "[The Na'vi] see a network of energy that flows through all living things. They know that all energy is only borrowed . . . and one day you have to give it back."[92] It is a deep connection that the Na'vi have to the forest. In a vision, Sully sees "a ring of glowing trees, which seem miles high. The whole image is bathed in spectral radiance. [He] looks down; his body and hands [are] transforming—fingers stretching into tendrils, legs becoming roots which spread outward across the ground, a thousand glowing dendrites which connect to the roots of the trees . . . ."[93] Sully is made a member of the Na'vi after his vision. As if to imitate what he saw in the vision, "All the members of the clan press

83. Ibid., 42–3.
84. Ibid., 44.
85. Ibid., 45.
86. Ibid., 46.
87. Ibid.
88. Ibid., 53.
89. Ibid. 64.
90. Ibid., 66.
91. Ibid., 78.
92. Ibid., 79.
93. Ibid., 86.

forward, crowding around and putting their hands on [his] shoulders, back, chest—hands upon hands—until he is connected to everyone."[94] Augustine explains this connectivity:

> What we think we know is that there's some kind of electro-chemical communication between the roots of the trees. Like the synapses between neurons. Each tree has ten to the fourth connections to the trees around it, and there are ten to the twelfth trees on Pandora. That's more connections than the human brain.... It's a network, global network. And the Na'vi can access it; they can upload and download data [and] memories....[95]

The third tree in *Avatar* is identified as the Tree of Voices. Neytiri and Sully

> run together into a stand of willows. Their trunks are as gnarled as bonsai. Long, faintly-glowing tendrils hang straight down in pastel curtains. Underfoot, a bed of moss glows faintly. It reacts to their footsteps with expanding rings of light.... The willows stir, responding to their presence. [Neytiri] holds up her hands, letting the tendrils caress her.[96]

She says, "This is a place for prayers to be heard—and sometimes answered." Meanwhile, Sully "puts out his hands and the tendrils play over his fingers, his palms, his forearms. His eyes go wide. [The viewer] hears the whispering of ancient Na'vi voices." Sully says, "It's like a sound you feel." Neytiri replies: "We call this utraya mokri—the Tree of Voices. The voices [are] of our ancestors, who live within Eywa." The woodsprites return and "circle around them, some alighting on their shoulders and arms. They stand, very close together now. Her eyes are intense, almost luminous. He feels drawn to them. But she pulls back a little." Then, Neytiri tells Sully, "... You may make your own bow from the wood of Hometree."[97]

The fourth tree in *Avatar* is located in the Well of Souls,

> a deep caldera one hundred meters [328 feet] across. It is ringed with enormous willows whose roots seem to pour down the sheer rock walls like candle wax. At the bottom, in a natural amphitheater, the [Na'vi] refugees are clustered around a central rock outcropping which forms a kind of dais and altar. Shafts of dawn light reach to the bottom of the grotto, lighting a single

---

94. Ibid., 88.
95. Ibid., 101.
96. Ibid., 88.
97. Ibid., 88–9.

willow—the Mother Tree. Ancient and gnarled, it grows in the center of the rock. Its roots spread down to the grotto floor, where they merge with the roots of the willows ringing the well—forming a braided mat resembling the surface of a brain. [Neytiri's mother] stands on the dais, leading them in a chant.[98]

She says, "Wise ancestors who live within Eywa, guide us. Give us a sign."[99] Meanwhile, the people "lift their voices in a song filled with tragic loss and yearning for deliverance."[100] Sully arrives flying and riding on the beast named Toruk Macto; this is the sign that he is their leader. Neytiri's mother "stands in a kind of trance amongst the tendrils of the Mother Tree. . . . [F]ine, hairlike threads have emerged from the roots and are gently spreading over Augustine's human skin"; she was shot in a battle and has died. Sully holds her hand and "watches her body being fused to the root-floor by a thousand connections." Augustine's avatar "is gently connected by the same questing root-cilia; they entwine with the queue and spread over the body. The grotto is dark except for the spectral glow of the willows. The chant continues, hypnotically." Neytiri's mother is "on her knees beneath the Mother Tree" and "writhes her arms in the trance state. . . ." Augustine's "eyes snap open. Her expression is amazed, as if seeing something so beautiful it can never be explained." She tells Sully, "I'm with her . . . ; she's real."[101] Augustine exhales and dies. The roots fall away from her human body and from her avatar.

In another scene, Sully returns to the Mother Tree alone. "He moves to the Mother Tree—gnarled, ancient, [and] majestic. The roots spread in all directions, like the center of the world. [He] steps forward. The willow-like tendrils sway toward him, moving in a breeze that isn't there. . . . He squats at the base of the tree." He says, "I've never done this in my life. And I'm probably just talking to a tree right now. But if you're there, I need to give you a heads up." The script states: "He looks up into the tree. The hanging tendrils undulate softly. It's easy to imagine a presence." Then, he says: "If [Augustine] is there with you, look in her memories; she can show you the world we come from. There's no green there. They killed their Mother, and they're gonna do the same thing here." The script states, "Woodsprites float in silence, moving around aimlessly." Sully explains that the battle is about to begin; "Neytiri approaches silently behind him, listening." Sully addresses the tree: "Look, you chose me for somethin'. And I'll stand and fight; you know I will. But I could use a little help here." When his prayer is finishing,

98. Ibid., 116.
99. Ibid.
100. Ibid., 118.
101. Ibid., 121.

Neytiri says, "Our Great Mother does not take sides. She protects only the balance of life."[102]

The Na'vi win the battle with the help of other tribes on Pandora, and the unobtanium miners are sent home, but Sully's avatar is severely wounded while his human body remains alive. He says, "There's a funeral tonight, and I don't want to be late. It was someone very close to me." The camera moves across "the concentric rings of people, all plugged-in and softly chanting"; this scene is meant to echo the one above involving Augustine.

> Neytiri, kneeling beside two figures on the dais—[Sully] and his avatar—lie head to head. Human [Sully] is wearing an exomask [used by humans to breathe on Pandora]. Both figures are still, hands folded, covered in translucent silken shrouds of rootcilia. . . . Neytiri removes the mask from [Sully's] human face. She gently closes his dead eyes with her fingertips. Then, [she] bends and kisses him. . . . Neytiri's hand comes into [the] frame, stroking his cheek.[103]

Then, Sully's eyes open. In other words, the Mother Tree has transferred his human intelligence to his avatar. He has been raised to new life with the Na'vi. In a scene before this last one, Sully hints at what would take place, stating, "New life keeps the energy flowing, like the breath of the world."[104]

102. Ibid., 128–9.
103. Ibid., 150–1.
104. Ibid. 150.

Other Trees

In the *Harry Potter* series of books and films, the Whomping Willow makes several appearances. However, its best showing is in *Harry Potter and the Prisoner of Azkaban* (2004). Harry Potter (Daniel Radcliffe) and Ron Weasley (Rupert Grint) crash Weasley's Flying Ford Anglia into the Whomping Willow, which violently defends itself and almost kills both Potter and Weasley. The following day some of the tree's limbs have to be bandaged. In another installment of the series, *Harry Potter and the Chamber of Secrets* (2002), the Whomping Willow destroys Potter's Nimbus 2000 broomstick when it falls into the tree's branches.

The tree is located on the grounds of Hogwarts School of Witchcraft and Wizardry. However, in *Chamber* it seems to be located near the training grounds in the courtyard, while in *Prisoner* it is located on a hill far from the school grounds. Its main function is to disguise the opening to the secret passage from Hogwarts to the Shrieking Shack. The Whomping Willow attacks anyone who comes close to the secret entrance. There is only one way temporarily to stop the tree from destroying whatever is in reach of its branches; located on the trunk is a particular knot which can be pressed to stop the attack.

Tolkien's Old Man Willow appears in *The Lord of the Rings: The Fellowship of the Ring* book, but it does not make it into the film version. According to the book, the hobbits begin to feel sleepy. "Sleepiness seemed to be creeping out of the ground and up their legs, and falling softly out of the air upon their heads and eyes."[105] Pippin and Merry fall asleep. Before Frodo succumbs, Tolkien narrates:

> He lifted his heavy eyes and saw leaning over him a huge willow tree, old and hoary. Enormous it looked, its sprawling branches

---

105. Tolkien, *Lord: Fellowship*, 134.

> going up like reaching arms with many long-fingered hands, its knotted and twisted trunk gaping in wide fissures that creaked faintly as the boughs moved. The leaves fluttering against the bright sky dazzled him, and he toppled over, lying where he fell upon the grass.[106]

The willow casts a spell upon the hobbits. Frodo, however, moves toward the river. "Half in a dream he wandered forward to the riverward side of the tree, where great winding roots grew out into the stream, like gnarled dragonets straining down to drink. He straddled one of these, and paddled his hot feet in the cool brown water, and there he too suddenly fell asleep with his back against the tree." Sam, who is not yet asleep, mutters to himself, "I don't like this great big tree. I don't trust it."[107] After a short interval, Sam discovers Frodo in the water with "a great tree root ... over him and holding him down." Sam pulled Frodo to the bank. Frodo says, "The big root just twisted round and tipped me in!"[108]

Frodo and Sam move to the other side of the tree to check on Pippin and Merry. Tolkien narrates: "Pippin had vanished. The crack, by which he had laid himself, had closed together, so that not a chink could be seen. Merry was trapped: another crack had closed about his waist; his legs lay outside, but the rest of him was inside a dark opening, the edges of which gripped like a pair of pincers."[109]

Sam and Frodo discuss what they might do to free Pippin and Merry. They settle on building a fire to frighten the tree to release their two companions.

> Quickly they gathered dry grass and leaves, and bits of bark; and made a pile of broken twigs and chopped sticks. These they heaped against the trunk of the far side of the tree from the prisoners. As soon as Sam had struck a spark into the tinder, it kindled the dry grass and a flurry of flame and smoke went up. The twigs crackled. Little fingers of fire licked against the dry scored rind of the ancient tree and scorched it. A tremor ran through the whole willow. The leaves seemed to hiss above their heads with a sound of pain and anger.[110]

This did not solve the problem. The tree merely tightened its grip on the two hobbits. Tolkien narrates: "The branches of the willow began to sway

106. Ibid., 135.
107. Ibid., 135.
108. Ibid., 136.
109. Ibid.
110. Ibid., 137.

violently. There was a sound as of a wind rising and spreading outwards to the branches of all the other trees round about, as though they had dropped a stone into the quiet slumber of the river valley and set up ripples of anger than ran out over the whole forest."[111]

Sam extinguishes the fire. Just as he and Frodo are about to try another option, Tom Bombadil, a character who is not incorporated into Jackson's film, comes singing and walking down the path near the willow. Sam and Frodo seek his help to free their friends from the willow. Bombadil identifies the tree as "Old Man Willow, naught worse than that."[112] Tom sings to the tree; then he breaks off a hanging branch and strikes the side of the willow with it. One crack widens, and Bombadil pulls Merry out of the tree. The other crack splits open, and Pippin springs out of the tree. "Then with a loud snap both cracks closed fast again. A shudder ran through the tree from root to tip, and complete silence fell."[113] Then, the hobbits accepted Bombadil's invitation to dinner in his home. The comparison of Tolkien's Old Man Willow to J.K. Rowling's Whomping Willow, especially in terms of violence, cannot be missed.

Finally, we have the trees in M. Night Shyamalan's *The Happening* (2008). The original screenplay, also written by Shyamalan, was titled *The Green Effect (2007)*. The opening credits of the film are displayed over white clouds against a bright blue sky while ominous music is heard. When the opening scene appears, the wind is rustling the leaves of big trees. The following warning signs appear for the first time: (1) there is confused speech by the character(s); (2) that is followed by physical disorientation (the loss of direction—characters walk backward while time seems to stop); and (3) characters commit suicide in multiple ways (such as stabbing, gunshot, hanging, etc.).

Elliot Moore (Mark Wahlberg), a high school science teacher explains what is happening to his wife, Alma (Zooey Deschanel):

> Our brains come equipped with a self-preservation mechanism to stop us from harmful actions. This is controlled by a combination of electrochemical signals in the brain. The blocking of neurotransmitters by certain toxins has been proved to cause hallucinations, asphyxiation, and paralysis. This new neurotoxin basically flips the preservation switch blocking neurotransmitters in a specific order causing specific self-damaging and catastrophic affects. Just how the toxin works .... It makes you kill yourself.[114]

111. Ibid.
112. Ibid., 139.
113. Ibid.
114. Shyamalan, Screenplay: *The Happening*.

The scenes with the wind blowing through the trees and, later, through grass in the country continue throughout the film heralding the release of neurotoxins by the trees in the northeastern United States. An unnamed nursery owner (Frank Collison) serves as one of the interpreters of the events in the movie. In one scene, he states: "I think I know what's causing this. It's the plants. They can release chemicals. Plants react to human stimulus; they've proved it in tests."[115] He continues to explain to other characters how plants have the ability to defend themselves when they sense that they are under attack. He states: "Plants have the ability to target specific threats. . . . We don't know how plants attained these abilities; they just evolved very rapidly. . . . Plants have the ability to communicate with other species of plants. Trees can communicate with bushes; bushes can communicate with grass, and everything in between."[116]

Much later in the film, after Moore and the nursery owner get separated from each other, even Moore figures it out through observation. He explains that crowds of people threaten the trees to release toxins. Every time that occurs, the three-fold scenario presented above takes place. Thus, the basic and simple thesis of the film is revealed and repeated over and over again. Just to be sure that the viewer gets it a scientist is shown being interviewed on TV near the end of the movie. He declares the events to have been acts of nature. He states that it was a warning that people are a threat to the planet. The trees are threatened by large numbers of people. When they are threatened, they release neurotoxins which confuse speech, cause physical disorientation, and result in suicide. The original title of the screenplay—*The Green Effect*—captured *The Happening* better.

Thus, trees reflect something of God. They share life with us on earth. Our relationship with them should result in awe and wonder which foster our spiritual transcendence. Trees, a kind of art, are spirit bearers that lead to our transformation. Trees get starring roles in Tolkien's books and Jackson's films. Lewis, too, liked to incorporate trees in his stories. Cameron raises trees to the status of goddesses, while Rowling and Tolkien before her displayed the violence of willows. And in many ways, Shyamalan brings us full circle. Trees on our earth are under attack; he asks us to consider what it would be like if they decided to retaliate.

Journal/Meditation: After considering trees in books and films, which is your favorite presentation? Why? What does that spur you to do?

---

115. Ibid.
116. Ibid.

Prayer: Ever-living God, the trees on the third planet from the sun in the Milky Way display something of you, LORD. As I share life with them, deepen my appreciation for the spiritual relationship that weaves together all of creation. Grant that the transcendence I experience now may lead me to transformation now and into eternity. I ask this in the name of Jesus Christ, your Son, who lives and reigns with you and the Holy Spirit, one God, forever and ever. Amen.

Other Books by Mark G. Boyer

History of St. Joachim Parish: 1822–1972; 1723–1973

Day by Day through the Easter Season

Following the Star: Daily Reflections for Advent and Christmas

Mystagogy: Liturgical Paschal Spirituality for Lent and Easter

Return to the Lord: A Lenten Journey of Daily Reflections

The Liturgical Environment: What the Documents Say

Breathing Deeply of God's New Life: Preparing Spiritually for the Sacraments of Initiation

Mary's Day—Saturday: Meditations for Marian Celebrations

Why Suffer?: The Answer of Jesus

A Month-by-Month Guide to Entertaining Angels

Biblical Reflections on Male Spirituality

"Seeking Grace with Every Step": The Spirituality of John Denver

Home Is a Holy Place

Day by Ordinary Day with Mark

Day by Ordinary Day with Matthew

Day by Ordinary Day with Luke

Baptized into Christ's Death and Resurrection: Preparing to Celebrate a Christian Funeral: Vol. 1: Adults

Baptized into Christ's Death and Resurrection: Preparing to Celebrate a Christian Funeral: Vol. 2: Children

The Greatest Gift of All: Reflections and Prayers for the Christmas Season

Meditations for Ministers

Waiting in Joyful Hope: Reflections for Advent 2001

OTHER BOOKS BY MARK G. BOYER

Filled with New Light: Reflections for Christmas 2001–2002

Lent and Easter Prayer at Home

Using Film to Teach New Testament

Waiting in Joyful Hope: Daily Reflections for Advent and Christmas 2002–2003

Waiting in Joyful Hope: Daily Reflections for Advent and Christmas 2003–2004

The Liturgical Environment: What the Documents Say (second edition)

Reflections on the Rosary

When Day Is Done: Nighttime Prayers through the Church Year

Take Up Your Cross and Follow: Daily Lenten Reflections

These Thy Gifts: A Collection of Simple Meal Prayers

Day by Ordinary Day: Daily Reflections on the First Readings, Year One

Day by Ordinary Day: Daily Reflections on the First Readings, Year Two

Mountain Reflections: A Collection of Photos and Meditations

Nature Spirituality: Praying with Wind, Water, Earth, Fire

A Spirituality of Ageing

Caroling through Advent and Christmas: Daily Reflections with Familiar Hymns

Weekday Saints: Reflections on Their Scriptures

Human Wholeness: A Spirituality of Relationship

The Liturgical Environment: What the Documents Say (third edition)

A Simple Systematic Mariology

Praying Your Way through Luke's Gospel and the Acts of the Apostles

Daybreaks: Daily Reflections for Advent and Christmas

Daybreaks: Daily Reflections for Lent and Easter

An Abecedarian of Animal Spirit Guides: Spiritual Growth through Reflections on Creatures

Overcome with Paschal Joy: Chanting through Lent and Easter—Daily Reflections with Familiar Hymns

Taking Leave of Your Home: Moving in the Peace of Christ

A Spirituality of Mission: Reflections for Holy Week and Easter

Bibliography

Abrams, M.H., ed. *The Norton Anthology of English Literature 2*. New York: W.W. Norton, 1962.
Adamson, Andrew, Christopher Markus, and Stephen McFeely. Screenplay: *Prince Caspian*. narniaweb.com/features/Prince-Caspian-Movie-Script.pdf.
"Adventures of the Great Hero Pulowech, or the Partridge, The." firstpeople.us.
Aesop's Fables. Translated by V.S. Vernon Jones. New York: Avenel, 1912.
Aldington, Richard, ed. *The Viking Book of Poetry of the English-Speaking World 1*. New York: Viking, 1941.
"Al Islam: English with Short Commentary." alislam.org/quran.tafseer.
"A Little Boy and His Dog, Beautiful Ears." firstpeople.us.
"American Forests: Native Americans and Trees." americanforests.org/our-programs/american-forests.
Andersen, Hans Christian. "Under the Willow-Tree." hca.gilead.org.il/under_wi.
Apsley, Brenda. *Tales from Hans Christian Anderson*. Manchester, England: World International, 1983.
Arnold, Matthew. "Requiescat." In *The Norton Anthology of English Literature 2*, edited by M.H. Abrams, 1031–2. New York: W.W. Norton, 1962.
Baltzer, Klaus. *Deutero-Isaiah*. Hermeneia. Minneapolis: Fortress, 2001.
Baring-Gould, Sabine. *Curious Myths of the Middle Ages*. New York: Barnes & Noble, 1994.
Bar, Shaul. "Trees in the Book of Genesis." *The Bible Today* 46:6 (2008) 383–90.
Bible Dictionary. "Marriage." lds.org/scriptures/bd/marriage.pl.
Blair, Robert. "The Grave." en.wikisource.org/wiki/The_Grave_(Blair).
Bloom, Harold. *The Gospel of Thomas: The Hidden Sayings of Jesus*. HarperSanFrancisco, 1992.
Book of Doctrine and Covenants, The. Independence, MO: Reorganized Church of Jesus Christ of Latter Day Saints, 1947.
Book of Mormon, The. Translated by Joseph Smith. Salt Lake City, UT: The Church of Jesus Christ of Latter-Day Saints, 1976.
Bovon, Francois. *Luke 2*. Hermeneia. Minneapolis: Fortress, 2013.
Bradbury, Robert. *The Hemlock Tree and Its Legends*. Philadelphia: John Duross, 1859.
Bryson, Bill. *At Home: A Short History of Private Life*. New York: Doubleday, 2010.

Bulfinch, Thomas. *Bulfinch's Mythology.* New York: Crown, 1979.
Burt, Virginia. "Healing Gardens as Transformative Spaces." *Faith and Form* 49:1 (2016) 22–3.
Caldecott, Moyra. *Myths of the Sacred Tree.* Rochester, VT: Destiny, 1993.
Cameron, James. Screenplay: *Avatar.* imsdb.com/scripts/Avatar.
Carola, Robert. "Johnny Appleseed." In *American Folktales, Myths, Legends,* edited by Leslie Conron, 213–14. New York: Madison Park, 2009.
Cavendish, Richard, ed. *Legends of the World.* New York: Barnes & Noble, 1994.
"Cherry Tree Carol." christmas-songs.org/song/cherry_tree_carol.
"Churchyard Trees." *The Saturday Review of Politics, Literature, Science, and Art* 104:2707 (1907) 330–31.
Clark, W.G., and W. Aldis Wright, eds. *The Complete Works of William Shakespeare 1–2.* Garden City, NY: Nelson Doubleday, no date.
Clarke, Chris. "How Did the Joshua Tree Get its Name?" kcet.org/redefine.
Clifford, Richard J. "Exodus." In *The New Jerome Biblical Commentary,* edited by Raymond E. Brown, Joseph A. Fitzmyer, and Roland E. Murphy, 44–60. Englewood Cliffs, NY: Prentice Hall, 1990.
Conron, Leslie, ed. *American Folktales, Myths, Legends.* New York: Madison Park, 2009.
Consolmagno, Guy. "Sci-fi Guy." *U. S. Catholic* 80:3 (2015) 35–38.
Count, Earl W., and Alice Lawson Count. *4000 Years of Christmas: A Gift from the Ages.* Berkeley, CA: Ulysses, 1997.
"Crocus as Fertility Daemon to the Mother Goddess, The." paghat.com/saffronmyth.
Davies, Simon E. "The Sacred Trees of World Mythology." ancient-code.com.
Dart, John, and Ray Riegert. *Unearthing the Last Words of Jesus: The Discovery and Text of the Gospel of Thomas.* Berkeley, CA: Seastone, 1998.
Delaney, Frank. *The Celts.* London: Book Club Associates, 1986.
Dharmananda, Subhuti. "Myrrh and Frankincense." itmonline.org/arts/myrrh.
Doctrine and Covenants. lds.org/scriptures/dc.
Doran, Robert. *2 Maccabees.* Hermeneia. Minneapolis, MN: Fortress, 2012.
"Dream Fast, The." native-languages.org/ojibwestory2.
Dunn, Jimmy. "Tree Goddesses of Ancient Egypt." touregypt.org/featurestories/treegoddesses.
Ehrman, Bart D., and Zlatko Plese. *The Apocryphal Gospels.* New York: Oxford University Press, 2011.
Eicher-Catt, Deborah. "Signs of Sacred Play: Musings on the Semiotics of Rainbows." *Listening: Journal of Communication Ethics, Religion, and Culture* 48:3 (2013) 224–239.
Faley, Roland J. "Leviticus." In *The New Jerome Biblical Commentary,* edited by Raymond E. Brown, Joseph A. Fitzmyer, and Roland E. Murphy, 61–79. Englewood Cliffs, NY: Prentice Hall, 1990.
Feldmeier, Peter. "What Is Spirituality?" *U.S. Catholic* 81:5 (2016) 20–24.
Flannery, Austin, ed. "Declaration on the Relation of the Church to Non-Christian Religions (Nostra Aetate)." In *Vatican Council II: The Conciliar and Post Conciliar Documents.* Northport, NY: Costello, 1987.
Fox, Jim. "The Legend of the Cedar Tree." powersource.com/cocinc/articles/cedar.
Francis, Pope. *Laudato Si' (On Care for Our Common Home).* Boston: Pauline Books and Media, 2015.
Frazer, James George. *The Golden Bough.* New York: Macmillan, 1922. bartleby.com.

Freeman, Mara. "Tree Lore: Oak." druidry.org/library/trees/tree-lore-oak.
Goodrich, Norma Lorre. *Merlin*. NY: Franklin Watts, 1987.
Gray, Thomas. "Elegy Written in a Country Churchyard." In *The Viking Book of Poetry of the English-Speaking World 1*, edited by Richard Aldington, 559–70. New York: Viking, 1941.
"Green Willow" Japanese Folktale. worldof tales.com/Asian_folktales/Japanese_ folktale_30.
Griffith, Jessica Mesman. "Organic Habits." *U.S. Catholic* 81:4 (2016) 12–18.
Grimm's Complete Fairy Tales. Garden City, NY: Nelson Doubleday, not dated.
Grundmann, Jena Walter. "Stephanos." In *Theological Dictionary of the New Testament*, edited by Gerhard Kittle and Gerhard Friedrich, 615–36. Grand Rapids, MI: Wm. B. Eerdmans, 1971.
Hageneder, Fred. *The Meaning of Trees: Botany, History, Healing, Lore*. San Francisco, CA: Chronicle, 2005.
Haley, R.D. "Johnny Appleseed: A Pioneer Hero." In *American Folktales, Myths, Legends*, edited by Leslie Conron, 215–19. New York: Madison Park, 2009.
Hall, Manly P. *The Secret Teachings of All Ages*. Los Angeles, CA: Philosophical Research Society, 1977.
Harrison, G.B., ed. *Shakespeare: Major Plays and the Sonnets*. New York: Harcourt, Brace, & World, 1948.
Hartin, Patrick J. *A Window into the Spirituality of Paul*. Collegeville, MN: Liturgical, 2015.
Hedrick, Charles W. *Unlocking the Secrets of the Gospel according to Thomas*. Eugene, OR: Cascade, 2010.
"Hemlocks." reed.edu/trees/TreePages/TSUG.
Herzberg, Max J. *Myths and Their Meanings*. Boston: Allyn and Bacon, 1984.
"Hotho." firstpeople.us.
"How Raven Brought Light to the World." firstpeople.us.
"How the Conifers Show the Promise of Spring." firstpeople.us.
Ions, Veronica. *The World's Mythology in Color*. London: Hamlyn, 1974.
Jackson, Peter, Fran Walsh, and Philippa Boyens. Screenplay: *The Lord of the Rings: The Two Towers*. imsdb.com/scripts/Lord-of-the-Rings-The-Two-Towers.
Jacobs, Joseph. "Jack and the Beanstalk." In *The Annotated Classic Fairy Tales*, edited by Maria Tatar, 131–44. New York: W.W. Norton, 2002.
Johnson, Luke Timothy. *The Gospel of Luke*. Sacra Pagina 3. Collegeville, MN: Michael Glazier, 1991.
Jung, Carl G. *Man and His Symbols*. London: Aldus, 1964.
Karris, Robert J. "The Gospel According to Luke." In *The New Jerome Biblical Commentary*, edited by Raymond E. Brown, Joseph A. Fitzmyer, and Roland E. Murphy, 675–721. Englewood Cliffs, NY: Prentice Hall, 1990
Kaur, Ramandeep. "Sacred Trees Worship in India." mapsofindia.com/my-india/india/sacred-trees-in-india.
Kodel, Jerome. *Lamentations, Haggai, Zechariah, Malachi, Obadiah, Joel, Second Zechariah, Baruch*. Wilmington, DE: Michael Glazier, 1982.
Lewis, C.S. *Prince Caspian*. Harmondsworth, Middlesex, England: Puffin, 1951.
Littleton, C. Scott, ed. *Mythology: The Illustrated Anthology of World Myth and Storytelling*. London: Duncan Baird, 2002.

Masterman, E.W.G. "Mulberry Trees." *International Standard Bible Encyclopedia*. Grand Rapids, MI: Wm. B. Eerdmans, 1939. internationalstandardbible.com.

———. "Terebinth." *International Standard Bible Encyclopedia*. Grand Rapids, MI: Wm. B. Eerdmans, 1939. internationalstandardbible.com.

McGinley, Phyllis. *A Wreath of Christmas Legends*. New York: Macmillan, 1964.

McKenzie, John L. *Dictionary of the Bible*. Milwaukee: Bruce, 1965.

Meir, John P. *A Marginal Jew: Rethinking the Historical Jesus 5*. New Haven, CT: Yale University Press, 2016.

Meyer, Gabriel. *In the Shade of the Terebinth: Tales of a Night Journey*. Leavenworth, KS: Forest of Peace, 1994.

"Mink and His Uncle." firstpeople.us.

Moore, Gerard. "Let Justice Find a Voice." *Worship* 90:3 (2016) 206–24.

Mowe, Sam. "Why Play with Koans: An Interview with John Tarrant." *Spirituality & Health* 19:3 (2016) 62–6.

Murphey, Cecil B. *The Dictionary of Biblical Literacy*. Nashville, TN: Oliver-Nelson, 1989.

Murphy, Roland E. "Canticle of Canticles." In *The New Jerome Biblical Commentary*, edited by Raymond E. Brown, Joseph A. Fitzmyer, and Roland E. Murphy, 462–65. Englewood Cliffs, NY: Prentice Hall, 1990.

"Native Americans and Trees." americanforests.org.

New American Bible, The. Washington, DC: Confraternity of Christian Doctrine, 1970.

New American Bible Revised Edition, The. Washington, DC: Confraternity of Christian Doctrine, 2010.

O'Connor, M. "Judges." In *The New Jerome Biblical Commentary*, edited by Raymond E. Brown, Joseph A. Fitzmyer, and Roland E. Murphy, 132–44. Englewood Cliffs, NY: Prentice Hall, 1990.

O'Day, Gail R., and David Peterson, eds. *The Access Bible: New Revised Standard Version with the Apocryphal/Deuterocanonical Books*. New York: Oxford University Press, 1999.

Official King James Bible Online, The. kingjamesbibleonline.org.

"Of the Surprising and Singular Adventures of Two Water Fairies Who Were Also Weasels, and How They Each Became the Bride of a Star, Including the Mysterious and Wonderful Works of Lox, the Great Indian Devil, Who Rose from the Dead." firstpeople.us.

"Okteondo and His Uncle, the Painter, or, Winter Delaying Spring." firstpeople.us.

Partridge, Tim. "Yew Trees and Their Inter-relationship with Man." ancient-yew.org/mi.php/trees-in-mythology/79.

Peck, Catherine. *A Treasury of North American Folktales*. New York: Book-of-the-Month Club, 1998.

Pelikan, Jaroslav, ed. *Sacred Writings, Volume 3, Islam: The Quran*. Translated by Ahmed Ali. New York: Book-of-the-Month Club, 1992.

———. *Sacred Writings, Volume 4, Confucianism: The Analects of Confucius*. Translated by Arthur Waley. New York: Book-of-the-Month Club, 1992.

———. *Sacred Writings, Volume 5, Hinduism: The Rig Veda*. Translated by Ralph T.H. Griffith. New York: Book-of-the-Month Club, 1992.

———. *Sacred Writings, Volume 6, Buddhism: The Dhammapada*. Translated by John Ross Carter, Mahinda Palihawadana. New York: Book-of-the-Month Club, 1992.

Polizzi, Nick. "Sacred Medicine Trees of North America." thesacredscience.com.

"Princess Raven." firstpeople.us.
Quran. intratext.com/IXT/ENG0027/_P2L.HTM#46.
"Raccoon Story, A." firstpeople.us.
Renewed Heart, The: The Art and Architecture of the Archabbey Church of Our Lady of Einsiedeln. St. Meinrad, IN: Abbey, 1998.
Roberts, J.J.M. *First Isaiah.* Hermeneia. Minneapolis: Fortress, 2015.
Roman Missal, The. Collegeville, MN: Liturgical, 2011.
Roman Pontifical, The: Dedication of a Church and an Altar. Washington, DC: United States Catholic Conference, 1989.
Roman Pontifical, The. "Rites of the Blessing of Oils and Consecrating the Chrism." Totowa, NJ: Catholic Book, 2012.
Ronell, Ann. "Willow Weep for Me." lyrics.net.
Runge, Philipp Otto. "The Juniper Tree." In *The Annotated Classic Fairy Tales*, edited by Maria Tatar, 158–71. New York: W.W. Norton, 2002.
Ryken, Leland, James C. Wilhoit, and Tremper Longman III, eds. *Dictionary of Biblical Imagery.* Downers Grove, IL: InterVarsity, 1998.
"Sacred Trees: Arbutus (Madrone) Tree." arbutusarts.com/sacred-trees.
Schwartz, Howard. *Gabriel's Palace: Jewish Mystical Tales.* New York: Oxford University Press, 1993.
Segal, Robert A. *Myth: A Very Short Introduction.* Oxford: Oxford University Press, 2015.
Shakespeare, William. "Macbeth." In *The Complete Works of William Shakespeare 2*, edited by W.G. Clark and W. Aldis Wright, 792–815. Garden City, NY: Nelson Doubleday, no date.
———. "Titus Andronicus." In *The Complete Works of William Shakespeare 1*, edited by W.G. Clark and W. Aldis Wright, 1–26. Garden City, NY: Nelson Doubleday, no date.
Shapiro, Rami. "Roadside Assistance for the Spiritual Traveler." *Spirituality & Health* 19:3 (2016) 19–20.
Shyamalan, M. Night. Screenplay: *The Green Effect.* 2007. mnightfans.com/up-content/uploads/2013/06/the-green-effect.pdg.
———. Screenplay: *The Happening.* 2008. springfieldspringfeild.co.uk/movie-script.php?movie=happening-the.
Sill, Gertrude Grace. *A Handbook of Symbols in Christian Art.* New York: Collier, 1975.
Smith, Huston. *Religions of Man, The.* New York: Harper & Row, 1986.
Smith, William. *Smith's Bible Dictionary.* biblestudytools.com/dictionaries/smith-bible-dictionary/palm-tree.
Spirit World, The. The American Indians. Alexandria, VA: Time-Life, 1992.
Suffness, Matthew, ed. *Taxol: Science and Applications.* New York: CRC, 1995.
Tatar, Maria, ed. *The Annotated Classic Fairy Tales.* New York: W.W. Norton, 2002.
Taylor, Mark Lloyd and Alissabeth Newton. "Praying at the Edge: Theology of an 'Emergent' Anglo-Catholic Sunday Evening Eucharist." *Worship* 90:3 (2016) 246–69.
Taylor, Richard. *How to Read a Church: A Guide to Symbols and Images in Churches and Cathedrals.* Mahwah, NJ: HiddenSpring, 2003.
Tennyson, Alfred Lord. "In Memoriam A.H.H." In *The Norton Anthology of English Literature 2*, edited by M.H. Abrams, 817–924. New York: W.W. Norton, 1962.

Tolkien, J.R.R. *The Lord of the Rings: The Fellowship of the Ring*. Boston: Houghton Mifflin, 1954.

———. *The Lord of the Rings: The Return of the King*. Boston: Houghton Mifflin, 1955.

———. *The Lord of the Rings: The Two Towers*. Boston: Houghton Mifflin, 1954.

"Tree Symbols." warpaths2peacepipes.com/native-american-symbols/tree-symbols.

Tresidder, Jack, ed. *The Complete Dictionary of Symbols*. San Francisco, CA: Chronicle, 2005.

"Uncle and Nephew." firstpeople.us.

Waite, D. Byron. "Up and Down the Hemlock." wemett.net/hemlock/history_history.

Walsh, Fran, Peter Jackson, and Philippa Boyens. Screenplay: *The Lord of the Rings: The Fellowship of the Ring*. imsdb.com/scripts/Lord-of-the-Rings-The-Fellowship-of-the-Ring.

———. Screenplay: *The Lord of the Rings: The Return of the King*. imsdb.com/scripts/Lord-of-the-Rings-The-Return-of-the-King.

"Wisdom of the Willow Tree, The." firstpeople.us/FP-Html-Legends/TheWisdomof theWillowTree-Osage.

Witcombe, Christopher L.D.E. "Trees and the Sacred." witcombe.sbc.edu/sacredplaces/trees.

Wolff, Hans Walter. *Joel and Amos*. Hermeneia. Philadelphia: Fortress, 1977.

Wordsworth, William. "Yew Trees." In *The Norton Anthology of English Literature 2*, edited by M.H. Abrams, 146. New York: W.W. Norton, 1962.

Wright, Addison G. "Ecclesiastes (Qoheleth)." In *The New Jerome Biblical Commentary*, edited by Raymond E. Brown, Joseph A. Fitzmyer, and Roland E. Murphy, 489–95. Englewood Cliffs, NY: Prentice Hall, 1990.

Yeats, William Butler. "Baile and Aillinn." best-poems.net/William_butler_yeats/ baile_and_aillinn.

www.ingramcontent.com/pod-product-compliance
Lightning Source LLC
Chambersburg PA
CBHW071241230426
43668CB00011B/1531